Settlers' Children

Rural children playing "Cut the Pie," Morton County, North Dakota, 1942. WPA photo. Reprinted with permission of University of North Dakota Libraries, OGL 264-54.

Settlers' Children

Growing Up on the Great Plains

By Elizabeth Hampsten

University of Oklahoma Press : Norman and London

Publication of this book is made possible, in part, through the generous support of The McCasland Foundation, Duncan, Oklahoma.

Library of Congress Cataloging-in-Publication Data

Hampsten, Elizabeth, 1932–
  Settlers' children : growing up on the Great Plains / by
Elizabeth Hampsten. — 1st ed.
    p. cm.
  Includes bibliographical references (p. 247) and index.
  ISBN 0–8061–2342–7
  1. Children—North Dakota—History. 2. Rural children—
North Dakota—History. 3. Child labor—North Dakota—
History. 4. Frontier and pioneer life—North Dakota. I. Title.
HQ792.U5H26 1991
305.23′09784—dc20   90–50689

To the North Dakota Coalition of
Abused Women's Services
and Bonnie Palecek, its founding leader.

Contents

Preface

This book owes its beginnings to the many people in North Dakota who wanted to tell me of their childhoods and persuaded me, as soon as I began to listen, that they were reciting more than anecdotes. For a number of years I had been reading letters and diaries of North Dakota settlers. No sooner had I begun looking in such obvious places as the state library manuscript collections than people began telling me of people they knew who kept letters, or they would bring me papers from their own families. Before long I found myself speaking about these writings to audiences around the state at events sponsored by the state Humanities Council, library boards, or civic organizations. We met in auditoriums, church basements, store fronts, living rooms, and back rooms of cafés, and I would not necessarily be the one doing the most talking. Invariably the testimonies of ordinary lives I was bringing provoked more. People wanted to talk, and what they told almost always included stories of childhoods. It is the urgency with which such stories were told that drew my attention, an urgency that I think comes from several desires, some possibly contradictory.

These are "good stories"—exciting or funny or sad, but invariably moving. They are stories important to the tellers, who don't want them lost, perhaps hoping that one more telling will prevent that loss. But they were being told, it sometimes seemed to me, with feelings of anger and rejection, and no wonder: who in their right mind would want to endure so much hardship again, let alone put children through such brutality? This was the puzzle for me, the seeming contradiction between hallowing events whose details more often than not were harsh, ugly, and destructive. How were people viewing their past, I wondered, what did they make of it, and how had they transformed that past into the rest of their lives?

Historical changes also change the climate of the stages of people's lives. The late nineteenth-century settlement period in North Dakota must have been an exciting time for men who came alone to "prove up" before sending for brides or families, and for young couples who ventured forth together. As people settled in, and had children, and grew a little older, situations for them could change. Women's lives became appreciably more difficult and precarious for lack of medical and other services in their childbirths, and for the difficulty of caring for young children under often primitive conditions. For children whose health was good, whose parents could feed and clothe and provide them with schooling because their own lives were sufficiently prosperous and calm, for such children, childhood appears, by many accounts, to have continued as a spirit of freedom and adventure that the parents had begun. And the ambitions of many parents that their children prosper better than they encouraged fairly adequate and extensive urban and rural school systems, libraries, basketball and hockey teams—all conditions generally favoring the young. For children born into poverty or into economically harsh households, growing up in North Dakota, by their own account, could be fairly grim. But at any rate, as long as there was land to move to and an expanding economy, North Dakota was a good state in which to be young.

A hundred years later much of that has changed. North Dakota is no longer a state of young people. These "outmigrate" because they find no opportunities within the state, rural schools close and consolidate, towns are left mainly with the elderly, and from some everyone has moved away. North Dakota is both a very wealthy and a very poor state, rich primarily in the productivity of the land, but poor in what its citizens realize from it. A consequence to children, in the 1980s and 1990s, is that the poverty of state government has steadily reduced the quantity and quality of educational and social services. But more damaging, I expect, is a reduction in the value given to the young. You would think children are not liked much these days, for increasingly they are growing up under physical and emotional conditions of great stress. Child abuse and child neglect rise, and the prizing of children, the delight in them and what they can do, this joy appears to decline. Such on-going deprivation must have its roots, I have to suppose, in experiences and attitudes that go deeper than the vagaries of seasonal economic conditions.

The phenomenon is hardly unique to North Dakota. Children are suffering throughout the United States because of government planning against their favor; nevertheless, the case of children's history in North Dakota—taking advantage of the state's relatively small population and short span of immigrant history—may be especially illustrative in suggesting ways that attitudes of one generation influence the economics, politics, and thinking of another.

It also must be said that the new hardships for children in the state are not entirely overlooked, for there certainly are individuals and agencies, in addition to families themselves, trying their best, with heroic compassions to attend to children. Honoring them is the hope of the dedication of this book.

In addition to individual people named who made manuscripts and other materials available to me, I thank the staffs of the Historical Society of North Dakota in Bismarck and the Institute for Regional Studies in Fargo, North Dakota, and Dan Rylance and Colleen Oihus and the staff of the manuscript room of the University of North Dakota Libraries, all generously helpful. Friends and colleagues have been important in the progress of this study: Everett Albers, Gretchen Beito, Suzanne Bunkers, John Crawford, Florence and Thomas Clifford, Ellen Dute, Byrd Gibbens, Jean Guy,

Eleanor and Richard Hale, David Hampsten, Ursula Hovet, Jim McKenzie, Sheryl O'Donnell, Marcia and Bernard O'Kelly, Stephanie Prepiora, Lillian Schlissell, Kathryn Sweney, Frances Wold, Mary Youngs. Bjorn Benson read pages at every stage, a contribution of imagination, patience, and fortitude perhaps best appreciated by those who have done the same for other books.

ELIZABETH HAMPSTEN

Grand Forks, North Dakota

Settlers' Children

1

Westward "for the Children"

In eastern North Dakota, the beginnings of the settlement past still are recent enough to be talked about by the people who experienced them as children and cherish their memories. They want to praise. At the same time, these sons and daughters of turn-of-the-century homesteaders, farmers, shopkeepers, teachers also tell of a great deal of suffering and deprivation. But those details typically are brushed aside in some deprecating version of it-was-tough-but-we-made-it —half bragging, half ashamed. That part of the story, which reflects a degree of rural poverty that now we hardly imagine, surely has been at least as crucial in forming ideas about regional history as the more flamboyant successes—railroads, towns, and farmsteads. Tough times, however denied, meant hunger and cold and exhaustion; they produced little in the way of art or literature or scholarship; they denied medicine and education and other sustaining comforts; and they meant early deaths. The period has left a legacy that still is difficult to assimilate into the region's history.

What was it like for children in the first years of settlement? By their own accounts (or as close as we can come to them), what did they think of their childhood? I should like to see how people in the second generation perceived their experiences. By knowing more about how they remembered their settlement childhoods, we might gain a fuller sense of the history of regions and begin to reach the origins of some of the myths about our country. How people claim to remember their past or even how it was recorded privately at the time (in parents' letters or diaries) of course may not agree with other accounts, nor be supported by more public records. Nevertheless, the stories we tell ourselves are the ones we are likely to want to believe.

These settlement childhoods were not easy. Many parents said that they came west "for the children"—following the script of the American dream. They wanted to assure their children better economic and social opportunities than they themselves had had. For many, the "dream" did come true, and the children secured their way into middle-class businesses, professions, and modern farming. Yet such hopes that centered upon children contradicted other myths about going west to escape domesticity, or at least the rule of parents. Photographs at the turn of the century show cattle drives, threshings with scores of horses, or men and single women in bars and saloons. Children are not part of these scenes.

However, except for the "rush" for gold in 1849, moves west did include families with children. Children were used by real estate companies to advertise land sales. The Brown Company, of Bismarck, North Dakota, circulated photos of winsome young girls in pigtails holding enormous watermelons or standing in a field of pumpkins. One of their photographs shows a group of children in front of a schoolhouse, the caption pointing out how many more girls there are than boys and suggesting that the extra girls would be suitable mates for enterprising young men from the East. In North Dakota half of those who came into the territory are reported to have moved elsewhere, but half did stay, and among those were a great many who could say that their children had indeed found prosperity, even though large numbers of first-generation settlers ended their days still working very hard or saw their labors erased during the depression. Whatever their parents' limited success, often the children of first-generation settlers expressed gratitude, a sense of indebtedness, and a desire to praise the country they had been brought to.

What can we call these people? Few whose lives I am exploring probably were, strictly speaking, pioneers, for while they may have moved under fairly primitive conditions and felt they experienced some years at a subsistence level, not many were truly "first" or unique to their experience. Nor did they appear to think that what they were doing was radically different from what others were up to; in fact, their desire seemed to be to emulate and form ties with others of similar aspirations. Their initial solitariness was being repeated everywhere.

North Dakota, as representative of the Plains and the beginnings of the West, experienced a settlement history slightly different from that of the rest of the country, yet also enough like other regions that what people said happened here we can suppose was more similar than not to conditions elsewhere. The climate is as harsh as any in the contiguous states. The land is flat, though slightly rolling in the west; there are few native trees except along riverbanks. North Dakota was one of the last regions settled, climate and topography making it the least desirable in spite of fertile and easily cultivated soil. The state was settled by a higher number of foreign immigrants than came to any other rural state—most immigrants from Europe or the Far East preferring urban areas. Settlement patterns in North Dakota in the main follow those of Canada: several family members, acquaintances, and sometimes entire sections of villages moved together to a single place. Thus there are, commonly along railroad lines, Icelandic, Finnish, Czech, Polish, Norwegian, Swedish, Irish, Scotch, French, and English communities hopscotching from east to west. People came directly from these countries, rather than generation by generation across the United States, and still speak of going "out" east as well as west. "Back" means to the country of origin. In addition, many settlers, both from northern Europe and from states to the east, were very poor, with far fewer resources than, for instance, those who traveled overland to Oregon and California. Some lived their first years in boxcars and picked buffalo bones to sell at $18 a ton for fertil-

izer. But even such poverty, many report, was preferable to
the deprivations they were trying to escape from. For those
first years, then, strong memories and attachments to the
"old" country for those from Europe, and poverty in an in-
hospitable environment, could not help coloring how people
thought of their arrivals.

Searching for children's lives is not easy, of course. Children rarely leave a written record, and when they do write,
there almost always is a teacher or parent supervising their
pages and controlling what they say. Parents and teachers
seldom keep what children write (or draw). And, during the
years I am speaking of, adults did not usually describe their
children at length in the letters, diaries, and other private
documents that have survived. When more institutions became interested in children—in regard to education and
schools, labor legislation, social services, health and medicine—their publications seldom asked children to speak for
themselves. But while sources are scarce, they are not non-
existent, for I think one can come to at least some understanding of a history of childhood in the settlement West by
reading what parents and other adults have said about children in their care; what institutions like orphanages and missionary societies publicized; and what elderly people have
written or spoken of concerning their childhoods, typically
the most specific portion of oral or written reminiscences.

Such a focus on children might also, I hope, suggest the
manner in which personal and cultural values have been
transmitted from one generation to the next. For instance,
we hear the West referred to as the "new" land; change and
newness are supposed to be at the core of pioneering. Yet
the newness settlers most uniformly embraced was economic, the hope of being richer than they had been wherever they came from. Other parts of their "old" lives they
were reluctant to change any faster than they had to, and
that reluctance toward change centered if anywhere around
children. Some Europeans resisted sending their children to
school where they would learn English and be weaned away

from the language and culture of their families, although eventually, of course, that happened.

The children whose lives I am exploring in this study fall into the category of the "obscure," as John Burnett describes them in his collection of life stories of English working people of the nineteenth century: "The poorest classes are always least represented, and we must accept that there remain some sections of society where voices cannot yet be heard by the historian." [1] My sources are various and nearly always incomplete. There are diaries or collections of letters in which parents write of their children, largely for the amusement of their own parents and other relatives, either bragging fondly about the children, especially when they are small, or complaining about the difficulties of managing them as they grow older. Here the attention is rarely on a child's inner life, but rather on the parents' relationship to their child and on the son or daughter's progress in physical development, school, and religious and moral training. In letters and diaries, adults, both men and women, write of children within the context of the rest of their own lives.

The reminiscences people write, usually in old age, and usually for the instruction of children and grandchildren, are half-public documents and meant to circulate, if not very widely. They attest to lives well spent, in spite of hardships; their purpose is like that Burnett found among working people in England: "to make a kind of sense out of an existence which might otherwise seem meaningless." [2] For settler children the "meaninglessness" was the drudgery and deprivation of daily living, but beyond that many elderly writers evoked larger aspirations of community-building, land development, and the like.

The writings typically begin with a childhood anecdote and almost always are most vivid in the earliest years—people write of first memories more clearly and more completely than of later events. In addition, earliest memories are apt more often than any other episodes to reveal negative details, as though the unflattering things that happened when one was young are not thought necessarily to reflect badly on the rest of a life. These personal manuscripts are usually short; often a younger friend or relative will have typed the work from handwritten sheets. They are not greatly different from life stories recorded from oral testimony: both forms sound oral and tend to be episodic and roughly chronological, and they dwell for the most part on single events—schooling, illnesses, jobs, moves, births of children, the deaths of parents and other family members.

Also likely to affect children in the settlement experience was many newcomers' relative lack of cultural curiosity about the place they had come to, an obliviousness that I would have expected contributed to entrenched racism and other expressions of ethnocentricity. I read of few settlers initially wanting to understand Indians (let alone disturbed about having displaced them) or reaching out to other groups of settlers of backgrounds different from their own. Wanting their children to honor and not to forget their past, people diverted attention as best they could from "new" forms around them, even as they considered themselves to be venturing into fresh territories. They did all they could to transform the strange into the familiar, converting Indians to denominations of Christianity, supplanting wildlife with plowed fields, and notably in the Northern Plains, forming towns and settlements with people from their same ethnic group. Norwegians stuck to other Norwegians, Lutherans sought out Lutherans and broke off from congregations subscribing to differing modes of Lutheranism. Children were likely to grow up in a more restrictive and less cosmopolitan atmosphere than their parents had—whether the parents had come from Europe or other areas of North America. The much-touted friendly and cooperative pioneer spirit does not often surface in private writings. Friends are people most like oneself, and strangers are viewed with suspicion.

Another impediment to our knowing as much as we should about the lives of children whose parents settled in the West is the overpowering expectation that this sacrificial "pioneering" had to have been successful, that prosperity was inevitable. Whatever the hardships of first-generation settlers, their children would have been responsible for asserting that such attempts had, after all, been worthwhile. James Marshall, tracing the nostalgic writings of the son of a failed homesteading family, writes that in his research he had "yet to locate one homestead narrative which candidly records dispossession by mortgage or other debt."[3]

The ambivalence with which many people who experienced western settlement regarded their childhoods cannot have been lessened by the ignorance with which adult settlers typically undertook the venture. Apart from the scarcity of roads and public transportation, and the initial lack of schools, churches, or supporting social services, few settling families had much of an idea about what awaited them. The lack of knowledge (let alone of money or job prospects) with which many were willing to start seems now quite astonishing. Letters received by the E. J. Lander real estate company in Grand Forks, for instance, ask for very basic information:

From Hoblersburg, Pennsylvania, March 20, 1891: Now I wish to come west, and what in your estimation would be the best plan to get hold of a farm? Does it require the ready money or is there any Government land to be taken up yet. Inform me as to crops whether good or failing, the soil what grains are raised, the prices of land per acre, what fruits grow there; tell me all about the climate, the duration of the summer season, the severity of the winter; inform me as the wages for different occupations, the prices of farm products, the hostility of the Indians, in fact give me a general knowledge to the above questions, if you will be kindly disposed and let me know at an early date.

From Bellefont, Pennsylvania, February 19, 1891: I would like to know what the crop plan is and if you think a man could get through with seven or eight hundred dollars in money with a small family and how near to a rail road and near to market and if the land is good.

From Bridgeport, Illinois, February 24, 1891: I have sold my firm here I am anxious to try a new country like that which you now live in so I write to you in regards to farming and what improved farms are worth and also unimproved, and whether a person can rent a farm by coming out there this fall and what rent to pay and what wages are worth there and also in regards to soil, water and climate and the generality of your country by so doing you will greatly oblige me and trusting it will not severely hurt you and that I may hear from you soon, I remain as ever yours.

From a manufacturer of cigars in Zylonite, Massachusetts, February 17, 1891: I organized about 50 German families all, except me, farmers, and some of them having a trade beside, as Carpenter, Mason, Plumber, Shoemaker, Brickmaker, Barber etc., with the intention to go to Grand Forks County. They are all steady workingmen of good character but without the capital to take land just now, and therefore I take liberty to ask your Honorable Board if, and to what number you could give, resp. secure work and shelter for us and our families. I send a copy of this letter to several Towns of your county, and I hope, if not work and shelter for all in your place, to have good result in your vicinity.[4]

While these writers (all men) needed to know about the "generality" of the new country—the climate, soil, wages, and the likelihood of "work and shelter" for families—they did not ask whether life would be tolerable for children and women. Crabapples, chokecherries, and wild plums are about the only fruit trees that grow in Grand Forks County; summers are short and winters dangerous. One might wonder whether an environment hostile to fruit trees may not also be less than hospitable to the survival of children. By 1891 schools, churches, and doctors were appearing in Grand Forks, but few of these amenities existed in the countryside. Children were intended to be an asset to farming, not the other way around. For, in the first years of settlement, what was done "for" the children often caused them severe hardship. The journey itself sometimes brought on deaths of children who might well have lived had they stayed where they were. Discovering a history of settlement childhood is complicated also by the relative impermanence of that settlement. People remained on the land, of course, wresting much of it from previous Indian settlers, but the history of the

West has been a shifting one. Populations that at first fanned out to farms, ranches, and prosperously booming small towns, a hundred years later have redistributed themselves to urban centers. Farmhouses stand as derelict as some of the villages they clustered around.

Studies of the history of childhood have usually evolved as extensions of the history of institutions connected to children: histories of schools and education, histories of labor, of medicine, of public welfare, and of the family. What we do not have are studies of children's perceptions—or as nearly as these can be approached—of the experience of growing up in the Plains and West in settlement years. Such a study inevitably also touches women's history, for it is obvious that children and women were important in each other's lives. Women bore and cared for children; their health and life-span were affected by children. Children provided career opportunities for women in teaching, social welfare, and other jobs and professions. Studies in women's history emphasize the effect children had on their mothers, female relations, and other women who came in contact with them. But might we see women differently when the focus is shifted to the children? We should wonder about the extent to which women's hardships under settlement conditions affected children, depriving them of basic care. Or, conversely, to what extent did some mothers manage to protect their children, to see that they experienced childhood as it was being cherished in more urban and middle-class environments?

Children do not necessarily recognize their parents' lives as separate from their own, yet in reporting what their parents "did" to them, they judge and evaluate that past, cherishing or denying it in their memories. In practical terms, a great many rejected their parents' establishments, for few of those children who had prospered from the removals were willing or able to remain where their forebearers settled themselves. Some stayed, of course. Do the judgments these children have made—some having stayed, others leaving their places of settlement, and, at this writing, many living into their eighties—reaffirm or cast doubts upon the wisdom of western settlement? Do they represent the rewards or the casualties of that grand experiment? Answers cannot be conclusive, but inquiring into children's lives may at least offer some useful observations.

2

Children at Work

Western settlement, especially settlement in the Upper Great Plains, created an anomaly in the history of childhood: it came in the years—between the middle of the nineteenth through the turn of the twentieth century—when in Europe and the eastern United States childhood was evolving into a time of its own. In longer-settled regions and in city suburbs, children were living under increasingly benign conditions, and fewer dying. What most distinguished them from children of earlier centuries was being kept apart from adult work and responsibility. Nineteenth-century children went to school instead of to field or shop. Free public education and improved nutrition, sanitation, immunization, and general health care was making life less precarious and brutal for all but the poorest children. Yet along with the urban poor, many children of rural households in the same years experienced fewer of these benefits, and children of the most recently settled rural areas benefited least of all.

Some of the children whose parents had made the most strenuous efforts of all on their behalf—the children of the so-called pioneers—may have experienced the greatest suffering of any. There are descriptions in parents' letters at the time and in childhood reminiscences of elderly people that can make us think they were written in the Middle Ages. Philippe Aries has remarked upon the absence of depictions of childhood in Medieval art: "It is hard to believe that the neglect was due to incompetence or incapacity; it seems more probable that there was no place for childhood in the medieval world."[1] No more was there in certain North American settlement households.

The household of Emilie and Charles Schumacher, for instance, seems to have been one with little room for childhood. In 1888 the couple moved from Chicago to Ashland Township, in Stutsman County, North Dakota. As young as they were able, the Schumacher children worked. The time something went wrong with the well, cattle had to be driven to a neighbor's farm a mile away:

This job fell to the three boys, Arthur age 7 1/2, Edward age 5, and Harry age 3 1/2. One day Alfred, who was not quite two years old, decided he would tag along. He had gotten about a quarter mile from the house when the boys discovered him following them. They told Alfred to go back home and then, typical of many young children, they paid no more attention to him. Later, when Emilie saw the returning boys, she noticed there were only the three older boys. She rushed out to meet them and to see what happened to the baby. The boys told their mother that they had sent him back home. A search was conducted and little Alfred was found safe and sound, asleep in a badger mound.[2]

Each of these children as they got older was required to pump water from a basement cistern into the kitchen, 100 strokes every day.

The account of the Schumacher family settling near what is now Jamestown, North Dakota, was written by a granddaughter, Dorothy F. Boldt Johnson.[3] Her desire was to memorialize these forebears as pioneers, but she does not conceal resentments some members of the family felt for the way they had been treated in the progress toward that settlement. Certainly Charles Schumacher achieved success, at least in the eyes of the local press, who wrote admiringly of him in 1908, when he was a candidate for sheriff (although he did not win election): "He is an example of what industry and stick-to-itiveness does, for he, like so many, came here in the early days with little more plausible than a smile, two strong hands and ability to work long and hard. Now he

owns a thousand acres, about 60 head of horses and the et-
cetera that go to make up a farming outfit—fine farm buildings and so little indebtedness than an average crop would
wipe it out and leave surplus."[4]

Charles Schumacher was born in Chicago in 1863 of German parents. He had worked as a laborer in a wholesale
house, and in 1884, age twenty-one, married Emilie Bischoff.
Four years later when he set out for the West, one of his
brothers tried to persuade Emilie not to follow him. According to Johnson, "He [the brother] knew that it would mean
much hard work for Emilie and thought that she would be
better off to stay in the Chicago area. Then too, he knew that
Charles was a very stern man and had a very bad temper.
He felt that on the prairie Emilie might be subject to harsh
treatment if things didn't go right for Charles."[5] When things
did not go right with the boys in the family, Charles treated
them with a buggy whip a merchant had given him in payment on an account:

Charles chose to keep this whip in his clothes closet, and if he
wanted to punish any of the boys for doing something wrong or for
disobeying him, he would say, "Go get the whip," and they knew
enough to bring it to him. He would require them to stand a measured distance from him as he would apply the business end of the
whip to the boy being punished. If the boy broke and ran, Charles
would crack the whip in the air, and the boy would return immediately to receive the rest of his punishment and possibly some additional lashing for having tried to run. Once having received such
punishment, they recognized who was boss, and from there on
knew that they had better mind. Charles was a large six foot with
blue, steel eyes. He was known to have a bad temper and the children learned very early in life that he was to be obeyed.[6]

The times had not been propitious either for these children
as infants, when the most ordinary care required extraordinary vigilance. During their first years in North Dakota
the Schumacher family lived in a one-room cabin, burning
straw and buffalo chips in a small stove, and they experienced one of the perils always threatening settlers. The night

of December 12, 1893, was particularly cold, and the straw
that was stacked for fuel next to the stove caught fire:

Emilie had put the children to bed in their overalls that night because of the severity of the cold weather. When the fire was discovered, Emilie and Charles and their hired hand, Max Naut, grabbed
the children in their blankets and made a dash for the barn. Upon
arriving there a headcount was taken; all four little boys, Arthur,
Edward, Harry and Alfred were accounted for, but the eight-day-
old baby girl, Clara, was nowhere to be found. Panic struck. A rush
back toward the burning house found Clara wrapped snugly in a
feather tick and sound asleep and safe in a snow bank where she
had been dropped in the panic.[7]

The more one hears of tales like that, as well as of work-
possessed discipline imposed on older children, the more
one is reminded of much earlier ages. It is as though in personal and family relationships the settlement experience
briefly leapt backwards through the centuries. On the whole,
the description of childhood in the Middle Ages that the historian Phillipe Aries gives is a positive, sympathetic one.
Youth was the period widely noted and prized, he says (as
we know it was in the years of western settlement), and until
the twelfth and thirteenth centuries, everyone, regardless
of age, was included in a single social experience. Ability
was what counted; so, if children like the Schumacher five-
to-seven-year-olds could manage watering cattle, it was
thought right for them to do so. Only later did children gradually come to be separated from adults—to be dressed differently and sent away to school. Aries draws attention to
the loss implicit in such progress toward childhood and
away from tasks and responsibilities the young had taken
on in earlier ages: the new childhood meant a break in contact with adults. The old childhood held on in some settlement households, it seems to me, and that break came late.
The work that children did hardly distanced them from
adults; their childhood was muted.

The increasing separation of children from adults is a process, however, that the psychohistorian Lloyd De Mause in-

terprets differently from Aries. De Mause calls the history of childhood "a nightmare from which we have only recently begun to awaken. The further back in history one goes, the lower the level of child care, and the more likely children are to be killed, abandoned, beaten, terrorized, and sexually abused."[8] While the work of De Mause and his followers has been controversial and hardly notes the effects of political, economic, and technological events, I have been struck by how often the violent history he describes coincides with recorded experiences of individual settlement children.

Education, or at least school attendance, for generations has been the key descriptor of childhood; childhood is equated with going to school. Neil Postman, a follower of De Mause, analyzes the connection between education and the separation from family.[9] Children go to school to learn to read, he says. In the small medieval communities, Postman points out, information was available orally, and equally to everyone, and medieval society as a consequence lacked either secrets or a sense of shame. As Peter Breughel shows in his paintings, ordinary human activity was displayed in front of children as before anyone else. Adults and children were not distinguishable from one another, at least in regard to the kind of information available to them. It was the invention of movable type in the late Middle Ages, Postman says, that brought about the existence of childhood. Print introduced secrets because, for the first time, information became available to some—those who could read—and unavailable to those who could not. Childhood was the period designated for learning to read, and for learning a new way of thinking along with the skill: in a linear, logical manner, conforming to the arrangement of type. Thus childhood came into being and led to adulthood, and print separated the two stages. Print brought about for the first time a consciousness of experience that depended on more than direct observation and oral speech. The printing press, Postman says, "gave us ourselves" and our sense of individuality. In this way childhood evolved as the protected period of time devoted to the gradual realization of that individual self.

In the Schumacher family, what might appear as a lack-
luster attitude toward education suggests that those children were not encouraged toward the individualizing effects
of print that Postman speaks of. The same year as his father
was reported running for county sheriff, Alfred, the sleeper
in the badger mound, was sent to Jamestown to board while
he attended high school. Telling of the experiences in his old
age, he still apparently felt the humiliation. Alfred lived with
a family named Mitchel; they owned a pool hall where Alfred also worked, and they accommodated the boy grudg-
ingly in their quarters over the pool hall, "where there were
three rooms, one where he [Mitchel] and his wife slept, one
where his daughter slept, and one used as a kitchen and dining room. There being no place for me except to sleep in the
end of the hall on the floor without even a mattress."

In 1919 the Schumachers moved to Fargo. Then, Dorothy
writes, "In 1925 Charles filed for divorce, after 41 years of
marriage to Emilie. Emilie counter-sued on the grounds of
cruel and inhuman treatment." She won and received the
two houses the couple owned in Fargo. In 1927 Charles married again but died of cancer in June the same year. "Before
his death, he called many times for his first wife Emilie, but
she refused to go to his side. One of the few children of his
that visited him in the last days of his illness was one of his favorite daughters, Esther" (the mother of Dorothy Johnson).
Charles was buried in a Fargo cemetery with no headstone.

Emilie Schumacher lived with her other daughter, Clara,
in McIntosh, Minnesota, until she died in 1953 at age ninety.
Dorothy summed up her grandmother's portrait: "In contrast to her large, tall six-foot husband, Emilie was only five
feet tall. She had blue eyes and beautiful curly dark auburn
hair. During the 41 years that she was married to Charles,
she did not live an easy life. . . . She was required to cook,
bake, clean, wash, iron, mend, tend garden, can for winter,
entertain and be a good wife." Her farm chores, in which the
children shared, included gathering and selling eggs, tending chickens and pigs, milking, separating cream and churn-
ing butter, rendering lard, and looking after a household of

sixteen people. Her granddaughter described Emilie's life as entirely defined by work and circumscribed by physical fear of Charles, the "large, tall six-foot husband," whose industry depended so much on hers and her acquiescence to him. The forebodings Emilie's brother-in-law felt if she were to join Charles in North Dakota proved all too accurate.

Dorothy Johnson includes a motif often appearing in settler narratives, the nostalgic glance back at a happy moment in childhood describing the grandparents who stayed behind. These memories dwell on comfort and the sense of being taken care of:

Emilie also told of how her grandmother Friedricke was at one time a cook for the Kaiser Wilhelm. She was referred to as the old Swede by her friends, but this grandmother also must have been a very kind and gentle old woman. To attest to this, Emilie often told the story about when she had her ears pierced. Emilie was not very old at the time, but she very much wanted her ears pierced, so one day on the way to school, she persuaded a young girl friend to do it for her. She told how badly it hurt, but she was afraid to go home, as she just knew her mother would be angry and scold her. Holding her hands over her hurting ears, she ran to her grandmother Friedriche for comfort. Her grandmother cleaned the wounded ears and kept Emilie with her that day until school was out before sending her home.[10]

Such memories of comforts—regular schooling, friends, nearby grandparents—make immigration and the move west appear retrogressive when we think how few of those simple pleasures were available to the Schumacher children once the family established itself in North Dakota. They were not poor, but Johnson reports almost nothing that mitigated the father's stern rule. These children, by the daughter's account, hardly felt the historical movement that was favoring other children in less newly settled regions. As father and husband, Charles Schumacher made the lives of his wife and children hard, and Emilie apparently was able to do little to mitigate his duress toward herself or their children.

In the Schumacher's Stuttsman County as elsewhere, family economics were not necessarily what determined the labor of children. Fairly prosperous settlement families saw to it that their children took part in the work of farm or ranch or town business. It does not seem to have occurred to them to do otherwise. They thought of work as a good in itself; they assumed it was good for children to work. In such families, children knew as much as anyone what went on in the family, in the family enterprise, and in the community.

Yet the importance to children of the work they did had to have been at least equaled by the importance of the amount of attention parents paid to them. Sometimes children who worked very hard received little attention from their parents; they appear at times to have been nearly forgotten about. But not always. Some parents managed with considerable care to focus on what their children were doing as they worked and to direct them to productive ends. In the history of settlement, childhood work certainly is a determining factor, but so is the matter of attention paid to children, a quality that has been universally acknowledged as crucial in child raising regardless of economic status, social class, or historical period.

To be sure, while it was taken for granted that children worked, few speak of the fact. Private records of the settlement period no more than public ones acknowledge what children accomplished. *Work* was what men did; women, and then children, at best were credited with helping an operation along. Only now and then do farm children peek out from behind a mother's skirts, and even the mother was obscured behind the father's more official place:

We took food along to the fields and while the children played I worked with your father. The children and I, of course, would leave a little earlier in order to build a fire in our wood range and have a nice hot meal waiting for Papa. When we got home, I brought the cows in from the field and milked them and watered and tended our other animals for the night. Then I returned to the house to finish making dinner and put the children to bed. When Father came home, tired and hungry, dinner was ready for him. After dinner I finally had timé to do my washing for the children and prepare for the next day's baking. And so day after day passed by, becoming months and years.[11]

If ever there were a double work day, this woman performed it. Although the mother says little about the children—she refers to them collectively and does not mention even how many there are—the children were bound to know much about how the farm maintained itself. And they were bound also to be serving an apprenticeship as they followed their mother around. She speaks companionably about them— "the children and I, of course"—and although she does not dwell on them individually, as though her sequence of days were too complicated, these children sound looked after and thought about.

But work was not always a companionable experience for children, nor was the institutional history of child labor in the United States much other than an affirmation of the brutal history of child-rearing that De Mause described. We have known a long sequence of failed legal efforts to control child labor. For decades, U.S. law, charitable agencies, and schools quarreled over what was best for children, with the result that advocates were never able to overcome the opposition that prevented the enactment of federal child labor laws and the constitutional ratification of a child labor amendment. This issue, the work that children could be allowed and expected to do, impinged too strongly, people argued, upon parent-child relationships, most particularly for parents and children on farms, and it would appear that the threat of denying to farm parents the labor of their children (or not allowing them to decide how much their children would work) was the single most effective impediment to child labor legislation. Other means, of course, have evolved to protect children, such as the minimum wage, compulsory school attendance, immunization, and hospital birthing, but the refusal of farmers and farm workers to accept direct governmental intervention on the agricultural work of children suggests a good deal about how children were thought of until well into the twentieth century.

Charity organizations showed a steadily increasing public interest in children from the mid-nineteenth century onward. The number of state-supported orphanages and private charities for children accelerated after the Civil War. In 1867 New York established a State Board of Charities; in 1869 Michigan began free public education; in 1874 the New York Society for the Prevention of Cruelty to Children was organized, and the next year children in New York State were removed from public almhouses. By 1891 Indiana had County Boards of Children's Guardians to care for dependent children. These appointed and unpaid boards were under the control of county commissioners in cooperation with the state Board of Charities, an instance of the gradual movement of the public care of children from private to government responsibility. In 1899 New Jersey established a State Board of Children's Guardians. By 1929, thirty-four states had children's code commissions, the first having been established in Ohio in 1911 with duties to coordinate the administration of children's laws and suggest new ones. The White House Conference on Child Health and Protection, convened in 1930, published a report recommending principles that state administrators of child welfare programs should follow. The texts of laws, congressional hearings, newspaper reports, and journalists' essays about children in the United States since the Civil War that are compiled in Robert Bremner's *Children and Youth in America: Their Labor History* attest to a contentious history. The very thought of children brought passionate arguments: federal versus state control, prominent advocates for children against each other, agriculture and manufacturing interests against any limits on child labor. Parents who were unwilling to lose children's incomes argued that laws about children violated the sanctity of the family.

In 1907 Congress authorized an investigation of child labor, something Theodore Roosevelt had been urging in his annual messages since 1904. He had proposed also that "a drastic and thorough-going child-labor law should be enacted for the District of Columbia and the Territories,"[12] but it never was. In 1906 a bill "to Prevent the Employment of Children in Factories and Mines" was pigeonholed in committee, even after an amendment passed that would have limited its application to the District of Columbia. The National Child Labor Committee, formed in 1907 and committed to state regulation of child legislation, did not endorse the bill. In 1914 the committee drafted the Keating-Owen Act,[13] "An Act to Prevent Interstate Commerce in the Products of Child Labor and for Other Purposes." It passed on September 1, 1916, and Grace Abbot (1878–1939) was appointed director of the Child Labor Division of the Children's Bureau in charge of the administration of the law. But it was in effect less than a year (September 1, 1917, to June 3, 1918) before the Supreme Court declared it unconstitutional on the grounds that it did not "regulate transportation among the States, but aims to standardize the ages at which children may be employed in mining and manufacturing with the States"—the same verdict as in *Hammner* v. *Dagenhard.*[14] The act set fourteen as a work age limit; it limited children between ages fourteen and sixteen to an eight-hour day and six-day work week, and to the hours between 6:00 in the morning and 7:00 at night, but it was struck down on the grounds that "the goods shipped are themselves harmless."

The successful challenge to Keating-Owen tells us something about the lives of rural children and more generally about attitudes toward children when they came into conflict with economic interests. Southern textile manufacturers fought hard against the bill, claiming that farm children would be the last to benefit. The publisher of the *Southern Textile Bulletin*, David Clark, testified in the Senate. While not going so far as to claim that mill children were not harmed at all by mill work, he pointed out that not even proponents of child labor laws were willing to challenge the assumption that children on farms ought to be obliged to work. Clark said:

The proposition of the National Child Labor Committee is that the cotton mill boys and girls are injured by working in the mills. That is the basis of their claim, as I understand it. They also claim that the second generation is going to show the effect of this injury. Now, as a matter of fact, the second generation of the cotton-mill people in the South are better physically, better looking people than the first generation that came from the mountains. I have here a few photographs which I desire to pass around among the members of the committee, showing some of the children of the operatives. . . . Before they came to the mills they had worked on the farms, where they had worked longer and harder hours. . . . The parents of those children had worked on the farms before they came there to the mills. . . . My theory is that the work in the mills is not as hard or as injurious as the work on the farms. The promoters of this bill have not the nerve to include the farms or even to refer to the farms.

Even before the law was challenged, a few journalists took up the issue that Clark had raised but that lawmakers and child welfare proponents had not been willing to. Writing in the *New Republic*, Owen R. Loveboy spoke of the weakness of state regulations, the power of sentimental mythology, and the resulting continued illiteracy that marked lives of rural children untouched by Keating-Owen:

Assuming that this law is effectively enforced, how far does it reach? Only 150,000 children will be affected. The other 1,850,000 children are left untouched. No federal law can reach them. They are the wards of the several states: the young hawkers of news and chewing-gum in our city streets; the truck-garden conscripts of Pennsylvania, New Jersey, Ohio, Colorado and Maryland; the cotton-pickers of Mississippi, Oklahoma and Texas; the 90,000 domestic servants under 16 years of age in our American homes; the cash-girls in department stores. . . . The delusion that every small street peddler is supporting a widowed mother dies hard. . . . From the sugar-beet fields of Colorado, from the berry fields of New Jersey, Maryland and Delaware, from the onion beds of Ohio, from the tobacco fields of Kentucky and from the hot cotton fields of Oklahoma and Texas, the cry of the children ought to make itself heard. But they are mute. They have not tasted liberty. Without complaint they step into the ranks of the 5,000,000 illiterates to grope blindly through a land of plenty.[15]

The case that nullified the child labor law was one brought on behalf of the father of two boys, aged fourteen and sixteen, who worked in cotton mills in North Carolina (where twelve was the minimum working age). Roland Dangenhart asserted that his sons would lose their jobs if the law went into effect, and therefore the result of the act "would be to deprive the boys of the their right to pursue the occupation which they and he had selected for their life work and to deprive him of their earnings."[16] Six years later the older of the two sons was interviewed—he was twenty, married, and the father of a child:

Look at me! a hundred and five pounds, a grown man and no education. I may be mistaken, but I think the years I've put in in the cotton mills have stunted my growth. They kept me from getting any schooling. I had to stop school after the third grade and now I need the education I didn't get. . . . From 12 years old on, I was working 12 hours a day—from 6 in the morning till 7 at night, with time out for meals. And sometimes I worked nights besides. Lifting a hundred pounds and I only weighed 65 pounds myself. . . . But I know one thing, I ain't going to let them put my kid sister in the mill, like [my father is] thinking of doing!
    She's only 15 and she's crippled and I bet I stop that![17]

Another attempt to control child labor at the federal level failed in 1922 when Congress passed a 10-percent "tax on profits from child labor entering interstate commerce" in response to the rise of child labor during the First World War. The tax was declared unconstitutional for much the same reason as the Keating-Owen bill had been, and it was in effect only between April 25, 1918, and May 15, 1922. In 1924 several groups, including the American Federation of Labor, the National Child Labor Committee, and the Consumers' League, supported a child labor amendment[18] that was approved by both houses of Congress but ratified by only six states by 1933. The amendment read: "The Congress shall have power to limit, regulate, and prohibit the labor of persons under eighteen years of age." It was opposed by manufacturing and states-rights groups, including the Woman Patriotic Publishing Company, an organ of the Antisuffrage Association, on the grounds that it would lessen competition for labor, give jobs to bureaucrats, and punish states that already had strict laws. It also would give encouragement to "Communists and socialists striving to establish governmental control and support of the entire youth of the Nation, which is the basic tenet of Communism," according to a petition to Congress (May 31, 1924) from the Woman Patriotic Publishing Company. California, Massachusetts, Nevada, North Dakota, Washington, and Wisconsin were the six states whose legislatures had petitioned Congress to submit the amendment. The *Manufacturers' Record* for September 11, 1924, painted a scary picture of what would happen to family and farm if the amendment were to pass:

You must bear in mind that this Amendment takes entirely from the parents the right to have their children, sons or daughters, do any work of any kind so long as they are under 18 years of age. Those who are backing this amendment distinctly state that the intention of the bill is to prevent the employment, for instance, of any boy under 18 years of age in any farm work of any kind. It was specifically stated by one of the most active promoters of this scheme that this was intended to keep boys under 18 years of age from driving up the cows, or hoeing the vegetables, or doing any work of the character even for their own parents. Under that bill the mother would have no right to teach her daughter to do any housework whatsoever, whether it be the sweeping of floors, or the washing of dishes.[19]

Whether or not proponents of the amendment "distinctly stated" that the amendment was to keep children from tending farm animals "even for their own parents," opponents mentioned children on family farms more often than did those who wanted to regulate child labor. All documents in Bremner's history referring to farm children consider only the children of migrant workers, not the children of farm-owning families. Thus an article called "Neglected Children of Migrant Workers" argues that migrant children suffer for lack of friends, neighborhood, and community ties, as well as for missing up to five months of schooling. Their very isolation, however, their parents saw as a prime economic advantage:

Parents take children of all ages to the country, though the largest number are from five to sixteen and most of them work. Little tots under five go with their mothers into the fields or remain at the house in charge of another child acting as "little mother. . . ." The major reason families migrate to the open country is work; work with its contribution to the family income; work without restrictions for all members of the household, young and small, old and large. . . . The work children may do in factories and mills is regulated by school and child labor laws, not so for children of migrant workers.[20]

Even members of women's groups who had worked hard on behalf of child labor legislation and felt rebuffed as women for the failure of the amendment to pass thought of its application to agriculture only in regard to migrant workers. Thus Lucy Johnson Bing wrote that the amendment should not exempt agriculture (by which she meant paid field work) because of "the growth of the factory system in agriculture where children are employed in large groups at piece work by a boss who does not own the land nor feel any concern for the children he works, as in the onion, beet and cotton fields."[21] She also resented the implication some detractors were making that the defeat of the bill was a defeat for women, merely because women had worked for its passage: "To be interested in public welfare movements is considered sentimental. According to many, sentiment may be permitted and even encouraged among women in private life, but is not to be permitted in government."[22]

"Sentiment" of this nature hardly affected children on farms, who did not call even as much attention to them-

selves as migrant children in the "factory system of agriculture." If parents, fathers particularly, asserted parental rights
to have their children employed and collect their wages,
how much more proprietary were parents about having children work in the home enterprise, where farm and home
were undistinguished from one another. We shall see, in
three fairly prosperous families interviewed in the course of
one of their member's compiling a family "history," that
children worked hard in a store, hotel, and farm regardless
of the families' relative wealth. These parents could not
imagine what else one might do if not work. Work, not play,
was what children "did."

Mary Margaret French

Yet the move west was not regressive for all children, even in
North Dakota, where the settlement of farming areas came
late in comparison to the rest of the country. There were
children, typically of parents in the professional classes,
who did not work to help support the family and who received the kind of care and attention, luxurious by comparison, that was becoming usual among the urban middle
classes. These children consequently appear more removed
from the adults around them than rural working children.
They remind us how, in settlement areas, it was possible for
very different child lives to take place side by side. While
some children survived precariously in sheds and sod
houses, others played with dolls and wore stylish clothing.

In 1919, Mary Margaret French was a seven-year-old in
Grand Forks, best friends with Bettina Bush, age nine. Their
fathers were physicians, and Dr. French the founder and
dean of the university's medical school. Mary Margaret and
Bettina's games imitated adult domesticity in a special play-
room the little girls had to themselves. Some sixty years
later, Mary Margaret French wrote:

What fun we had playing dolls! Bettina had a regular doll family,
twice as big as mine. Her oldest daughters were twins: Geraldine
and Genevieve, who soon became bosom friends with my oldest,

Dorothy. Then there were Dearie and Hazel (they were big dolls), and Blanche and Bluedy, and Betty and Reddie, and Sammy, and the baby Dottie Dimple. Always at Bettina's house there was a special room for dolls, which could be arranged just as we wanted it and left that way. Bettina and I were sisters, devoted mothers, who delighted in our brilliant and adorable children and worried about their health and their naughtiness. Bettina wrote stories about her family and had a whole sheaf of typewritten pages. I wrote one, too, in little-girl long-hand, about Emeline and the cow.

When the Bushes moved away, we continued our play for a while in letters. Here is a part of one, signed "Auntie Bet": "My darling sister: You don't know how pleased I was to get your letter, or how the children clapped their hands over the nice little letters from Emmie and Dot. The children miss their cousins so much. We are all fairly well except Sammy who has a heavy cold. I have to wrap him in flannels and smother him with camphor at night, for I fear he may develop croup; he has a slight tendency that way. Bluedy is outdoors nearly all the time roller skating. The children enjoyed Christmas very much. Baby liked it best of all, I believe. She couldn't remember last Christmas, and her eyes were simply starry when she saw the tree. The children had such a fine time marveling over her delight in her stocking. Sammy rather startled me the other day by remarking cheerfully, 'Gosh, I'm hungry.' He certainly is growing fast." [23]

French catches the phrases of middle-class urban parents and dramatizes the separation of children from adult concerns, one that working farm children would not have been likely to experience. Nor would they have had the leisure to mimic work in play.

Martha Gray

Martha Gray was another only child in a medical family, her father a doctor in army posts on the upper Missouri River between 1866 and 1870. In her old age she told stories to the small grandson of a cousin about what it had been like to be a little girl on army posts. It may be that to please the little boy she overemphasized somewhat the pleasanter details of her babyhood; nevertheless, she describes a life that conforms to the period's upper-middle-class suburban norms, one that did its best to translate them however awkwardly to the exigencies of a frontier post. Martha was about two and a half in 1867 when the family was at Fort Buford, North Dakota.

I was lying on a bed in our big tent under a mosquito net and the heat and glare of the midsummer was intense. My mother was fanning me and coaxing me to sleep. . . . Another time, at night in the same tent, I was in my mother's lap. A shaded candle was lighted and she held me under the hooded waterproof cape she was wearing to protect me from the cloud of mosquitoes. There was great confusion outside, and the endless beat of Indian drums came to my ears from behind the stockade. My father in his shirtsleeves kept coming at intervals to soothe my mother's crying, telling her he did not think there was any real danger of attack, that he had several wounded men just brought in and must be at the hospital.[24]

Social class and her parents' affections protected Martha from mosquitoes, from her mother's fears, from possibly attacking Indians, and also, one can assume, from questioning the existence of army posts at all. At the next, Fort Stevenson, Martha again was spared some of the rigors of post living: "The new fort was a mere aggregation of tents at the time, but the boats were beginning to bring materials and civilian workmen for the permanent post. We lived in a comfortable hospital tent with a wooden floor. My father unpacked his box of books (without which he never changed posts), my mother her linen and silver and they settled in."[25] Normalcy, at least an approximation of residential living, denotes her safety.

"The Childhood" is the name Richard Coe gives to a literary genre that he has defined as "an extended piece of writing, a conscious deliberately executed literary artifact, usually in prose . . . but not excluding occasional experiments in verse, in which the most substantial portion of the material is directly autobiographical, and whose structure reflects step by step the development of the writer's self; beginning often, but not invariably, with the attainment of a precise degree of maturity."[26] This narrative moves from unawareness to awareness and stops when the child the narrator remembers has turned into the adult the writer knows him or herself to be. The child who is the subject of The Childhood, Coe maintains, "is as alien to the adult writer as to the adult reader. The child sees differently, reasons differently, reacts differently," and inhabits what Coe calls an "alternative" world.

While neither Mary Gray Wales nor other writers included in my study are as self-conscious or as self-aware as the professional writers Coe refers to, his analysis of this narrative of childhood can be useful in reading informal letters and reminiscences. Coe's observations about adult alienation from childhood may help to explain, for instance, Mary Gray Wales's manner of backing off into generalization and even sentimentality in the midst of certain memories. Thus using an abstract and passive voice, she says she "became conscious of the landscape" at an early age. Describing a drive with her parents onto the prairie in a light spring wagon to see prairie flowers, she personifies the flowers, and speaks about herself as though she were a passive observer: "It was a beautiful morning after just the right amount of rain. The short grass had grown green and the lovely little things were holding up their heads. I was jumped down from the wagon and stood looking at them. I recall blue and yellow flowers, but no red ones." Next, the family "drove to an Indian agency at Fort Berthold, perhaps to see a sick person. There was quite a collection of tipis, women, and children with their little bows and clay toys, and the women held up eggs to sell. I began to learn Indian names. I used a sort of chant: 'Minnerconjou, Brule, Black Feet, Uncpapa, Mandan, Arikaras. But Arikara are best.'" She abstracts and transforms into landscape, into a "view" for the eye's aesthetic contemplation, what she remembers experiencing.

Indians, in Martha Gray Wales's descriptions, are mainly decorations on the landscape or menacing forces for non-Indians to contend with. She seldom described individual Indian persons. Indians attacked some soldiers cutting wood on a river bottom: "I remember the excitement of everyone from the post rushing to the plateau and hearing the firing of the mortar." The event was a spectacle; she did not, apparently, wonder whether anyone had been hurt, nor why Indians objected to the soldiers' woodcutting. Even when she tries to praise, she sounds rather at a distance: "The little clay figures of animals made by the Indians, one in particular, a beautifully modeled buffalo, I remember." [27] A boat arrived in the spring—"our main link with civilization"—and Christmas parcels included a wax doll for her. "Through Tonak Mary [a woman from Fort Berthold whom her mother had hired to do housework] the Indians heard of my doll, and often while playing with it on the floor, the windows would be darkened, and I would look up to see dark faces peering in to look at 'Waxy,' as I called her. My father was offered buffalo skins, beaver pelts, and other valuable things for it, but I was never asked to make that sacrifice." In the writing, Indian culture is in opposition to "civilization," and Indian personality masked behind "dark faces"—yet one is not certain how much of this language repeats general prejudices of the time, or to what extent it accurately reflects her own feelings.

The Grays' years on posts along the Missouri came just before major battles broke out between Indians and army troops. Her father took Martha to Yankton so she could see some of the Indian chiefs with whom the United States ostensibly was carrying out negotiations: "I remember some of them—Spotted Tail, Red Cloud, American Horse and Sitting Bull. My father was anxious to have me see these famous men and often drove my mother and me over with him. We used to have photographs of them taken as they sat outside the agency building and I felt sorry for them as they looked as though they felt it an indignity." [28] A few Indians might represent famous relics, but Indians in general produced fear, making Martha Gray wonder whether, after all, she was as safe as she wanted to think she was. She writes of having read a journal entry of General de Trobriand:

"'Only their tribal quarrels and jealousies saved the lives of the stockaded garrison of the upper Missouri.'" She added, "I must have absorbed some of this feeling for I carried the fear of Indians deep in my consciousness for a long time after leaving Dakota."[29] On hearing of Custer's fate: "I remember standing perfectly still and the blood pounding in my ears. It was almost as bad two years later when I was a big girl of fourteen at Fort Riley, Kansas." On that occasion she heard of the death during General Mackenzie's campaigns of a lieutenant who "used to play with me in Texas and taught me to waltz." Although direct hostility does not appear in her mention of Indians, Martha Gray Wales does seem to assume that in a violent episode they are the enemy, and the ones at fault:

I remember an Indian boy who was found near the post nearly dead from eating poisoned meat thrown out for the wolves. He was cared for at the hospital, but that was too rapidly filling with our men, so my father brought him home and made a bed for him in the lean-to and said, "We will keep him until he is able to go back to the agency, and he can help get the wood and water in." Idle words as it proved in the end. My mother had made a lemon pie for next day's dinner and left it in the kitchen for over night. Next morning, no John with the wood. He had vanished along with the filling of the lemon pie scooped out by hand.

The consciousness of childhood is replete, certainly, with images of safety—our parents' laps, the streets, the houses, and special refuges in them we remember. For Martha Gray the protection given childhood had its military applications:

I had a room of my own [at Fort Sully], and was promoted to a half-past seven bedtime, and by eight I was just settling down to sleep when 'Tat-too' sounded. It was a pleasant cheerful call and made one feel safe and cozy thinking of the soldiers gathering in their barracks and the big gates being shut for the night. . . . If I waked in the night the Sentry's call, "Number 1, twelve o'clock and all is well," or whatever the time was, kept me from feeling too lonely in my own room. Number 1 was the sentry post near our house.

In emergencies, it was the small safeties she remembered. Once crossing what the Grays thought was a frozen river on the way to Yankton Martha fell out of the wagon and through the ice into shallow water on a sandbar: "I remember perfectly thinking 'Papa will find me, I must be still.'" (He did, and hauled her to shore.) "My father wrapped me in his coat and we drove home where I was wrapped in hot blankets and was soon myself again."[30] Her memoir closes with a description of "the remarkable fortress of Ft. Wood" in New York harbor, her father's last post: "It was built in the nineteenth century and is still preserved by the government as a perfect example of medieval defense engineering. Its little inner parade ground now holds the Statue of Liberty. I came into my fairy story age while living myself in a castle with moat and drawbridge, port-cullis and parapet, and I always imagined the princes and princesses living just there." She has indeed narrated her life like a fairy tale, herself the princess rescued often by her father and reassured by the bugler.

Martha Gray's four years on the upper Missouri River, which could not have been greatly different from what it was to live in New York harbor, suggest how successfully some parents could maintain upper-middle-class habits on the frontier. It took a little longer—Christmas mails arrived in the spring—but the Gray's time in Dakota was an adventure with an end in sight, in contrast to the years other people spent, unable to leave once they had arrived on the frontier. The habits of a social class, and her parents' relative wealth as well as their watchful and affectionate natures, made Martha Gray's infancy on Missouri River army posts little different from the increasingly protective idealization of childhood in upper-middle-class urban America in the late nineteenth century.

3

Schooling Mostly Meant Doing Without

For many settlement children, school, not play, was the opposite of work, but for most, work was more taken for granted than school. Children who were too young to work might be sent to school (possibly with the added advantage of having them out of the way). Children who were sickly or not "handy" also might not be begrudged schooling. Some, at their own insistence, persevered through the grades of the one-room schoolhouse and went on to high school, boarding in town and working to pay their way in what sound like heroic efforts. For the very few, higher education in emerging colleges and universities offered escape from rural living altogether (and still does).

Some ambitious children, if their hopes were thwarted—who dreamed, they said, of going to college, entering professions, and seeking their fortunes in cities away from North Dakota—turned to teaching school, sometimes before they themselves had finished high school. Teaching, a way to help a family through financial hard times, was often looked upon as a stopgap, a deferring of ambition until better times. But for the most part, according to those who wrote about being pupils, or teachers, or both, school did not seem to suggest an intellectual experience one might associate with education. What school seems mainly to have represented was relief from work, the company of other children, and some attention from well-meaning if often harried teachers with little education or training. Carrying water, stoking stoves, baking potatoes in the stove, playing games in the schoolyard, these images suggest that children are remembering a little leisure and feeling of being looked after. Ethnic groups differed as to enthusiasm for education. Norwegians and others of Scandinavian heritage generally were known to favor schooling. Germans from Russia were reluctant to have their children spend the day speaking English. They thought schools alienated children from work, from the German language, and from the home family and culture generally.

The story of Hazel Miner, the "Angel of the Prairies," has become a myth in North Dakota expressing both personal sorrow and a community's ambivalent responses to schooling as well as the entire settlement experience. Deaths of children call into question the great experiment in migration. According to the *Children's Home Finder* (the publication of an orphanage in Fargo) for January 15, 1921, Hazel (age sixteen) and her younger brother and sister had been on their way home from the consolidated school near Center, North Dakota, in mid-March of 1920. The buggy overturned, and the children were unable to right it. It was very cold. Hazel put the children (aged nine and eleven) "in the shelter of the upturned sleigh" and covered them with her own coat. As the *Home Finder* described the scene: "The fierce wind blew the blankets and clothing off the children, and in trying to protect them she lay down partly on top and partly on the side of them, and with her benumbed hands tried to hold the blankets over them." The horse, still attached to the traces, did not move. Hazel died, and the children were found the next afternoon. The *Home Finder* finds an illustrative moral: "Hazel Miner, this guardian angel of the prairies, covered with a thick sheet of ice, gave up her own life to save her brother and sister. Such are the simple annals of a plain young girl from a prairie homestead, who freely gave her life for others. How like the Christ, who died to save lost mankind." Then follows an appeal for the organization of "Hazel Miner Circles," whereby schoolchildren could give money toward the orphanage building fund. (The sadness of it all: children whose own voyages to and from school were every bit as precarious as the Miner children's being asked for money to benefit other children whom nobody much wanted.)

And yet there are additional slightly different versions of this episode (as well as other accounts of the same storm).[1] According to the local newspaper, the *Center Republican*, someone said the horses were going in the wrong direction; the children's father had come to the school in another buggy and told the children to wait while he went into the school before starting home. They did not wait: there is the question of whether the horse bolted or the children disobeyed their father. (The horse was reputed to be very gentle.) The brother, then nine years old (he died only recently), said in an interview that the two younger children had begged Hazel to get under the blanket with them and she refused. Hazel had taught Sunday school and was admired by younger children—did she have Christian martyrdom on her mind? A woman said that she had been four years old when the children were brought to her family's house once they were found. She remembered Hazel's outstretched, frozen arm scraping along a curtain when they brought her in the front room. There was talk, according to one contemporary news account, of establishing a memorial fund to build a hospital in Center; later the family decided they preferred a large engraved stone.

The anguish of the family, indeed of a whole community, is more than enough to account for Hazel Miner's being memorialized (there are at least two local ballads about her death). But the myths that have evolved, which are less about Hazel than about wanting to believe in an Angel of the Prairies, surely evoke complex and ambivalent feelings about children sacrificed to a venture that was supposed to be on their behalf.

But of course not all children attending rural schools were at such risk as the Miner children. Hazel Satterthwaite Evans has written about the same storm of 1920, when she was attending country school in Mountrail County with seven other children between the ages of six and nine. Margaret Weidert was teacher. As part of her duties she "carried the lignite coal [a soft surface coal abundant in western North Dakota] from the coal shed on the north end of the school-house, along the west side of the school, in the door on the south and then the length of the school house back to the northwest corner where the furnace-like stove was located." The account Hazel Evans gives of the storm as she remembered it shows that some parents and teachers took sensible and courageous precautions to protect children who traveled some miles to school—even though the physical conditions of the school might necessitate the teacher's hauling fuel in so inconvenient a manner as confronted Mrs. Weidert:

The morning of March 16, 1920, was cloudy and snowy, so my father, Ben Satterthwaite, took us three girls to school on horse-back. He and Ruth, age six, rode on Teddy and Esther and I rode on Brewster. By late forenoon a strong wind was driving a heavy snowfall from the southeast with rapidly falling temperature. Mrs. Weidert began carrying coal from the coal shed into the school house and piling it behind the stove. She intended to get enough in so she wouldn't have to replenish the coal supply during the night as she was intending to keep us school children in the school house overnight [teachers routinely were advised to be prepared to do so in case of a storm]. In mid-afternoon, the fathers of the three families arrived at the school house at about the same time, and there were no telephones in those days. They decided to load the bundled up pupils and teacher into Mrs. Weidert's sled, cover them with blankets and take them to the Uran home to the northwest of the school. Mr. Curren returned to his home. Mr. Satterthwaite went with Mr. Uran. One of the men walked ahead of the team and followed the fence line while the other drove. By doing this they arrived safely at the Uran home without getting lost or turning over. The teacher and pupils then spent the night at the Uran home. Mr. Satterthwaite returned home to the east of the Urans by letting his saddle horse take him there. This was the same storm in which Hazel Miner lost her life while saving her brother and sister near Center as they attempted to return home from school that same afternoon.[2]

Ben Walsh

Education seems to have fit rather casually into the experience of some rural children (at least before the days of compulsory attendance). Life stories appear to take the turns they do in large part because schooling was so scant. School was a brief interlude for so many; if education might have made a difference no one will know because few had that choice.

In 1980, Ben Walsh, of Courtenay, North Dakota, wrote an essay, "I Attended a Country School." Walsh is appreciative of efforts made on behalf of the earliest children to live in rural plains regions, but he recognized limitations:

A comedian once defined a country school as a building built for the purpose of depriving a child of an education. While I concede that there is much truth in this glib statement, I cannot agree with it in its entirety. I clearly recognize the disadvantages and shortcomings of such a school, yet it also had its positive side. Let me tell you about such a school I once attended as a small boy not long after the turn of the century, when Teddy Roosevelt was in the White House and Babe Ruth was in short pants.[3]

Walsh describes the building: three windows on a side, outdoor toilets and a barn behind, classroom and cloakroom at the entrance, with a shelf for drinking water. "Beside the pail, on the same shelf, stood a wash basin, but to my knowledge it was never used."

Walsh's eye is more critical than most:

In my memory they still exist—the big stove in the center of the room that kept us warm (at least on one side) during the long winter months; the bell, the broom, the books, the battered globe, and the coal scuttle piled high with lignite. There were the desks, little ones for the little kids, big ones for the big pupils, bearing the carved initials of boys long since men. They were perhaps more skilled with the knife than with the pen. They had left their mark before going forth to carve their way in the world, helped perhaps, by the smattering of education they acquired in that humble building.

Children carried noon lunches of bread and syrup in syrup pails. Smells distinguished school houses, and the seasons: the smell of rodents nesting under the building in warm weather; in winter "the permanent smell of coal dust, coal smoke, food and feet"; the barnyard smells from children who had done morning chores before school. An incongruous detail, he found, was the presence of books: "Along one end of the room was a small library. Yes, a library in a country school shortly after the turn of the century! It was put there through the efforts of some long-forgotten teacher who had tried (and failed) to bring a little of the outside world into our lives. Like the wash basin in the entrance, I never saw it used." Children from the house nearest the school brought water in an open pail, but in cold weather that would freeze: "Therefore, during the winter months there was no water carried, and the pupils simply went without—something they were used to doing many times, and in many ways, during their young lives." The limits, not the expansion of opportunities is the prevailing sense of these recollections.

Walsh describes sympathetically the lot of farm children: "They were born into hard work and hardship. . . . They learned, while still very young, that what they wanted they must first earn, or do without," and while they gained much from the experience of classroom and playground about how to get along with others, "they were destined," Walsh says, "never to have an education." Education was not valued in their time and place; work was what was important, and education merely a distraction from work:

These young people were being raised in an era and a locale where complete indifference prevailed toward education by parents. Children old enough to work were allowed to go to school only after the farm work was done for the season. After the last bundle was threshed, and the last furrow turned, they could go to school, if they so desired. In most cases the young boy or girl wished to go, not that he or she valued education any more than the parents, but because the pupil wished to join in the fun and games at school.

Even in winter they knew they must do the farm chores before and after school—or they could stay home, no one cared.

Ben Walsh's parents did believe in education, however, and his father served on the school board, readied the schoolhouse when a term was to start, and "would hitch his driving mare to the buggy and drive around the neighborhood spreading the sad tidings that school would open next Monday morning." But this also would be threshing season, when parents were not willing to loose their children's labor. "School was for lazy people. As a result many an irate mother poured forth her wrath (sometimes in a strange and foreign tongue) upon this meddlesome neighbor who was forever trying to educate her children." Only children too young to work were willingly sent off. As to school attendance laws, Walsh says, "they didn't penetrate the farming communities."

Teachers appeared no more promising than the buildings or parental attitudes. They were usually young single women, Walsh observed, teaching in country school either to move onto something better or because they could find no better job or were looking "for romance and adventure and often found it." A teacher's contribution to the community tended to be less intellectual than social: she could count on high status and popularity at dances, basket socials, and other events ("Many a humble farm hand paid what amounted to nearly a month's wages for the fleeting pleasure of eating supper with the school marm"), but low wages accompanied scant education, and her effectiveness as a teacher was judged, Walsh writes, by the gifts she gave at the Christmas program. "On that night the teacher who passed out the biggest sacks of candy, the largest oranges, and the reddest apples was judged the best teacher. . . . Her chances of being rehired often depended upon her generosity that night."

Yet Ben Walsh concludes fairmindedly that for all their shortcomings, country schools, "should be viewed with the reverence and respect that they deserve. It was these humble little buildings, scattered over the desolate prairies, that brought the first gleam of enlightenment to the child of the isolated farms of a half century ago." Meager as the education they offered was, it gave a child "a better chance of success than had he not attended school at all." Finally, Ben Walsh allows himself for a moment the pleasure of nostalgia: "Many a senior citizen today [he was writing in 1980], as he sits alone with his thoughts and watches the jet age world speed by, may think of the slower and quieter life of his youth. And perhaps, if his memory serves him well that day, he may see, once again, through the mists and shadows of time, the shabby little building where he first learned to read, and for a moment he is a boy again."

Gabriel Lundy

Almost anything more than a few scattered months of rural school could signify an energetic "pursuit" of education. A pursuit could hardly have been more strenuous and unremitting than that of Gabriel Lundy, who in 1953 retired as head of the Department of Agricultural Economics at South Dakota State College in Brookings, where he had begun to teach in 1926. Gabriel Lundy was born in 1886 on a farm six miles from Parker, South Dakota, his parents having immigrated from Norway. Four years later they returned to Norway with the four youngest children, leaving two older boys in the United States. "However, some time before 1895," the autobiographer writes, "Mrs. Lundy, unfortunately, was left alone with their indebted farm and the children."[4] The mother paid farm debts and returned to the United States to her brother in Niagara, North Dakota (near Grand Forks). She homesteaded eighty acres, gradually acquiring more land in partnership with her older sons.

For Gabriel, prospects were not promising, as he laconically reports: "Gabriel [he writes about himself in the third person] became the employee of a Norwegian tenant farmer, who did not see any benefit in sending his kid employee to the public school. But he did supply him with a couple of blankets for sleeping on the hard and cold kitchen floor." In the summer he did carpentry work and took a correspondence course in building construction, the beginning of a strenuous academic career. "But an intense desire to read and study in school induced him to attend the public school in Petersburg, North Dakota, two short winters," during which he supported himself with janitorial work. His fourth grade teacher, Grace Wheeler, encouraged this seventeen-year-old pupil and advanced him to the sixth grade, but that year he managed only forty-seven days of school and never reached high school.

However, he did not give up. In 1906, at age twenty, he enrolled in the subpreparatory class at the agricultural college in Fargo, again supporting himself as janitor. After three years, he transferred to the university in Grand Forks, where his mother bought a house nearby. He studied German and Norwegian and took extra courses at the Model High School. After two more years of janitorial work, he graduated in 1914 and accepted a teaching position at South Dakota Normal in Spearfish. The next year he went to graduate school at the University of Wisconsin in Madison, achieving an M.S. degree in agricultural economics in 1917. The same year he was married to Asta Mathilda Mikkelson, who also had been a student both at Fargo and in Madison. Asta was twenty-four years old; her parents also farmed.

After a year in the army in France (1918–19) Gabriel Lundy joined Asta's brother in banking in Warwick, North Dakota, but the bank failed, and in 1926, after a refresher course in economics at the University of Minnesota, he returned to teaching, accepting the position at Brookings. Gabriel Lundy reviewed his life with equanimity:

Looking back over life as a whole, Gabriel Lundy can say: With enjoyable family relationships, satisfactory employment, friends and informative reading matter life has been interesting. Quite early in life Gabriel Lundy was anxious to read a lot on various subjects, and not very many years after his Lutheran confirmation his ideas changed which led him to join the Unitarian Church in Boston. Eventually he joined the Unitarian group in Brookings, South Dakota.

We can only imagine how his life may have differed had he resigned himself to the farmer who gave him a blanket to sleep on but kept him away from school. A kindly rural schoolteacher, the availability of janitor work, the existence of "sub-preparatory" programs that assumed college students would not have had high school educations, no doubt the encouragement of other instructors along the way— these made Gabriel Lundy's own doggedness "to read a lot on various subjects" eventually bear fruit. Yet he did so by rejecting not only the Lutheran Church, but also the work-centered agricultural life to which he appeared destined.

Ellen Dute

The effect of rural schooling was complex. Children of the very first settlers were not likely to have school at all unless their mother or a close neighbor taught them in their home. Once state schools were established, they might only be in session three or four months, between seasons of farm work and excluding months of the worst winter weather. For some children, whatever time they managed in school was more than they would have experienced without the rural schools, however rudimentary their facilities and the teacher's abilities. It was a respite from unremitting work at home. For other children rural schooling was memorable mostly for its limitations. Education has been the way to leave a rural setting; a rural education alone prepared one, however, only for teaching in rural schools, in a sort of self-perpetuating cycle. Ellen Dute, who taught for many years in the Grand Forks schools, began her teaching career in rural schools and before that attended rural schools herself. She describes those two early school experiences and appears to accept the hardships of both fairly uncritically. Her story begins with the hardships of her parents before she was born:

My mother must have known what marriage was like, for from the time she was eight, she frequently was hired for some days after a woman had given birth to a baby. The money was given to her parents. Later her parents built quite a good sized house, but my mother did not long live there. I was born in a tar shanty in Union Township, Grand Forks County. I was the fourth child in the family, two sisters and a brother. The home had three rooms, a kitchen, livingroom, and a bedroom, which eventually had three double beds, for before we moved from this place two more children were born, my sister Rose was a year younger, and a little brother. Sometimes during the winter, the kitchen was closed to save fuel, and we lived in two rooms.

Her growing up included illness and deaths of siblings, the heartbreaks of poor health in rural areas:

When my little brother was seven months, we came down with scarlet fever. I remember taking sick, crawling into bed, turning my face to the wall, and wanting to be left alone. Two of my sisters also took sick, and my little brother, who died. My memory records the part of the funeral. When a man who I thought had a very ugly face picked up the small casket in which the baby brother lay, and I wondered that my parents permitted that man to carry the baby away.

As they appear to have for many, Ellen Dute's school memories are mainly of physical hardships and humiliations, a casual stop to going to school altogether, and kind but hardly experienced teachers. School was an interlude to farm work:

I started school one fall, but recall nothing of those first few months; we lived two miles from the school but shortened the distance by going cross the field. A heavy snow came one day and the north wind was cold. My older sister walked ahead of me. We had not gone far when my garter loosened and the stocking came down. My sister trudged ahead but would not stop to help me with my garter, and either I feared to be left behind or my hands were too cold to fasten the garter. I cried all the way home. After that my mother kept me home from school. The next fall my sister, Rose and I started school together. In spite of short terms and later when

I often stayed out, at first to herd cattle and in the spring to help in the fields. I loved school, and though the teacher was but a high school graduate, plus some preparation for teaching, she was a good teacher, for both of us were passed into the second grade before the school year was over, so that we finished the eight grades in seven years. We had to pass state examinations in order to graduate.

When we finished I thought my school days were over, and for a number of years, spring, summer, fall found me working the fields. We had no tractors in those days, and so I drove horses, four for many implements but five for plowing. I froze in the spring and the late fall, and suffered the heat of summer. The implements I handled were the plow, the drag and the disk. One summer I cultivated corn, cut hay and raked it. In harvesting I ran the binder and in emergency the corn binder. In cold weather, when plowing, I walked all day behind the plow in order to keep warm, for North Dakota late fall days are cold and windy.

She does not explain how it happened that her parents "sent [her] to school to prepare for teaching," but so it was, and she became a teacher in a school not very different from the one she had herself attended:

About the time of World War One, North Dakota passed a law that all children must pass the eighth grade or remain in school to their sixteenth year. Whether these were the conditions which meant a shortage of teachers, I do not know, but Valley City Normal devised a course of 10 1/2 months for country school teachers. In the fall of 1916 my parents sent me to school to prepare for teaching. It was during my attendance there that the U. S. entered World War One. The course was an intensive course of all we needed to teach in country school teaching, plus methods of teaching this. At any rate my first grade learned to read before they moved into the second grade. And we taught the alphabet and phonics.

Teachers' accounts, like Dute's, frequently tell at length about difficult travel by train, wagon, and foot; complicated but ill-defined arrangements with boards and superintendents; and the work of making schoolhouses habitable. Few that I find mention studies or actual teaching:

My first school was near Gackle. I went by train as far as Jamestown where I stayed overnight and Sunday my cousins who had a car took me to the school, a distance of 40 miles. The County Superintendent had hired me, and when I arrived in September no one knew that school was to begin. I got in touch with the school board and some of the parents to let them know school was to begin. Board members cleaned the school house Monday so the school did not meet on Monday. This was a German-Russian community, first generation immigrants. The schoolterm was seven months. In the homes were no English books, foreign language was spoken in the home. For this reason school progress was slow. I recall being warned about the kind of books which could be used since the only English books in the homes was the Sears Roebuck Catalogue, which to these poor, somewhat isolated children, was truly a "wish book."

This beginning introduced me into a situation no inexperienced teacher should have to deal with. The building was small with seats which could accommodate thirty-four children, but thirty-seven appeared. This was because though one family who sent five children to this school belonged to another district, but sent their children to this school because their school was situated farther from their home. What to do with the extra three was the problem. Every country school had what was known as a recitation bench, a long bench. Three of the children used that and when writing was required, they knelt on the floor using the seat for a desk. Children came from foreign speaking homes. This meant they needed to learn the language in order to learn to read. I was amazed at how quickly these six-year-olds learned to speak English.

There were no screens on the windows, so the flies were drawn by the children's lunches, always carried in empty syrup pails. There were rough youngsters who knew rough discipline at home, and keeping the school so that the children could study was a problem. About a month after school started the superintendent came to call and she told the children in no uncertain terms that those belonging to another district must attend their own school. Apparently the parents felt her authority for the children no longer attended.

A country school teacher was her own janitor, keeping the school clean and building the fire, carrying out the ashes, bringing in the coal, and often chopping the wooden logs so that they would go into the stove. Since the fire never held through the night, the teacher went early so that the school might be warm when the children arrived. As the nights grew colder, the flies which were on the ceiling and walls were very cold. Once a good fire was burning, I would sweep down the flies and throw them by the shovel into the blazing fire.

The teachers who had no degree were forced to spend a week at a center for lectures on teaching. The board had promised to paint the school during that week and they did. But November was bitterly cold. The board had burned all the prepared wood so I began chopping new wood. But worse than that, the desks were scattered over the school yard, some in the barn. Those outside were frozen to the ground and I used an ax to loosen them. All the children's books were thrown in a corner of the school. By the time the children arrived, the place was warm and the desks in their place. However, they had to sort out their own belongings. My salary was $65 a month.

The dreary part was the weekends. On Saturday as Seventh Adventists, they spent the entire day in church, and I was left to myself. Then Sunday, they seemed to work as vigorously as any other day. I never knew which I dreaded more, the beginning of the week and the burden of that school, or the long lonely weekend.

A second time illness and death at home interrupted, and Ellen exchanged teaching for nursing:

Shortly after Christmas or perhaps before Christmas, sister Clara came down with scarlet fever. Right after the New Year, my sister Ethel came down with scarlet fever as well, as [did] my mother and my sister Esther. Ethel became sick on a Wednesday and by Saturday afternoon she died. The doctor said that the illness had gone to her kidneys and this was the reason for her death. We were quaranteed and this meant I could in no way return to teaching, so I sent in my resignation. In the meantime we had instituted certain measures to keep those still well from being exposed. For instance, Ed never took care of those who were sick. The dishes for the sick were isolated. Beds were brought down and placed in the living room. We had no indoor plumbing, so that all water had to brought in from the outside and all slops carried out. We were fortunate to have a cistern for rain water under the dining room, so that soft water need not be brought in. Since both Rose and I were immune to the disease and so apparently was my father, we three divided the night watches among ourselves; Rose stayed up until midnight; then Dad watched until 4 AM when I took charge.

That Saturday when my sister died is graven on my mind. It was bitter cold and lots of snow had fallen. I had gone outside to look for clean snow which seemed to soothe the fevered sick with their sore throats. I got Ethel a spoonful of this and in touching her felt the coldness of death beginning; because of that, I hurried to the kitchen to heat some water. This Ethel took and when I asked whether it felt good, she said "Yes," and that was the last rational word she spoke in my presence, for she seemed to be sinking into a coma. The doctor had been called in the morning, but because of bad roads he did not arrive until about 4 PM. All day I was on edge, perhaps fearing Ethel would die before he arrived. Naturally, her case was so far gone that the doctor paid little attention to her and rather gave his attention to the other sick people. Shortly after his departure, Dad and Ed began to dress to go out to do the chores, and Rose to prepare for supper. I took up my vigil at Ethel's side. In just a short time, I noticed a distinct change in Ethel's breathing. Dad was called who took her pulse, saying she was dying and shortly she breathed her last.

The next fall I began teaching the school attended by my younger sisters and brothers. Early in November I came down with the 1918 flu epidemic. Schools and churches were closed until the first of the year. All but my dad were in bed with the flu on November 11, when the Armistice was signed. My older sister, Lillian, who was in Bismarck in nurses' training, delayed because of flu at the hospital. She was home to take care of us. And Dad, who seemed immune to almost every disease, looked after the chores. The year passed quietly. As usual, I helped in haying and harvest time.

The fall of 1918 I went to teach a country school near Anslem. The year before, three teachers had tried to teach unruly children, but quit, unable to handle the children. In my contract was a stipulation that if I could handle the school, my monthly salary would be increased by $5 a month, from $80 to $85. By now my plans for going on with my education were firmly decided, so that every penny possible was saved and banked. There was tension in the school, primarily caused by five children from a very poor family; the father was known to drink too much, therefore the children were looked down upon by other more respectable children. That may have been one reason the other children looked down upon them. They were the only children who tended to be rebellious. I tried the carrot and stick method and for the most part succeeded in keeping the school in order. But one always needed to be on guard. Therefore, I refused the contract offered to stay another year.

One day during the winter a heavy snow storm developed. I managed to walk to school that morning, but the storm became more violent as the day wore on. The children of but one family dared the weather; the family lived only one half mile from the school and the father brought them. There was little danger of getting lost, since a fence ran along the one side of the road. By noon the father came to get the children and urged me to go with them fearing if I tried the mile and a half, I should be unable to make it. I stayed there over night. The next morning came, clear and cold and I walk[ed] the half mile to school. It was almost impossible to get into the school since the shovel was inside. But I managed and start a brisk fire. Then I went out, first to shovel a path to the school, and then to clean out the two toilets so that entrance was possible and doors could be closed and opened. On returning to the school house, I was startled to see that the stove pipe, which ran the length of the room, was red hot, as a result of the fire. I hurriedly put on the damper so that the red stove and pipe would cool off.

I wish to comment upon my reaction to those children I tried to teach. There were a few I seemed never quite able to win to full co-operation. The loss was theirs and mine. Fortunately, the majority of the children were always with me, and that was as important for discipline as anything I could do. One observation about children: their acceptance and affection toward me gave the pleasure of teaching. Their ability to forgive and forget always impressed me. Would that we adults could be that willing to give affection and trust inspite of our faults.

Ellen Dute did earn enough money to continue her education, at Ripon College in Illinois, working for her board with a family, and in the summer at a golf course restaurant. Although her biographical pages do not continue past these college jobs, college and teaching degrees presumably made possible her teaching eventually in schools in larger towns. But her years as a child and young woman typify connections between attending and teaching in rural schools.

Stephanie Prepiora

Wanda Koskydyn writes a column called "What's Happening in Caldwell" for the *Progress,* of Caldwell, New Jersey. She began the one for November 4, 1982, "On a recent Saturday afternoon, I had a most pleasant surprise. My doorbell rang, and there stood Stephanie Prepiora, who I'm sure many of you remember. Stephanie—also fondly remembered as 'Miss Prep' or just plain 'Prep' to her close friends—had a medical lab behind Bruce Drugs, next door to Grunings for many years." Stephanie Prepiora was in New Jersey on a visit from Minto, North Dakota, where she had grown up and returned to after a long and successful career as laboratory technician and manager. The Caldwell *Progress* columnist accompanied her on a tour of the town, meeting old friends and viewing new buildings. "Our last stop for the day was a must—St. Catherine's Infirmary on the Caldwell College campus—where Prep worked closely with Sister Georgine Marie and Sister Mary Roland. To her delight, they were both there. Everyone had a happy visit." Her clipping file is growing, for in the *Walsh County Historical Society Newsletter* for December 1984 there is a picture of Stephanie standing behind a birthday cake. She was being honored for her service as membership chair of the historical society and curator-manager of the museum in Minto, North Dakota. Such recognition—being the subject of a newspaper feature and receiving tribute for volunteer work —is not restricted to small towns, yet this notice expresses profound social achievement, a ritual of approval and admiration for making the American dream come true after all.

For many, it did not. How it happened that someone from Minto, now (in the late 1980s), in her eighties managed a thriving professional business in the East was thanks in part to her escape (not too strong a term) into education and professional training. Education, more than was accorded her brother and sister, made possible each of her moves. Stephanie's education and experience have marked also her return to Minto in 1971, when she helped develop the Walsh County Historical Museum and found her place in the town again.

Stephanie Prepiora wrote an essay about her parents for a Walsh County, North Dakota, commemorative book. Her parents came, separately, from Poland, lacking, she says, education, money, and knowledge about the United States. Her father, George Przepiora (Stephanie dropped the *z* in the spelling of her own name), "in 1886, at the age of sixteen, crossed the ocean only to be turned back to Europe at Ellis Island because he did not have enough money. . . . Upon his return to Europe he remained in Germany where he worked and saved enough money for a second try. This time he succeeded in meeting all requirements." He worked in coal mines in Scranton, Pennsylvania; at the Carnegie Steel Mills in Pittsburgh; in Michigan iron mines; and as a lumberjack in northern Wisconsin, where he and a friend "first heard of North Dakota and its harvest fields." Arrived in Ardoch in the midst of a hailstorm ("They thought the walls of the box car in which they were riding would collapse"), they walked after the storm to Warsaw, where they were hired in the wheat fields. Her father worked hard under sparse and uncomfortable conditions. Machinery was powered, of course, by horses, which also had to be fed and cared for. He and other men spent much time cutting and hauling wood in the winter. More than a little exasperation enters the narrative of her father's life:

Housing and food and what was required of the "hired man" depended on the humanity of the farmer or his wife or both. There were those who treated him as a member of the family, being allowed to eat with the family and sleep in the house. There were also those who treated him like something less than human. He was allowed to come into the kitchen for his food which was usually inadequate and second rate. Except to eat, he was not allowed to remain in the house but was given a place to sleep in one of the other farm buildings. These buildings had no heat or light and, regardless of cold or blizzard, this was his only refuge. Mr. Przepiora experienced both but did not remain long with the family whose aim seemed to be to exploit him.

George Przepiora soon learned English and passed examinations for naturalization.

Stephanie's mother was Frances Gawlowicz, who came to Warsaw, North Dakota, from Poland in 1895 when she was in her early twenties to be housekeeper to her cousin, Francisek Gawlowicz, priest of St. Stanislaus Church in Warsaw. Frances's mother had died when Frances was seven years old, and she was brought up by other relatives. She came well qualified to be housekeeper to a priest of a thriving parish, Stephanie says, and evidently lent style to the rectory:

Mrs. Przepiora, while still in Poland, had, on her own initiative, learned the art of cooking. Prior to coming to America she was employed by one of the nobility of Poland who entrusted her with the keys to the estate and treated her like a member of the family. She was responsible only for preparing the main meal of the day which included no dish washing or cleaning up. Special help was hired to clean the dishes and pots and pans used in preparing and serving a meal. She was also responsible for all food preparation and service for special social or political functions.

Not long after she arrived in Warsaw her fame as a cook spread throughout the area. She was called upon to cook not only for the Bishop and visiting clergy, but also dinners sponsored by persons seeking political office. When she cooked for political gatherings she would make herself scarce so that the politician's wife would get credit for the excellent food. She served many a wedding breakfast to young couples who traveled distances for the marriage ceremony.

Frances gardened, raised poultry, and kept a cow. She also acquired citizenship. Both parents had filed homesteads in Roseau County, in northwest Minnesota, seven miles from the town of Leo, along the Red River, and after their marriage at St. John's Church, Pisek, on May 23, 1898, they moved to their two 160-acre plots, a wagon trip of three

days. They lived in the wagon until a tarpaper shack was built. Frances and George Przepiora farmed in Minnesota for six years, "acquiring a degree of success through much hard work," then in 1905 bought farm land and moved to North Dakota, near Minto. Stephanie writes that her mother had said "when she walked inside and saw the condition, she wept. There were mounds of hay on the floor which apparently had been used as beds and every kind of rubbish and litter was there. She spent days and weeks of hard work to make the place liveable." Gradually they rented and bought more land, constructed better buildings, "and things generally began to look very hopeful." There were five children; Stephanie is the middle child.

But soon began what Stephanie terms a series of disasters amid these hopes of prosperity. In 1913 four of the children came down with diphtheria, and two died. When prices of farm produce rose during World War I, the Przepioras bought two more farms. By the mid-1920s, land prices and interest rates increased and prices of farm produce declined, and the Przepioras, like others, lost land and suffered further setbacks because of drought and grasshopper plagues. Nevertheless, Stephanie's parents were able eventualy to buy again most of their land and continued to live on the farm. George died in 1949 at age seventy-nine, and Frances in 1956 at eighty-three. Their son Frank kept up the farm until his death in 1982.

Except for their mother's distinctive cooking, the children's lives on the Minto farm were probably fairly typical for families in similar situations:

My sister and I each got one doll. We were not over-indulged with toys and play gadgets of every description as we used our imaginations and improvised. We made our own doll house, buggies, etc. out of paper which became very real to us and we loved them; we never much asked for store-bought toys. My brother being a boy was given skis, skates, a bicycle. Only boys were given those things, not girls. Quite early in life we became aware that there was not an abundance of money and that there were things we could not have which we accepted as a fact of life. We were thrilled on Christmas morning if our stocking had an orange and some nuts and perhaps a surprise package with some practical wearing apparel. This on top of the wonderful foods which my mother made; she was an excellent cook, added up to a perfect holiday. My parents preserved some of the Christmas customs of Poland.

Farm children worked hard, for the farm operation was diversified and included a variety of animals as well as crops. Stephanie was expected to herd cattle:

What a bore waiting for a cow to fill its enormous stomach; even the dog who came with me would get bored and run home. As we grew older more work was required of us, as was of all farm children. We milked the cows, helped clean the barn and chicken coop, fed animals and poultry, bailed and stacked hay, shocked grain, helped with the plowing, helped with housework and cooking. When the family bought a threshing machine my sister and I worked in the cook car—hours from 4 AM till 10 PM if you were finished. It meant three large meals and two substantial lunches—the lunches consisted of meat sandwiches and a sweet as cake or doughnuts. We baked bread, cakes, pies, and cookies daily, and did the wash; we dug potatoes, carrots for meals, picked peas, tomatoes and all the vegetables used for meals, brought in wood for the stove and all water used. Threshing would go on for many days and sometimes if a rainy spell came it could last for many weeks.

But her memories are not entirely of boredom and drudgery: "We loved the spring when new colts and calves arrived. How we would pet them and spoil them. I especially loved the colts. There were baby chicks, turkeys, ducks and geese all requiring work but it was a work of love and all pleasures."

She described her country schooling, benign, if not intellectually progressive:

We walked 3/4 of a mile to school except in bad weather when Dad drove us. It was a one-room one-teacher all grades school, a real mixture of ethnic groups. Three families were Irish, two Czech, one

German and one Polish. We were the youngest and smallest of the group and were often picked on because of that. Teachers changed yearly, some good, others not caring. Some had a real discipline problem with the 17- and 18-year-old boys who came to school when the farm work was done. We had no play equipment on the school ground but we chose teams and played base ball, steal chips, tag, drop the handkerchief, ante ante over, and many other games.

In an essay written in 1976, Stephanie described teachers:

Teachers came in all shades and varieties. There was always a new teacher every year which one had to adjust to. Some were good, some were mediocre and one was especially cruel. She was so cruel in fact that no matter how well you knew your lesson, everything left you when called upon to recite. I was so afraid of her I cried every morning when I had to go to school. My first year at school was very pleasant. We had a lovely, kind teacher and because I was the smallest in the school, she mothered me, often hugging me and giving me an occasional kiss. This embarrassed me very much because the bigger kids teased me. For the most part, the teachers were on a man hunt. They were more intent on getting a man than imparting any knowledge onto us.[5]

Stephanie Prepiora's life came to differ from her parents' and from her brother and sister's. Frances and George Przepiora were marked by "hard work." Hard work brought them the success and prosperity they sought, and hard work marked the home life of their children, Stephanie included. But she challenged her parents by insisting upon attending school after the eighth grade:

Very few went to high school for a number of reasons. Children would have to live with a family in town and most farmers couldn't afford to pay for the board and room or for the room with cooking privileges. Many were needed to help with farm operations and there were those who did not care to go. In addition, it was commonly thought in those days that men, if possible, should get the education—that women did not need it because they would only get married anyway. Many a girl was denied an education because of that kind of thinking. I would not be denied a high school education and raised such a fuss and storm that the folks finally gave in much to the annoyance of some of their friends. That was the cornerstone of my future.

That future led, fifty years later, to the medical laboratory Stephanie Prepiora organized and directed in Caldwell, New Jersey—the subject of the *Progress* columnist's article—but it took some years to achieve. At the high school in Minto, Stephanie majored in pedagogy. "With an emphasis on Pedagogy," she wrote, "one was eligible to teach in a country school upon graduation [in 1922], which is what I did. Few went on to college, and especially few women. It was not deemed necessary then for a woman to have a higher education. So unless one turned to school teaching, there was not much else for a girl to do except perhaps to get married." For the next four years, she taught at three different country schools in Walsh County. The first had a dozen pupils, the second twenty, and the third "up to forty-five pupils in the winter months when the older children were no longer needed at home to help with the farming." Language had crucial importance in the schools: "This was a Czech community where Czech, for the most part, was spoken in the home, and children learned English when they came to school and soon were bilingual. I too was born of immigrant parents (Polish) and have been bilingual all my life."

She enjoyed the teaching—the children were not difficult to get along with, and the town friendly with house parties and dances. But, "Walking to and from school I would often wonder what lay beyond the horizon and the circumscribed world I knew." She began penetrating that horizon by enrolling at the Kahler School of Nursing in Rochester, Minnesota (affiliated with the Mayo Clinic), because "nursing sounded humanitarian and interesting." That led to the Chicago Lying In Hospital for training in obstetrics and pediatrics, services not then available at Mayo's. The hospital was in the poor, black, and crime-ridden section of South Chicago, where, Stephanie claims, her farm upbringing served her well: "At the dispensary a doctor, an intern and a nurse went to the slum districts (mostly Black) to deliver babies at home. The conditions where these people lived are indescribable—the poverty—many people living in two or three rooms. It would take a book to describe it all. After the baby was born, the nurse had to make a call there for eleven days to take care of the mother and baby and to instruct the mother in the care of the baby."

Stephanie was not daunted by South Chicago: "Having come from a farm I had no fears of traveling alone in these areas or in going into the hovels where these people lived. I simply assumed that all people were good." She graduated in 1929 and was employed by the Mayo Clinic to give radium treatments, then spent several years in private nursing in Milwaukee. After two more years of training in X-ray and laboratory work, with two other women she started a school lab in Utica, New York, to train students as technicians, but the partnership did not work out, and in 1936 Stephanie went to work for a doctor in Caldwell, New Jersey. "Here I set up a complete laboratory, learned electrocardiography, took x-rays, worked in the office during office hours, helped in deliveries and surgery, and did nursing. It was a well rounded experience working with a top notch physician and other doctors who acted as his assistants." And she "saw everything that New York's Broadway had to offer."

But four years were enough, and she next accepted a position with the Merck Chemical Company of Rahway, New Jersey, to set up a laboratory in their employees' clinic. After six years there, she joined a two-year research project on anemia in pregnancy conducted by White Laboratories of Newark and then worked for two years at the Medical Center in Jersey City. While she held these laboratory positions, Stephanie attended night classes, first at Columbia University and then at Seton Hall University in South Orange, New Jersey, where she graduated with a B.S. in biochemistry in 1949. The following year she studied at Cornell with Dr. Papinacleau of pap-smear fame. It had taken her five and a half years to complete the degree. Her next venture, in 1950, took place again in Caldwell, establishing her private medical laboratory:

I remember going to Newark to register the title of the lab: Caldwell Medical Laboratory. It was the Christmas season and everyone on the trolley was talking about Christmas. I wondered if I was doing the right thing or should I just forget the whole thing and get excited about Christmas like everyone else seemed to be. I did not change my mind. Over the Christmas holiday, I spent my time writing announcements of the opening of the lab and making out orders for necessary equipment, chemicals, etc.

The practice grew and prospered. Doctors sent patients to her for tests instead of to hospitals; she made house calls and kept office hours, and soon expanded into larger quarters with more employees. "Serving the doctors and the people of that community were the happiest and the most rewarding [times] of my professional life, which covered a period of twenty-five years. You became a very necessary part of a community, rendering a much needed service." But success called for another move and expansion, which she was unwilling to do, so in 1971 Stephanie sold the lab, "one of the most difficult decisions of my life," and returned to Minto.

Certainly Stephanie Prepiora, like her parents, worked very hard, but it would appear that no amount of hard work alone would have led to managing a laboratory; she could not have done that at home in Minto, nor could she have done it without the various nursing programs and college night classes, however protracted that educational progress came to be. Extraordinary effort was required for her to have the professional and business career that she achieved, and she probably could not have done it without leaving North Dakota.

Stephanie's older brother and sister did not leave. The *Walsh County History* briefly summarized their careers: "Emma, their eldest daughter, remained on the farm, as many farm children did, where she was so essential to the survival of the family. Frank, their only son and present

owner of the land, also remained on the farm where he
worked from childhood, first with horses and later with tractors, tilling the soil." Stephanie speaks of their lives in relation to her own:

The children living in town had an advantage over farm children
because they could easily avail themselves of a high school education since they could stay home and do so. The farm children had
distances to travel (I had four miles) so for them board and room
had to be provided with some family in town for which the parents
had to pay. Many farm families would love to have given their children an education but simply could not afford to do so. My brother
and sister fell into this category, plus the fact that they were needed
on the farm. They did not go beyond the 8th grade except for some
special courses [Emma attended Concordia College, in Moorhead,
Minnesota] although both were avid readers and self-educated; in
knowledge and intelligence they did not have to take a back seat to
anyone. My sister was a gifted artist and my brother had a good
knowledge of world and local history. He was often a guest on the
local radio with stories of local history and settlements especially
of this area. During all my endeavors, my family always stood behind me and encouraged me.

Emma was eighty years old when she died in 1979. Frank
Przepiora died in 1982, at age eighty-one. Stephanie and her
brother and sister appear both typical and unusual for their
time and place. None of the three married—fairly unusual
among farm families. But it is less unusual that Stephanie,
having decided upon an ambitious professional career com-
bining business and nursing, should not have married, for
many women of her generation who succeeded in careers
found that they had to choose not to marry. Nor was it unusual for Emma Przepiora, the eldest, to be the one to stay at
home to help, even though she had begun college. For her
and Frank, the depression came at just the time to affect the
personal choices they made. On the whole, Stephanie writes
as if she feels fortunate in what she has done and grateful to
her parents for not interfering:

If they had completely disapproved there is no way I could have gone, being almost four miles from the nearest high school. It is true that I insisted in a positive way that I was going to high school, and my parents must have seen it my way, in spite of the general consensus in those days that a girl did not need a high school education because she would only get married anyway. She was expected to stay home and learn housewife duties from her mother or she would hire out as a servant girl to some wealthier home. In spite of the negative thinking and influences in those days, I did graduate from high school and feel it was the corner stone for my future.

She appreciates her parents, "who by example and by word taught me the values of life which we were to follow such as honesty, respect for the law and those in authority, value of hard honest work, and all the values as listed in the ten commandments although at no time did we wear our religion on our sleeves." Another good influence was the radio, just then coming into use. "Radio opened up a new world and made me curious and anxious to see and experience first hand some of these many wonders. One of my greatest thrills dating to radio days was my first broadway show in New York when the lights dimmed and the curtain went up just as had been described on radio."

Stephanie did not leave Minto because she was unhappy in the country; she reports some very happy moments at the farm in Minto when she was about three years old: "The farm had a big white house, unlike the small one we had lived in. My sisters, brother and I were so intrigued with the house that we chose to walk rather than ride so we could inspect the new house and yard. The yard had a big pond which contained water all summer. The pond was big enough, so my dad built us a small row boat which we paddled in the pond. Ducks and geese also spent many happy hours there."

All in all, George and Frances Przepiora may be said to have achieved the purposes for which they left Poland and ventured to North America and North Dakota—"to avoid compulsory military training and seek a better life." Their experiences were like those of many others: they worked hard and protected their children as best they could. But it took an extraordinary child and extraordinary effort to accomplish anything other than continuing the farm that the parents had started (although even that, given bad weather and bad economic times, was no small accomplishment). For Stephanie Prepiora as for so many others in North Dakota and similar agricultural regions, other accomplishments almost invariably necessitated leaving for Minneapolis, Chicago, and the mysterious urban East. Her return is less usual, but the effort she has expended on the community of Minto through the historical society is not unusual among women especially, who, after active careers in larger cities, find themselves in a small rural community. Much of the social and intellectual life of Minto is found at the historical society, and at its center is Stephanie Prepiora.

4

Children in Danger

"It Seemed As If All Fun Was Taken Out of Life"

Immigration to America, particularly to the homestead farms and ranches of the Midwest and Far West, is typically cast in heroic postures. There were dangers, of course, from sinking ships, disease, accidents: one could die of starvation, be killed by Indians and marauders, become lost in the wilderness, kicked to death by a horse, or burned in a fire. Nevertheless, accounts tell us, the West was won because rather than in spite of the selfless sacrifices of brave men. And yet, except for the early solitary explorers, it was not single men only, but also families who moved to the West from Europe or the eastern United States, a decision typically and primarily made by married men, who put themselves in danger, to be sure, but also exposed women—and children most of all—to a more precarious existence than they had known before. Sea voyages; overland journeys by train, by wagon, and on foot; the construction of housing and barns; farming; working on railroads, lumber crews, or mines—all these activities posed even more danger to children than to their parents, for children were participants in, as well as observers of, their fathers' work.

The drastic move to a "new" land endangered worst of all those children who were not closely guarded within a family. Private records make clear that the death or abandonment of one or both parents made it considerably less likely that their children would live out adult lives. The toll could be quite extraordinary. William Pickwell's dissatisfaction with the butchering trade in England, we shall see, ultimately brought about six deaths in his immediate family by the time he had reestablished himself as a teamster in Salt Lake City. Reading settlers' accounts or the remembrances of their children, one can be amazed at the casualness with which these very dangerous journeys and removals were undertaken. Was it courage, foolhardiness, or merely ignorance of what was in store that prompted the ventures so driven by need?

Even people who emigrated because they thought themselves poor or politically oppressed—who intended to better themselves by going to the West—often were taken aback by how dangerous the New World turned out to be compared to what they had left in the Old. Physical dangers always were very real on ocean voyages and during settlement, especially for children. Children died on board ship, in house fires, and from other calamities that would not ordinarily seem severe enough to kill adults or even injure children if adults were with them:

While father had applied for citizenship, and entered request for homestead we were billeted at the Chamberlain farm west of Obarion. Here we were again to see the perils of fire on the prairie. The Hare family who lived less than two miles from us had gone to town and the older children played with matches, the house was set afire and the three children were burned to death before neighbors arrived on the scene. I remember the ghastly description of the mother telling how the baby had been tied in a high chair and they dug the bones out with a pitch fork. This occurred in February when the ground was frozen so hard that burials were often postponed till spring and remains had to be covered and protected from predatory animals.[1]

Parents grieved unendurably at the deaths of children, and mothers most of all:

A son, my brother, named Fillip, was born in Russia and died on board ship enroute to the U.S.A. After arriving in the U.S.A. he was buried in a Boston, Massachusetts, cemetery. My sister, Mary, was born on the same ship while at sea. My mother told of many small children dying enroute to the U.S.A. After seeing how the first deceased children were buried at sea, the mothers would not report the death of their children. They kept it secret so the deceased children would be buried on land."[2]

Germans who came from Russia often confronted severe dislocation; many found the change from southern Russia to the Plains regions of the United States (or of Argentina, Australia, and Canada, where members of this group also settled) particularly disquieting. Germans had begun migrating to South Russia in the seventeenth century. Catholics and Baptists wanting to avoid conscription into the German army had answered the call to populate the agriculturally rich countryside east of the Caucasus in exchange for free land, exemption from taxes and conscription, and other benefits. By the time of the Russo-Japanese War in 1904, however, these Germans were conscripted anyway, and afterwards increasingly harassed and persecuted by the Bolsheviks. Many of those who did not leave the country were sent to labor camps in Siberia. But for all the subsequent suffering of those who stayed in Russia, many who did leave looked back on their *dorf* (village) communities as prosperous havens compared to America's harsher climates, rougher farming terrains, and isolated homesteads (each family was required to "prove up," that is, live on their own 160 acres instead of going out to the farms from communal villages.)

Monsignor George P. Aberle's book, *Pioneers and Their Sons: 165 Family Histories,*[3] describes Roman Catholic parishioners in and near Dickinson, North Dakota, most of them first-generation German immigrants from Russia. These family stories summarize the careers of men; they name the wives, mention the accomplishments of sons, and give the names of husbands the daughters married. By "pioneers," Aberle means males, fathers and sons. Some entries begin with lyrical descriptions of the land they left behind:

It was not always easy for our pioneers to leave the country of their birth, especially for those who were well-to-do. The climate conditions of South Russia were ideal; the seasons were almost equally of three months each, and the soil was exceptionally good for agriculture and horticulture, where all the small grains and the semitropical fruits and the various kinds of table and wine grapes were raised. It was a land where every colonist, farmer and artisan had his own orchard and vineyard. Every farmer had his own watermelon patch, and the pumpkins of South Russia were world famous for their size. It took two strong men to lift the large ones from the ground onto the wagon.

Aberle described Kandel, a colony of the Kuttchurgan Valley on the Danube. He admired the town's

orderly, neat and clean streets, their snow white stone and sundried brick homes, and their magnificent orchards with a dozen varieties of pear and apple trees, at least one or two kinds of plums, cherry, peach and apricot trees, besides a number of varieties of mulberry trees in the yard. . . . When all these fruit trees and the famous acacia trees, orchard after orchard, colony after colony, were in bloom, the air, as it were, was filled with perfume, and a person sensed a little bit of the garden of Eden. . . . Young Jacob attended school at Kandel where he learned both the Russian and German languages. Realizing that there are better opportunities in the United States for themselves and their children, Mr. and Mrs. Adam Mack left the county of the Czars and came to Dickinson in 1902.

Aberle glides rather vaguely over people's reasons for leaving such apparent prosperity in favor of "better opportunities," if indeed he knew why they left; in any event, in western North Dakota, the father, Adam Mack, worked as ranch hand, and both he and his son mined coal. This particular family established themselves in Dickinson, evidently, but they do not seem to have found "opportunities" much better than what must have been available in the prosperous villages they left. If there were political motivations for the move, Aberle does not mention them. The accounts in *Pioneers and Their Sons* mainly describe nostalgia for a past that the narrators, as children, could not have known very well. The portraits nevertheless place that past in a country of origin where people were safe; where children felt cared for, even if, as with Germans in Russia, they were becoming increasingly threatened by Czars and then by Bolsheviks.

And yet these children who thought back about their childhoods sometimes betrayed regret, in spite of whatever promise the move might have had for their parents, and eventually for themselves. Another Aberle pioneer, the father of Magdalena Heidecker, worked on the railroad near Dickinson and was away from home much of the time. Magdalena's mother despaired of bedbugs: "Mama wasn't used to being alone so much and became lonesome for friends and family in the old country. She often cried, saying, 'Is this all there is to this golden new world? We can't even get a good night's sleep without getting the blood sucked out of us.'"[4]

Marie Johnson Enochson

Looking back, settlers repeatedly followed episodes about how well they were cared for in the places they came from with grim tales of what befell children as soon as they arrived in America. Thus Marie Johnson Enochson described Aadalen, Norway, where she lived until age four.[5] Her grandmother had nursed an infant cousin whose mother died:

I went over to her to watch the baby at his job nursing, and she sent a stream of breast milk into my face. . . . Grandmother was 50 years old when that baby was born, and it was up to her to take care of the baby as well as the rest of the family, whether the baby or she got much rest; and what was just as bad, the baby's pitiful crying, so to quiet and pacify him, she gave him her breast, and let him nurse, and it came milk in her old breast, and she nursed him and weaned him as his own mother would have done had she lived. People from far off came to see; they heard about it but they had to see for themselves before they could believe.

In retrospect such care was especially amazing. Letters soon arrived from an uncle in America, saying that if Marie's father "only was in America all things would be fine." The family took his advice and left Norway, but in young Marie's memory, "things" became less and less fine. The trip took nine weeks, the uncle did not meet them in Quebec with money as promised, and to complete the journey, the family was forced to sell everything they had with them except their food. They went to Chicago. There they camped on the wharf, and the first episode in America that Marie described is this: "My little brother died there on the wharf by the lake, June 27, 1868. Now I don't know if you will believe it or not, but I did mourn for that brother of mine, it hurts yet when I think of it. I can see him lying in Mother's lap, when all of a sudden he cried, I want to go to Father, and as Mother laid him in Father's lap, he passed away." From the point of view of young Marie, care and safety of children were left behind in Norway.

Christine Hinderlie Reinertsen

At least in the short run, Christine Hinderlie Reinertsen experienced less happiness after immigration to South Dakota, than she had before. Growing up in Haugesurd, Norway, Christine was cared for in a meticulous household:

When I was about four years old I began to learn to read. My grandmother lived with us, and our uncle lived upstairs. Uncle Johannes had been attending a seminary. He wanted to become a minister, but was taken sick with a cold and it settled in his spine. T.B. But before he got so bad that he had to be in bed and twice I had to go upstairs every morning (had to have a clean dress on and hair combed just so) with my book, and he taught me to read. Whenever I saw a word in a newspaper I asked what it was. When I was five I could read any book or paper, but could not start school until I was six years old. Then I had to cross the big bridge that connected the island we lived on with the mainland. It was called Haugesurd. On very windy days Papa had to go with me as I was apt to be blown off. Once I remember my new hat blew off way into the water.[6]

Christine took part in daring athletic pranks calling for physical courage, and like many secure children, she claimed she hardly knew fear:

While living in Norway right by or on the North Sea we used to lie on our stomachs all day fishing crabs, etc. Papa had a big storehouse, he was a cooper by profession and had an arrangement where he could have barrels and from ships loading from our storehouse. Often we children would see that the chain was securely fastened and take hold of the big hook and take a good start from way in the room and go way out over the water and back again. Never thought of being afraid.

In 1884, the year she attended public school in Haugesurd, the family prepared to leave Norway for America. The day before their departure, on May 17, "All the school children were to march to Harold Stotten (the monument of Harold Haarfager). I had been there many times but this was to be so grand to march with all the children. But it rained so hard all day that we could not go. A few weeks before this our auntie took us children over there, and brought a picnic lunch along. She wanted us to remember that monument." These trips had their effect, for Christine associated them, even the one that did not take place, with the comfort and safety of Norway. When the family left for Rotterdam at four in the morning, "people sat along the mountain cliffs waving handkerchiefs." Holland impressed her: "Stayed there about half a day. It must have been that for young girls came dressed in almost like a nurse's uniform—blue dresses and white aprons and capes. They had brushes and mops with long handles. One washed the whole front of buildings (brick), windows and doors and sidewalks. It surely was clean there." All these images attest to affection and care of persons as well as property.

But as soon as the ship left Holland, Christine grew apprehensive:

Mama was down below arranging our beds. The boat was just gliding from shore when one with a mouth organ in one hand and holding a girl in another, and many more couples started jumping around. I thought surely they were going to jump overboard. I ran below and told Mama to come, for they surely were going to jump into the sea. When she came up she said, "They are dancing, child.

Don't look at them." Had read about dancing but never seen it before. Of course saw plenty of it before we got off the ship in New
York. I also remember that I was so worried on the whole trip that
some one would get lost.

Her fears notwithstanding, the sea voyage was relatively
pleasant and uneventful: "We had pretty nice weather nearly
all the way." Her tenth birthday came on a day they saw
"three large icebergs quite close and the ship was going
slowly for they said there was danger of running into them."
She thought she saw a polar bear on one. There was a single
very stormy day when people were told not to go on deck,
but "there was so much seasickness down below it was impossible to be there so I sat and crocheted all day in the stairway leading up to the deck, so I could feel the fresh air. Was
not sick once."

Arrival in New York was a fearful experience for ten-
year-old Christine, although no actual harm befell anyone
in the family: "Came to Ellis Island I think it was the 6th or
7th of June 1884. It was almost like a big cattle corral or
yard—the different steamers used different corrals or yards.
Everybody started in calling and shouting to come outside
as they would show them where to go." A man distributing
Bibles "told Papa not to listen to all those shouting for they
wanted to fool you out and would rob you; we were only to
go when the agent (ours) came. We were surely like cattle
driven. Did not understand a word." The Johnson family
managed to make their way to an uncle living in Red Wing,
Minnesota, with whom they stayed a month before moving
on to South Dakota.

She experienced severe dislocation in the isolated rural
settlements of Minnesota and South Dakota: "Everything
was new and queer to us who were used to living in a town.
We were the last Norwegians on the west in the Norwegian
settlement. A mile west of us were Russians. We went to
school with them. They could not speak any more English
than we could. They had lived here many years. The teacher,
Norwegian, told the school that we had to speak English—

when on the school grounds and in school." Compared to
her rope-swinging days in Norway, Christine felt afraid much
of the time in South Dakota: "I forgot to tell you how deathly
scary was the first year. We were afraid of snakes, gophers,
etc. Had never been in the country much in Norway. Remember once I was going on an errand to Rev. Norby's our
nearest neighbor. Had to go through some thick dead grass.
Heard something coming in the grass behind me. Never
looked back but gave a kick, felt something and when I was
going back there was my pet cat dead. He had followed me. I
surely felt bad."

After a year, her father was ordained and "accepted a call
to Kingsbury Co., North of Lake Preston, S. D." Then the
family's fortunes changed drastically for the worse: "Had
been there only one month when Mama died from exposure
while moving from Turner Co. to Kingsbury Co. We moved
in uncovered wagons. Slept under the wagons. We all got
sick but Mama got it worst. It seemed as if all fun was taken
out of life. Struggled there five or six years. Had to get used
to burning hay and straw. Quite a change from what we
were used to." Acquiring a parish no doubt meant progress
in Christina's father's career, but it cost the life of her mother,
and the journey from one county to another contrasted
sharply with the earlier send-off from Norway and the relative luxury of the sea voyage as far as Holland. In fact, it is
difficult to visualize the second move, which sounds rather
carelessly conceived.

Once her mother had died, the rich details of Christina's
writing fall away. She has less to say about events: "Our
schools in the country where we lived were very poor," she
writes, without describing them any further. Even so, in
1889 she attended Augustana College, working for her board
at the president's house, and in 1890 Brookings College, not
returning to Augustana until 1893. "It was then I met papa.
Were engaged in summer of 1893 and married 1896 in the
fall." College and marriage brought Christina to a safer and
more prosperous way of living; she achieved, we might say,
the promotion to the middle class that is the American dream.

But in those first years the journey away from Norway had led to greater physical danger, worse schooling, and deeper poverty than Christine says she had ever known before. The last move caused her mother's death. Whereas Norway, by contrast, Christine remembered as the place where an aunt and teachers had taken her to see a monument so that she would remember it.

Torkel Fuglestad

The name of the village, the farm, and the family all are Fuglestad. Torkel Fuglestad was born March 13, 1856, in the mountains of western Norway on a farm "with thirteen or fourteen milk cows, two horses, and sixty to seventy sheep." His reminiscences contrast the strict, but valuable education and upbringing he experienced in Norway with the mendacity and violence he discovered when he immigrated to the United States. He describes the military school he attended at eighteen at Kristiansend in lengthy and fond detail:

It was a state school. Everything was free, including three meals a day. The only items we had to supply were our underclothes. If we wanted a lunch (coffee) we had to pay for it ourselves. They gave us a few "ore" (pennies) with which to buy writing material. The school was a good one, and we had to be diligent if we were to keep up. To the best of my memory we had lessons in twelve different subjects, about one half of them military instruction. If we wanted to take the examination we had to take required courses.[7]

There were one hundred students ages eighteen to twenty-one, and in addition to military drill and academic subjects, there were religious classes "to prevent our becoming heathen." The boys marched to and from church services. The gymnasium was an important center of activity and prowess:

Whenever we were dismissed for a rest period it was as if one loosed a flock of calves. Some began to dance, others strolled back and forth studying their lessons, but the majority rushed to the gymnastic apparatus—rope, bars, and ladders; others leaped over the "horse." This was made of wood and was overstuffed with a

leather cushion. It was about five feet high. This was the real test
for the boys' muscles. Some of the bigger and stronger fellows
could never leap up on the horse, but many of us, even some of the
smallest, could leap over the horse even with a man sitting in the
saddle. A few did somersaults resting the head in the saddle, making
a leap and alighting with bowed knees and fine balance on the mat
on the other side.

Fuglestad recounts a number of incidents about military
school that illustrate the abuse boys suffered at the hands of
unscrupulous officers. He tells of being among "ten thousand men gathered to war against each other" on the Swedish border in 1876, when he was underage, and describes,
during that week's campaign, King Oscar coming among the
troops and joining in a dance. Torkel Fuglestad concludes
this section of his narrative: "Readers please pardon the fact
that I have discussed these reminiscences from military life.
I am now cured of militarism"—a change of mind that came
about, he explains, when his sons served in World War I.

In 1883 Torkel and his wife, Abigail, "packed up and journeyed to America . . . not because it was my wish but because it was God's will, and therefore it was for my good." It
also was a bad period economically in Norway. Torkel had
lost his job at a foundry that built steamboats and turned
down his father's offer that he take over the farm. The couple
settled near Valley City, North Dakota, but before arriving
there, Fuglestad tells of several unfortunate episodes, one
no more than an hour after docking in New York: "I had
bought a loaf of rye bread and we still had some butter from
Norway. We were sitting on a bench with our backs to the
wall and were eating. The bread lay on the bench between
us. I was about to cut another slice, and reached and felt the
empty bench. We got up and looked about, but the bread
was stolen, so to say, from under our noses. And among the
others, likely stood the thief amused at our surprise." Later,
someone stole the ball of yarn Abigail had beside her while
she knitted.

He tells also a strange story about a Finnish woman being

in labor on board ship and no one paying attention to her until Fuglestad called a doctor. The ship docked, and the woman was taken ashore, leaving her baggage and two-year-old daughter on board unattended when the ship set sail again. No one claimed the child, so Abigail took care of her for a few days until, at another port, the child was claimed by "two young ladies" who said they were taking her to her father. (The account does not explain where they were for the ship to be calling at so many towns.)

Once in North Dakota, however, matters improved, and the Fuglestads filed for a homestead, reporting nothing worse then an encounter with a skunk. But Abigail was less sanguine:

And the Mrs.? Well, just this one time in all these years did I see her lose courage in the economic strife and turmoil. I came out. There she stood quite downcast. She pointed to the sod-house and said, "See what people have to live in here. If we had the money I would go home at once." And she meant it. She had come from a well-to-do childhood home in Norway, where there was enough of everything, and this, of course, did not appear inviting. But when we visited settlers toward the Cheyenne River, she met acquaintances from the neighboring parish in Norway. They had been here a couple of years and had made somewhat better arrangements. As a result she became as interested as the others and has never again given evidence of retreat.

Abigail's experience was undoubtedly repeated countlessly, especially by women who had made the extraordinary removal to please (and remain in the company of) their husbands. Not surprisingly they often had second thoughts, but they reconciled themselves and saw "things" get better. Torkel's observations reflect also a remorse that men felt more often than is usually reported at having subjected the women they cared for to hardships and disappointments.

Mary Burch Klaus

It was highly probable that people would die under the strains and dangers of extraordinarily ambitious undertakings. The relative lack of effort to prevent injury and help weaker persons make less surprising the deaths of mothers, which added so drastically to the precariousness of children's lives. So often did mothers die, in fact, that describing their deaths developed into a literary art, as though an elaborate composition might make up for the life and keep husbands from asking whether the "sacrifice," as it was often called, was worth it. These writings almost never consider whether the death might have been prevented, nor typically do they describe the woman herself. The deaths of mothers, if one trusts reports of surviving children and husbands, were described as a greater hardship to the remaining family, broken by the loss, than to the woman who had died. The attention is all to survivors, the husband who lost a companion (and worker) and the children who were left without the one person who primarily fixed her attention on them.

In the 1950s, Delia Klaus wrote a sketch of her parents' coming in 1896 from Bessarabia, Russia, to the Richardton area of western North Dakota. Her father, John Klaus, had served in the Russian army. He and her mother, Mary Burok, were married in 1894. Delia was three and a sister nine months old at the time of migration. Delia's writing principally described various jobs her father held in Hebron and Richardton, the small sheep farm he bought near Spring Creek, threshing his first grain harvest, and sheep-dipping arrangements. Then she wrote about her mother:

That summer Dad and Mother done a lot of haying, as my mother mowed, and my dad hauled it home and stacked it. At that time he had around 300 head of cattle to feed. All went fine till my mother took sick that fall. Dad went to Richardton to get our winter supplies. He was gone on that trip about 4 days as it was a long trip with team and wagon. While he was gone Mother took quite sick. Before he went to town she had asked him to buy a few boards to make us a larger table, as the one we had was quite small. Dad said on the way home something kept telling him he would not use that lumber for a table.

After arriving home he found Mother very sick. She and us three kids had stayed alone while he was gone. And only two weeks later our dear mother passed away on December 5, 1905. We had just got some new neighbors that summer, and they were at that time with us. It was Mrs. Percy Brooks, her brother, and sister in law who came with tears on the cheeks and put their arms around us and said I am very sorry, here are three little children without a mother, and our dad was down on his knees beside her bed praying and crying. That very night our dad and this good neighbor took that lumber and made our mother a coffin. The ladies washed her, and with Dad's help they dressed her with the new clothes he had just bought her, not knowing that would be her last. Very early next morning Dad and our neighbor loaded our dead mother on the wagon, bundled up us three kids, little sister Rozalla only 3, and Julianna 7, and I Delia was 9. Then he hitched up his faithful black team of horses and started out for grandparents, my dad's folks.

That trip was about 50 miles. There was a lot of snow, but Dad had no sled, therefore had to use the wagon. The horses were very tired. Poor Dad prayed, and cried pitifully all the way. We reached there way after dark. Everyone was very much shocked over the sudden death of our mother. The next day Dad and my uncle drove to a little country store where Dad bought some black cloth which they covered the coffin with. With white ribbon they made a cross on the top, and a lady Margaret Fisher put three nice paper roses on which she had made, and the day after that the funeral took place in a little country church just north of where Zap now is located. After the funeral we three stayed with our grandma and our Dad returned back all by himself into the empty sod shack.[8]

Many families who tried to move and resettle at the turn of the century found they were living in a constant crisis at a time when, for the poor, ordinary days could be marginal enough. Men and women who were poor and who made these extraordinary migrations, in large part, as they said, "for the children," sometimes found it very difficult to give children even minimal care. As we have seen, they sometimes were not able to give them even as much care as those children had received wherever the families came from. Women worried all the time, if we believe what they wrote; some grew nearly frantic because it was so difficult. Such worry may have numbed families, for in spite of the constant anxiety women felt for their children, we hear tales of calamities that could only have been brought on by incompetence. The causes and the effects of deaths in families were various and complex; they reveal public as well as private attitudes and strategies for coping. Deaths of infants and mothers could cause greater displacements than the moves themselves, and deaths of infants could occur in a clutter of improvisation: "Twin girls born on the 3rd of January. Both were so small they could fit into a shoebox, according to Aunt Lizzy. They were born on the farm and in order to keep them warm, they laid them in cotton and placed them on the open door to the kitchen stove oven. However, all attempts to keep them alive failed and they both died within five days of their birth."[9]

The main subject of writings about death was the larger community, an emphasis that deflected attention away from the person who had died—the more so if she were female. The writers in 1942 of a "Historical Sketch" of the Ringsaker Lutheran, United Norwegian Church (twelve miles northeast of Cooperstown, North Dakota) described how six deaths in 1881 precipitated complicated real estate dealings for a cemetery. The land acquisition appears to have interested the writers of the church's history more than the loss of parishioners (a woman and several children):

On November 8, 1881, this little flock was reminded how uncertain is life when Mrs. Anna Nelson Svartberget (Anna Andersdatter) 48 years old, was called away, and in the fall of 1882 five children passed away during the diphtheria epidemic. There it was that it became necessary to get a place of burial, and Ole Olson Bjornstad was appointed to ask Carl A. Flisaram for an acre of land for a cemetery, which he (Flisaram) donated, but due to some error, ownership was not recorded, and the land was sold to some company, and later bought by Ole Pederson Overby. We read from the minutes of 1885-86-89-91 of the struggle to acquire title to this parcel of land. Mr. Overby wanted to give title, but times were hard, and the pioneers had to go through drought, rust, and grass hoppers, and he could not give title until he himself had acquired title.

Later we read from page 12 of Book two of the minutes of Jan. 4, 1894, that the cemetery and committee's work was finished, and that the land was "overdeeded" to Carl A. Flisaram, trustee.

Sarah Pickwell Reid

The children of immigrants hold memories of their first home, the one from which their parents removed them ostensibly in search of something better. Those memories often appear the more poignant because the first homes were so modest. The places they left, whether in Europe or elsewhere on the American continent, remain to these children havens of safety and comfort, populated with tender grandparents, attentive teachers, and relatives whose solicitousness could only have been magnified by the drastic lessening of attention the children felt they received as soon as they arrived in the new place. Many felt abandoned, often no doubt with justification, given the arduous demands made upon adults by the rigors of travel and settlement. Only later, when order had returned to the household and the children were older, were there signs that their generation might show economic improvement over their parents', improvements that were so important to the parents' deciding to move in the first place.

At age twelve Sarah Pickwell set out upon a journey that took her from her native village of Bolney, in England, first to Saint Louis, Missouri; then to Salt Lake City, Utah; and eventually to a ranch near Medora, North Dakota. The account she wrote could be the stuff of a romantic novel of the late nineteenth century, full as it is of hair-breadth escapes and "affecting scenes." A typescript of sixteen pages titled "Reid Family History" was compiled by her daughter, Sarah Ann Gertrude.[10] It is a fairly complex, somewhat puzzling, and partly literary document. The first ten pages appear to be fairly close to what Sarah Pickwell had written herself; the later ones, the daughter explains, are her own summary, adding reminiscences and commentary. The first of the two parts of the "Reid Family History," about Sarah Pickwell's

childhood and early marriage, follows the mode of sensational sentimental fiction: children die, starve, are beaten,
suffer from exposure and overwork, and are cared for by no
one, least of all by the parents who abandoned them or died.
But unlike popular novels of the period on these themes,
which she appears to be imitating, Sarah Pickwell's account
of her early life contains no moral; in it virtue does not tri-
umph—indeed virtue is not mentioned—and no hero saves
the day. Sarah Pickwell did marry, but she does not claim
her husband as a reward, and for a while, her life after marriage was almost as physically precarious as it was before.
Her life story lacks also the threat of sexual ruin, so necessary to sentimental fiction; she reports no menacing seduc-
ers, no threats to her virginity. No man along her travels
proposed marriage, let alone an illicit sexual liaison. In good
time she married William Reid, a stage driver. Two primary
ingredients of sensational popular fiction—sexual menace
and rewarded virtue—are missing from Sarah Pickwell's
narrative.

She writes with formal echoes of sentimental fiction but
omits sentiment in a straightforward story of almost unre-
lieved suffering, but suffering that, unlike what we would
find in fiction, improved no one's character. Sarah claims no
moral superiority for herself; if anything, her narrative implies, less suffering would have made a better and certainly
a happier woman. Sarah appears to be adjusting her life
story to conform partly to what a "book" should be, or the
kind of book she was familiar with, the sentimental novel.
But she chose only plot outlines from the formula, leaving
aside lachrymose and moralizing effects. Her desire to emulate possibly was a way of making the writing respectable,
or endurable.

The second part of the "Reid Family History," the daughter's comments upon her mother's life, more obviously and
patriotically imitates American western adventure literature. Sarah Ann Gertrude casts her parents as western he-
roes: "Both had played their part well and had outlived the

Old West they had helped to civilize. There are no monuments to Bill and Sarah Reid, but no puny memorial of rock
and concrete could do them justice. Their monuments are
the waving fields of wheat and the sprawling cities that
an unconquerable pioneer spirit helped to make possible."
Such hortatory language is absent from the pages of Sarah
Reid, who did not write as though she thought herself a car-
rier of civilization.

The Reid family eventually lived in Medora, North Dakota, where Bill Reid became acquainted with Theodore
Roosevelt, "who came out to his ranch there every fall." It
was thanks to Roosevelt, according to Sarah Ann, that her
mother wrote about her life.

Roosevelt was a great admirer of rugged, western frontiersmen,
and he and Bill Reid went on many hunting trips together. Young
Wallace Reid worked for the Roosevelt Ranch for a time, and his
family came to know the future president well. One day Roosevelt
listened, fascinated, as Sarah told of some of her early pioneer experiences. When she had finished, the doughty politician pounded
his hand and declared that she should try and write down the story
of her life, if not for publication, then as a valuable record for the
inspiration of future Reid generations. Sarah did write down many
of her early adventures, and it is upon her narrative that much of
this story is based.

Whatever the stories that impressed Roosevelt, Sarah
Pickwell's childhood experiences had little to do with the
rugged western frontier; rather than inspire future generations, they are enough to shame those of the past. Sarah herself was neither a romantic nor a sensationalist, and she
opens the narrative matter-of-factly: "I am going to relate a
little of my life and experiences." These began in a working-
class English village, which offered a degree of safety and
protection that she never realized again:

I was born in the year 1843, August 11th, at Bolney, Sussex Co., England. There were seven children of us in the family—I was the
third oldest, my brother and sister left home at the ages of thirteen

and fifteen years to go out in the world for themselves. I was only about 8 years old then, but remembered it very well. The village we lived in was a very small place, but a very busy little place. There was an old lady that taught me to read and write, that was all the schooling I had. This lady had taught school about twenty years. When I was ten years old my mother said to me one day and the other children, we were going to America. Because business was so slack, we were to look for a new location.

(The teacher did her job well, for Sarah's writing is literate as well as expressive. She wrote much as one would speak.)

William Pickwell's decision to relocate for business reasons could not have had more perilous results. He ran a butcher shop in partnership with a man in another village; his partner owed him money, and for six years Pickwell tried to collect the debt, to no avail. Finally he was promised the money on the day before the family was to leave: "Well the last day father sent my brother over three times to Jenners, but they did not get any bill. The next morning we left. Before leaving father threw all his day books and ledgers in the fire for he thought they were of no more use to him." But, like an ill-starred character in a fairy tale, he was to regret not guessing the perfidy of his partner:

We were all ready to sail on the 22nd day of November, 1853, when late in the evening of the 22nd as father was strolling about on the deck, there came a police officer and asked if there was a man named J. H. Pickwell on board. As father was standing near he came forward and said his name was Pickwell. The officer said you are my prisoner, and father asked on what charge was he arrested. The policeman said theft. Then he knew why Tom Jenner would not settle his little bill with father before he left.

The police would not allow Pickwell to see his wife, so he "sent her a message which with all her other troubles just prostrated her for a time." Mrs. Pickwell did not want to leave at all without her husband, but William pointed out that if she did not, they would forfeit passage money and had no place to live in the meantime; in addition, the magistrate assured him that in a few weeks he would be able to leave and catch up with his family on a "mail packet line steamer" (which in fact he did). The presence of her close friend Mrs. Starley (to whom William had lent money for her fare) reconciled Mrs. Pickwell to undertaking the journey without her husband, a comfort fraught with calamitous irony. She took sick, Sarah continues:

She neither ate, drank or slept, grieving all the time until she lost her mind, when we had been out about ten days at sea. I seen she was sick and nervous, but child like did not realize what was the trouble, we had all retired at the usual hour, I had been to sleep when I heard mother calling me. So got up and went to her, I found her unconscious but seemed perfectly satisfied when I was there. After several hours I thought she was asleep so went to bed again, had not been there long when she called me again I got up and went to her staying with her the rest of the night. My little brother James was sleeping with her, I took care of him. Mother was no better in the morning, our friends Starley did not seem to think there was any serious trouble with mother, and let her lay in that condition days, then called the doctor. It was too late after being unconscious four days she passed away in the evening. They sewed her up in some bed clothes laid her on a plank and slid her into the ocean.

Sarah, the oldest Pickwell child on this journey, blamed herself for her mother's death: "I don't think she had a cup of tea or anything to eat in all those four days. Neither Mr. or Mrs. Starley gave her a cup of any nourishment that I know of. She had not eaten enough to keep a mouse alive since we had come on ship board. So literally starved to death. I feel quite sure if she had been properly taken care of she would have come through all right for she was a healthy woman." A ten-year-old can hardly be blamed for not observing that her mother would starve to death without food. Remembering the event as an adult, Sarah neither exonerated nor overdramatized her helplessness: "I was ten years old knew nothing about sickness, as we never had any sickness in the family that I remembered what the result would be, but have since learned to my sorrow a great many times."

She learned another unpleasant fact: the Starleys had no intention of looking after the Pickwell children. They "did not take the least interest in us. They appropriated all our best provisions to their own use." This neglect took more toll on the family: "Five days after mother's death my baby brother grew weak for the want of proper food (and we had plenty of our own) but the Starleys had it all locked up. So I had to feed them on the ship's rations, and they were not very appetizing for small children, to say nothing of a sick child. A young strange lady took him thinking she could do more for him than I could, but he did not get any better and died in a couple of days." The Starleys' taking the children's trunk of food was the first of a series of abuses Sarah and her siblings experienced at the hands of adults ostensibly charged with caring for them.

Sarah Pickwell's next description reads like suffering romance fiction, but minus the moral tag:

Our rations were so slim that we all grew weak and could not keep anything in our stomachs. With our sea sickness and improper food grew very weak, soon after my brother died, we were all feeling very sick and hungry, we all went up on the deck and crawled into the large coils of rope around the main mast, all crying the little ones for food looked up to the older ones because they could not get food for the little ones. While we were there crying an old gray haired sailor came down the main mast, wanted to know what we were crying about. I waited for my older brother to answer him but he did not, so I said we were hungry. He said how is that, where are your father and mother. I told him my father was in England and my mother was dead, died on the ship, he asked who was looking after us I said that the folks that were with us had locked up all our food, that the little ones could eat, so we were all hungry. He said to John bring a large cup and plate and stay near the sailors' cabin every time the horn blows, and I will see you do not go hungry any more. Then he went away for it was against the rules of the ship for sailors to talk to the passengers.

John refused to go the sailor's mess with cup and plate "because he wasn't any beggar," but Sarah said, "I will not have those little ones crying for food when we could get some if we would go get it. So if he wouldn't go I would go myself." John did, and they ate well for the rest of the ocean voyage. They landed in Saint Louis on January 3, 1854, and Mrs. Gooding came to look after "the widows and orphans." The Pickwell children "found a very comfortable home there." The next day they were distributed to other households: Sarah to a family named Evans, Fanny to a cousin of Mrs. Evans named Dinwoodey, John to a family named Gordon. Two sick children, Thomas and Katherine, remained with Mrs. Gooding, who "done all she could for them but they grew worse and died. I never knew where they were buried." An ocean and river journey of two-and-a-half months cost the Pickwell family three children and their mother.

True to his hopes, Mr. Pickwell caught up with the remaining children in Saint Louis. It is possible that his removal from England was influenced by an interest in the Mormon Church: "My father wrote a number of letters to mother, but the President of the Mormon church at Saint Louis kept them until father came and then he told to his sorrow of the sad fate of mother and the children. Then he wished he had paid the bill unjust though it was it might of been the salvation of his loved ones," as indeed it might. "His troubles were not over yet," Sarah wrote, for her brother John was "very low" and the Gordon family no longer wanted to care for him. Mr. Pickwell took him to the hospital, but "he only lived an hour. Father said he never expected to see him alive when he took him there on Tuesday and when he went to see him on Friday he was dead and buried. Now all he had left of his family was Fanny and myself; he was prostrated with grief he could not do any work for some time." Mr. Pickwell roused himself sufficiently to want to "go to house keeping," but the Evanses dissuaded him, pointing to the expense, Pickwell's own intentions of moving to Salt Lake City as teamster in the spring, "which was very near now," and the fact that the two girls were "provided with homes for the present." Even for the time he was in Saint Louis, William Pickwell appears to have had little success in bettering the lives of his children. If he were aware of the abuses they suffered, Sarah did not report that he was able to do anything about their treatment. Meanwhile, "We passed on over to the next year without much trouble."

But trouble came soon again, when Sarah moved to the household of a Mrs. Edwards, who carried a strap with her to beat Sarah whenever she found her asleep. One morning when she was awakened with an especially strong beating, Sarah thought about what she "could do to get even with her." She took the children for a walk along Washington Avenue, the street they lived on:

There was a large lumber yard [on Ninth Street], well I thought now I will have a good sleep I put the children in a pile of lumber that was laid up to dry got in it myself and went to sleep, at about five in the morning [an hour that makes one wonder how much sleep the Edwardses' own children were allowed]. I woke up a few minutes to eleven, well I thought I have had a good sleep now I am in for it by a good beating but I don't mind that after this good sleep, took the children out and went home, there was no one there, they were both out looking for us, very soon Mrs. Edwards came in and wanted to know where I had been so long. I told in the lumber yard asleep, she said she would learn me to go out to sleep, she took her strap off her apron and laid it on my back pretty lively then she asked me if I would ever do it again, I said yes if she would not let me sleep in the house I must sleep somewhere else, then she went at beating me again was determined to make me promise and I would not do so. I said beat away until I have had a good sleep so she did beat until her husband came in and stopped her, he said the police would interfere if she did not stop, he asked me where I had been and I told him in the lumberyard asleep so I could not stand it any longer to keep awake, he said you must not do it again for we have been almost frightened to death about you and the children.

In April 1859, Sarah wrote that she "left for Salt Lake City to go to my father as he had sent money." He had arranged as well for her and her sister Fanny to travel with a family named Eldridge. Whether her father kept in touch directly with his daughters in Saint Louis, she did not say, but by this time he presumably was established as teamster in Salt Lake City, as he had intended. Payment for the girls' journey was to include space to ride in a wagon and meals. Yet Sarah made the journey alone: "My sister Fanny decided not to go and remained behind in Saint Louis, married Will Krumside in 1864 and in '65 gave birth to a son and died two hours later." That left Sarah the only member of her family, beside her father, to undertake the last stage of migration from England to the western United States and live to a relatively mature age (Sarah died at age fifty-eight).

The treatment Sarah received from people she had to depend on did not improve during the journey from Saint Louis to Salt Lake City. A steamboat took her to Florence City, "the starting point for the ox teams headed for Pike's Peak, as Colorado was then called, Salt Lake City, and California." Mr. Eldridge proposed that Sarah buy a handcart, but, Sarah says, "I told him no I would not walk and pull a hand cart across the plains although there were hundreds that did." A place was found for her with a widowed Mrs. Smith, who had several children. Like the many women under whose custody Sarah found herself, this Mrs. Smith took what advantage she could of Sarah—by insisting she walk almost all of the time, and later by trading so much of Sarah's share of provisions for her own family's use that Sarah had to buy more supplies along the way. "She became so disagreeable that I would rather walk than ride," Sarah wrote. But she made friends with a Miss Annie Hill, "then I did not find the walking very hard except in wet weather and stormy weather, for we were a jolly crowd having a good time." Many people were barefoot, Sarah noted, although she and Annie had good shoes, which they would have to take off each time they waded a stream. The people who had been paid for Sarah's trip to Salt Lake City subjected her to abuse almost as bad as what she had endured from families on board ship and in Saint Louis. Overland travel was precarious enough; it gave Sarah's tormentors added opportunities:

One day I was quite ill and not able to walk any further so told my friend Annie I would have to stop and wait for the wagons so I could ride as it happened that day ours was the last ten wagons of the train of sixty wagons. [She explains that the wagons were organized into six groups, which rotated their order so that no group would always be either first or last in the march.] My friend proposed to wait with me until the wagon came up for we always walked ahead of the teams out of the dust. I told her there was no use to wait as she would then have to walk in the dust, so she went on with the balance of the girls. When our team came along I asked Mrs. Smith if I could ride for I was not able to walk any further she said no for I was quite able to walk I said I cannot walk, and started to get in the wagon but she pulled me out backwards, then tried again with the same result, then I walked straight out from the road in the sage brush and had a good cry, then cried until I fell asleep and the train went by I never woke up until some tramping woke me up when I opened my eyes it was dark. And I was so frightened I could not move at first when I raised up I could not hear the tramping, so laid my ear to the ground and then I could hear it quite plainly. It seemed to be coming straight for me so I thought was some wild beast and crouched under some sage brush and waited in a short time I heard some one talking then I came out and spoke for I thought it must be some one looking for me from the train. It was the captain and a man that had seen me walk out and lie down. The captain came up and asked me what I was doing out there, why I was not with the wagons I told him I felt ill and so stopped for the wagon intending to ride but Mrs. Smith said I was able to walk. I felt hurt that I walked out and laid down, but had not intended to go to sleep, and had woke up when I heard them coming. He had brought his horse so he put me on it and we went to camp which was about six miles, for about half past two was when I stopped. If they had not come for me I never should of known the way to go on, and was as likely to gone the wrong way as the right. I discovered when I got to camp it was my friend Annie who had found out I was not in camp after getting her supper over went to Mrs. Smith's camp and inquired for me. Mrs. Smith said she did not know any thing about me. Annie asked if I was in the wagon she said she did not know then her youngest son a boy of 12 years told her I was left back on the road she then went to her sister who she was traveling with and her brother in law who went to the captain who then made inquiries about me. One of the men said he had seen me go out and lay down and would go back and show him where it was. The captain got his horse and this is how they happened to come after me. When we got to camp the captain told Mrs. Smith that if she ever refused to let me ride again he would tie her up to a tree and leave her on the plains, as I had paid my way to ride whenever I wanted to. But I never wanted to ride for she was more disagreeable than ever after that. And God knows that was needless.

It was a long and tiring journey. Sarah described the end of it gratefully: "As I came out of Emigrant Canyon on the bench a high strip of land I thought I had never seen so grand a sight the city down in the valley with its shade trees on each side of the streets and a stream of clear water from the north side of the town from the mountains coming down the town. The Great Salt Lake in the background it was really a grand sight to see to us poor weary souls." Her father, Sarah discovered, had married a widow with a daughter sixteen years old. "My father seemed very much pleased to see me and have me home again. I stayed at home for some time, then took a situation with a milliner." So ended Sarah Pickwell's journey, which had begun in Bolney, England, seven years earlier. Sarah wrote very little about her first year in Utah: "I stayed with her [the milliner] until I had a better offer out on the stage line at a place called Rock Ridge. There I was married to Wm. A. Reid November 17, 1860." She was seventeen years old.

With the report of this marriage, Sarah's narrative changes to the "western" adventures of a man who succeeded in spite of adversity, a story in which the primary antagonists were Indians rather than evil foster parents. Although Sarah was not always at the scene, she listened well and sometimes reported as though she had been there. This second, "western" part breaks absolutely with Sarah's life as dependent waif; there is no mention of any event or person from her earlier years, not even her father. Traditional western mythology predominates. Sarah did not challenge those values; she did not express objections, for instance, to the treatment of Indians by Anglo-European settlers or the U.S. Army that might suggest she connected the abuse of Indians with what she had suffered as a child at the hands of mendacious caretakers. Having modeled the story of her young life on one familiar kind of book, she now took up another. By focusing on William, she conformed to expectations that wives be less central than husbands.

Sarah Pickwell and her daughter were of two separate generations; they saw things differently. Whereas Sarah Pickwell may have had in mind, as she wrote, popular sentimental fictions about immigrant waifs, her account nevertheless remained unadorned. She wrote in the first person, realistically for the most part about what happened to her, although with no particular reflection as to what her experiences might have meant. But neither did she make a hero of herself; she did not write as though she thought she was unusual or her adventures extraordinary. However, when Sarah Ann took up where her mother left off, she shaped events into a heroic mode, western style. Sarah Ann's description of her parents preparing to leave the family they had stayed with at Fort Bridger and her explanation of how she came to contribute to her mother's writing set her apart, as a writer, from her mother:

They stood for a moment, surveying the endless plains and buttes of the surrounding country and reflecting on the joys and miseries of their frontier existence. This was the end of the Sarah Pickwell Reid manuscript but, of course, it was only the beginning of Sarah's and Bill Reid's life together. Whether the balance of the manuscript was lost or never written is not known, although we do know they continued with their frontier way of life. With a family to think of, Sarah faded into the background and her story evolved into a narrative of her restless husband and of the opening up of the West.

Sarah Ann has interpolated ideas and attitudes that she attributes to her mother, but which we had not heard Sarah Pickwell mention herself. It is the daughter who subordinated her mother in what she thought was primarily her father's story.

After some months at stage stations, the Reids returned to Salt Lake City. Sarah, knowing that she was pregnant, hoped the child she carried might be born in Salt Lake City—which he was, on October 15, 1867. The baby was named William James Reid. When William Reid was at the Three Crossings stage station on the Sweetwater River of Wyoming, the daughter wrote, "Life at a stage station was still a lonely existence, but now Sarah had her young son for company and the time went much faster." Yet Sarah nowhere had mentioned loneliness. It was as though Sarah Ann thought of her parents as partly fictional persons living in historical times.

It was during this period that the Reids met most of the famous army officers and frontier characters of the early 1870s. Mrs. Cody and her children lived with them for a time. Wild Bill Hickok was a special friend of the Reids also and visited often. Hickok was fond of children and no doubt bounced all of the Reid youngsters on his knee at one time or another.

Sarah evidently enjoyed companionship with William Reid (at least nothing is said to the contrary), but she told little about him in a personal way and certainly nothing to make him seem her rescuer. As a representative of the western success story that his daughter attempted to write, William Reid did not particularly conform: he played poker, he fled to the hills after wounding a man in a barroom brawl, and he moved his family every few years from one makeshift cabin to another—all details more true to actual lives than to the mythic ideal. The "unconquerable pioneer spirit" his daughter made much of did not always match facts. William Reid could be described as a fairly ordinary opportunist who found jobs where he could—most, unskilled and temporary. And Sarah, when she shared his ways, recorded no criticism of his habits or values.

Sarah Pickwell was an artful writer. She constructed her narrative by means of carefully repeated patterns. In the throes of disaster, for instance, she said several times that she may have been partly at fault for making trouble worse for herself. When conditions improved, she noted the fact, although without sentimental optimism. Her adventures until she reached Salt Lake City, as we have seen, consisted of a series of deprivations—of food, shelter, sleep, and of course the deaths of her mother and siblings. On the journey west she was nearly abandoned. Rescuers of sorts appeared each time, men in authority (ship captains, sailors, a husband who stopped his wife beating her, the man in charge of the wagon train). But their authority never lasted, and no one permanently improved her condition. What got Sarah through and ensured her survival was her tenacity; she did not rebel, but she stuck it out. When her brother felt ashamed to beg sailors for food, she threatened to go herself. Sarah Pickwell endured and survived, but she did not display particular ingenuity or passion about events, a flatness of style that makes her desire to "relate a little of my life and experience" sound true.

The absence of either parent, and certainly the death of a mother, drastically worsened children's lives. (Not until the 1960s did divorces outnumber deaths of parents in the United States.) Mrs. Pickwell did not want to leave England and be cut off from her two eldest children—the thought of leaving "was very hard on Mother," Sarah wrote. It evidently did not occur to Mr. Pickwell that a journey to Salt Lake City "because business was so slack" might cost more than "a new location" was worth. It can be argued that nineteenth-century technology encouraged adventure and whetted desires for rapid economic gain while providing few safeguards, either physical or economic. The machinery of transportation, farming, mining, and other industries, and even of housework, to say nothing of medicine, could not keep up with the burgeoning ambitions many held for new lands and new lives. Adventure outran safety. Men who directed these ventures appear to have given extraordinarily little thought to elementary protection for the weak. Ship passengers were required to provide their own food on transatlantic journeys, and individual homesteaders had to "prove up" with a house on their land. Poor settlers might have had an easier time had shipping companies fed them along with the sailors, or central farming villages been allowed, on the European model. The obsessive individualism of the "unconquerable pioneer spirit" Sarah's daughter touts brought suffering to many.

"Distressing Cases"

The *Children's Home Finder,* the publication of the Fargo (N. Dak.) orphanage, routinely published affecting scenes in the lives of poor children. In July 1921 administrators explained that they did not have room to take boarding children: "We cannot be unconcerned when deserted wives and widowed mothers come to us with tears in their eyes, and tell us they will go insane if they cannot find some way to have their children cared for while they work out to support them." The April 1919 issue reported "A Distressing Case": six children in their care while the parents were being held "on the charge of murdering their eldest daughter." A crippled son of fourteen had been locked up and starved. "Some of the children are very pretty, and all are of a happy and lovable disposition. The morbid curiosity shown by some of the people who crowded about the children while in Jamestown and since they came to the Home has been nauseating, and we had to decline to permit people calling just to gaze at them." In October 1920 there is reported "A Sad Case" of a Russian family named Krywornezh "broken up by the insanity of the mother." She had taken her five children in the middle of the night "onto the wastes of the Bad Lands, leaving the three-year-old near the house when he could not walk so fast." She returned with the other children, but the youngest had disappeared, his remains discovered three weeks later four and a half miles away. The writer remarks: "Their father is a typical Russian or Ukrainian peasant—hard working but incompetent to take the personal care of his children." Sad and distressing cases were not respectors of class, although class was respected in treating them:

We desire to confer or correspond with some high-grade family in Fargo who have a desire to give an adopted daughter a first-class education. We know a girl, almost a young lady, from an aristocratic family, who by misfortune needs just that kind of a home. She is a fine girl, and way beyond the ordinary child thrown upon its own resources. She will make a daughter for some well-to-do family home who will grace the best home in Fargo or any other place. She is a fine scholar, a good thinker, high-spirited and proud, with the best Virginia blood in her veins, and a Christian girl. Only those who can furnish the highest grade references need write. She must have a college education before she finishes [August 15, 1916].

The Children's Home, we can assume, was no more snobbish than the general population; it merely reflected general hostile attitudes toward the distress of poor children, as well as the actual precarious physical conditions of those children.

The surge of new economic opportunity in the nineteenth and early twentieth centuries was made possible by improved technology in transportation, the dislocation of Indian people, urban industrialization, expanding populations, and more ambitiously democratic ideas. These and other drastic social and intellectual changes all affected children. Children were the intended beneficiaries of most family moves, but in the short run many bore the brunt of conditions that did not make allowances for them. Eventually, better nutrition, medicine, housing, and schooling caught up with the rural frontier, but in the meantime children's deprivations, instead of giving pause to the entire fever of expansion, became objects of sentimentality and romance. Even children themselves could succumb to such lures. The *Youth's Companion*, for instance, was sufficiently disturbed by what lay in wait for children who might on their own take on the romance of the rugged west that the chief inspector of the New York police, Thomas Evans, wrote an article called "Runaway Boys." He was disturbed, he wrote, by the "large number of runaway boys" whose cases had come to his attention, and he thought the probable cause of their behavior lay in "trashy and sensational novels and newspapers." He hoped to discourage more young readers from running away:

Many of the runaway boys who come to New York provide themselves with a proper outfit in which to go West and fight Indians. This is a favorite fancy. They want pistols and big broad brimmed hats and other equipment, and then they intend to set out on an expedition against the red men. . . . There is another class of boys who leave their homes on account of really cruel treatment on the part of their fathers. Brutality is not too strong a term to use in describing the conduct of some fathers toward their children. And when boys have been almost driven away from home in this way, it is not to be wondered at if the father is glad rather than sorry and not disposed to take much trouble in searching for the fugitive. . . . I remember one instance of undoubted brutality, in which the boy repeated his charges against his father face to face with him, in my office. The father became so incensed by what was unquestionably a truthful narrative that he was unable to restrain himself and lifted his hand and struck his son in the face. I had him arrested immediately.

But, Chief Inspector Evans concluded, he lost track of the case. In the history of Plains and western settlement, the lives of all too many children were lost track of.

5

"Though I Am Young, a Little One"

Parents' Preoccupation with Their Children

We know that children had to be out there, in the settlement West, but just where is hard to tell when we mainly hear of men's activities with other men—building railroads, mining, logging, cowboying. Photographs show scores of horses and men at wheat harvests, on cattle drives, men crowding saloons and street corners. These pictures give the impression that any children in the households from which the men emerged somehow took care of themselves until they too reached productive adulthood. In fact, young ambitious men and women claim to have gone west precisely to get away from domesticity, or at least from their parents. Adventure, physical daring, endurance—these were not challenges meant for infants and children. In the new lands, we are led to believe, there was little room for thinking about children, even though family groups in fact were dominant among settlement populations. To what extent did the idea of "home" depend upon children and women? Did men who lived apart from them entirely glory in all-male company, or did they too attempt to fabricate female-associated semblances of home? How children became accommodated to new settlements may suggest also how "frontier" evolved into "home."

Isabella Dickie Fraser

But of course many did think about children, and many women who wrote about their experiences thought about their children unceasingly. Virtually without exception, women's letters, diaries, and reminiscences demonstrate that children were of overwhelming concern to their mothers. Women thought of little else, and almost all other activities—social relationships, farm work, paid employment, even church-building—took place in the context of child care. Children always were on women's minds; husbands sometimes only now and then. But that does not mean that women necessarily felt victimized by childcare, although some certainly were. As an example of someone who made deliberate negotiations in planning her life around the care of two boys, and no more, there lived in eastern North Dakota a witty and tough-minded Scotswoman named Isabella Dickie Fraser:

I was married on January 3rd to William Fraser 1879 in Old Deer at the home of my mother in the village of Stewartfield by the Rev. Dean Rankin of St. Drustan's, and left for our new home in Aberdeen where he was working in the Rubislaw Quarry. I was not infatuated with marriage, but made up my mind to make the best of it, and my husband did not seem to miss anything of my affection. He did not make much money at his work and we had a kind of precarious living. Then we had so many talks, and made up our minds that if we had to have children, that we could not raise them, and then we thought if we could raise the money we would go to America.[1]

The Frasers had two boys while they lived in Aberdeen, but because William was not able to make enough money, and Isabel, as she explains, "did not take well to being poor," he emigrated to North America.

Once William left, Isabel wrote, "I did not feel very bad as I had my babies and mother and they occupied my time." William did well enough at his work managing a farm in North Dakota to send $100 for her passage: "It was a venture my Mother did not approve of, and she tried to advise me against it, but she had brought me up always to do my duty and so I had to get a ticket for myself and one for the boys."

The trip was arduous, and the arrival rather confirmed her mother's skepticism: "We landed at last at the farm. I was anxious to see the people that I had to work for. We were dumped out of the wagon at the door of a sod shanty. I looked again. After living in Scotland for thirty-four years in houses built of granite, to be brought to a sod shanty. I thought where is all the wealth that they brag about in America. However I made up my mind to make the best of my new home."

Her little boys were Isabella's main concern on the journey and continued to be on the farm, where things were strange and the children constantly underfoot. "I did not wish my boys to be kept down altogether. Nor lose their individuality altogether and I did not have their father to help me, he was out on the farm all the time only at meals and they were in bed when he was in from the farm." Although she praised his honesty and hard work, William was at best on the edges of her life. She enjoyed working for the Wilsons, then she heard that they planned to go to Cleveland for the winter: "I would be all by myself. . . . I was quite pleased when they went. It was a quiet winter and snow on the ground. William drove them to town, and it felt so good to be alone."

But she was not alone very much, for she made a name for herself in the neighborhood by delivering the babies of other women, although she had no more herself. A Mrs. McLoud asked for her: "My husband was out at a neighbor's threshing. It was snowing, quite a blizzard nobody at home but me and the boys. I knew I would have to take them with me. . . . I was there on the prairie miles from any one. However I made up my mind I would do my best. I had good common sense and knew how things would be done." All went well, the doctor arrived eventually, "and I won new laurels . . . it is a glorious sensation." For Isabella Fraser, words such as "duty," "affection," and being "infatuated with marriage" stand for the inevitability of pregnancy, although she says nothing about not being companionable with her husband. Isabella Fraser lived as she was expected to. She did her duty, as she expressed it, and she put her children first. Where it mattered, she controlled what happened to her and to them.

Mrs. Robert Goudreaux

The tenacity with which countless women focused on their children's survival sometimes comes to light in life stories that barely glance at the woman herself. A writer who signed herself Mrs. Robert Goudreaux submitted an essay about her parents to a Mandan Creamery contest called "Interesting Facts of the Pioneer."[2] She described her father, who was almost always absent, as the central character in the family, and appears to refer to her mother in a more secondary manner, even though it was her mother's efforts and ingenuity that devised opportunities for the children.

The father, Barney Lannigan, came from Ireland in 1860 and, after a stint in the army, homesteaded a hundred miles south of Bismarck. According to Mrs. Goudreaux: "In 1875, after living alone on his homestead for five years, he met my mother (I am one of the children) the daughter of Left Hand, a Sioux Indian" (she did not give her mother's own name). The couple farmed, and Barney Lannigan had a mail route. "About this time came the gold rush in the Black Hills, so he gave up the mail contract and in company with ten white men who were also married to Indian women, started for the Black Hills and stayed three months. He was the only one of the ten who returned to his family, the rest he never knew what became of." Nevertheless, he was not with the family for long: "After five children were born, he died, being unable to get medical aid. He was buried on his homestead, with nothing but a wire fence to mark his grave. The older children then were old enough to go to school, and with no schools there we had to move back to the west side of the river to the reservation where the Catholic missionaries were starting to build schools for Indian children. The homestead, after years of hard work, was sold for taxes."

While this daughter places her father centrally in the family, during most of her growing up he was absent. It was her mother who kept up the farm for the years Barney Lannigan was prospecting, cared for him when he was ill, bore and cared for five children, and returned to the reservation for the sake of their education. The daughter of Left Hand looked after her children first and always.

Inger Ford Grindeland

Thinking about their children preoccupied women regardless of their economic status or social class. Women who were moderately wealthy worried as much as those who were not. Rich and poor shared a concentration on childbearing and child-raising, and while it was difficult for any woman a century ago to speak or write openly about sexuality, writings characteristically reveal correspondents who knew and thought more about sexuality than they could say or act upon publicly.

Inger Ford married Andrew Grindeland in 1882 and moved with him from Big Canoe, Iowa, to Warren, Minnesota, where Andrew practiced law. In letters to her sister Ingeborg, in Iowa, written between 1882 and 1888 (and translated from the Norwegian by her son Igolf Brindeland), she tried to sound cheerful, but apprehensions come through—mainly about pregnancies and the care of her children. Besides missing her family, Inger worried about health, about establishing a Lutheran Church in Warren, and about her children's welfare over the years. Marriage isolated her. Soon after arriving in Warren, she wrote: "I have not been out all around town to take a look-see, as yet. I feel like a stranger and I don't like to go around alone. And Andrew can not take time off during week days to take me out. We have postponed it until some Sunday afternoon. . . . I am so happy that we bought 'Dr. Waltyhers Goodhousekeeping.' We read it together each one his share or part and to each other." [3] A year later, after returning from a stay in Iowa during which her first child was born, she wrote: "Well, now I have a real nice and beautiful home. You should see it. You can't realize how happy I am." And she added: "It seems that I am not living in this Red River country. We live right in the woods which will protect us from the stormy winds because the trees completely surround the house on all sides." New carpets pleased her, and she managed to "forget to get homesick" that winter:

And that God will grant us health and good fortune in addition to all this. You can just know how happy Andrew was when we came back to him again. And you should just see how happy he is with his little daughter. He can hardly leave her alone when he is home. . . . Often she sleeps for two hours at a stretch, and when she awakes she looks around and plays with her little hands. When she gets tired of that she begs me so tenderly and looks so prettily at me that I have to take her up. If she will stay healthy and well she will give us many happy hours with her.

The move to Warren undoubtedly was intended to benefit Andrew's beginning legal career, but Inger's thoughts returned to the mother and sisters she left behind.

Inger was constantly attentive to this infant who at most slept two hours at a time. Andrew evidently took little direct part in domesticity—that we infer from her gratitude to her sister and mother: "I am not able to express my thankfulness to you for all the kindness you showered on me, all the really nice things you did for me. Sometimes I feel so reticent and hold back. If I hadn't been with you folks when I was sick [giving birth to the child] I would not be as happy as I am to look at my little daughter." Referring to Andrew and the child: "He almost eats her up when he is home. She gets quite displeased with him sometimes when he fondles her too much" (November 20, 1883). "She has begun to play and romp around with her father when he is home, so much so that he can hardly control her. He plays peekaboo with her and she thinks it is so much fun that she is beside herself" (February 11, 1884). But for Inger, the child provided less pure entertainment:

Well, Ingeborg, I think it is truly a shame that I have not written before this. It seems that I am overloaded with things to do that I, yes I remember well what you said to me one time, and that was that you could hardly find time to sew for your own little ones, and I have to say the same for myself. Even though Louise is good, yet you know about how much time I have left to spare after I am finished with my housework. Lately I have sewed a dress for one of the most prominent ladies in town. And you can believe that I sat with trembling hands and could hardly get any sleep at night for worrying about that blamed dress.

A year later she and her sister each had given birth to another daughter (Inger had seven children in all):

It is with much happiness that I sit and write a few words to you. I am happy that you have overcome giving birth too, and hearty well wishes to you for your little daughter. You will never know how happy I am when I heard that everything went well. Lately, I have often dreamt about you, and many times my dreams were not at all pleasant, either. . . . You and I are not the ones who have it easy during pregnancy. Oh well, as long as everything goes well afterwards, then we soon forget the difficulties.

She urged her sister to keep the hired girl as long as she could "because it is not wise to boast about starting to work again too soon. I found that out this winter just past. Well now you have equalled me again; now we are equally rich that we each have two girls apiece." But both women had to contend with husbands who were disappointed that these infants were not sons. Inger wrote as though she and her sister endured childbearing and rearing alone and felt obliged to apologize to their husbands for not presenting male children.

The effort to establish a Lutheran church in Warren succeeded and was strangely connected to Inger's anxieties about childbearing:

I have just thought so many times how wonderful God plans. When I was carrying Synneva [her second child] I was often distressed and blamed myself so many times that I should have another little one so soon. But later I felt that God had planned it so and for the best. Because Anderson came up here, and as he said himself the

last time he was up here (at Louise's baptism), as he pointed to Synneva, "See, there, there is the beginning of Baptismal services
here." Now I know that if God had not brought her to us so soon,
perhaps we would not have gone forward so soon with church affairs. [n.d.]

Inger's letters are always cheerful, if formal (perhaps
partly because of translation), but over the years they also
revealed increasing desperation:

Ja, now one of my little ones is crying and I must stop. It seems that
there is no use to tell you how it is, because no one can know before
one has gone through it oneself. One believes he understands but
he does not know. The only thing that holds me up is that I have an
unusually kind husband. If he was not so helpful and trusting,
many times when I feel in the mood to break down and then I
would in no wise know what would become of me. I am not the
kind that takes everything lackadaisically or carefree, but the dark
side soon becomes clear to me.

Unhappily, "an unusually kind husband" did not dispel "the
dark side" that confronted her.

Inger visited her family in Iowa again during the summer
of 1888:

I did not think it would be so long before you should hear from us. I
could have just as well found time before but you know how it is
when one is tired and can only find time to sit down for a little
while but even so one does not always feel up to it to write a letter. I
am much troubled with rheumatism in my arms and hands so that
my hands shake almost away and also ache often at night so that I
don't know where I can find rest for them . . . Andrew spends most
of his time out in the countryside for whole weeks at a time. He has
purchased a horse and buggy so he can go and come as he pleases.
[October 24, 1888]

She could not do as she pleased, and moreover was alone
with the children for those same "whole weeks at a time."

Anxieties about her health, childbearing, and her children
continued, as in this undated scrap:

If it were not so, I think it would be my last. The doctor knows of nothing else for me except to give an emetic, but to take this is not so easy. It is very difficult before I can get anything up. I almost thought about how very tough it is for a mother to be as sick as I was, and with all the little ones standing round me. My little ones stood and looked at me and didn't know what they should think. Louise went around the house and says "Her is so sick her mamma" over and over again. When I got to feeling better and was able to go to the kitchen, then they were so happy that they didn't know what to do to busy themselves or what to find to do. The first that Louise said was "Now mamma is so kind, my girl mamma." Then they were hungry and thirsty because they had not had any food for such a long time, they filled their mouths with talk to each other of everything that came to their minds.

In four years could Andrew have so removed himself as to be unaware of her desperation?

Inger wrote often of childbirth, hers and those of other women. But for all her guilt and worry, her children were the subject about which Inger wrote to her sister with the most consistent enthusiasm: "Synneve, she is so little and short but thick and fat. . . . She promises to be a capable and beautiful child. And Louise also the same. The only difference is that Louise is so earnest and sober and quiet" (n.d.). Her greatest single joy was her friendship with her sister: "Have you thought about making a visit this summer? Bless me if you should. You could at the same time rest up for a while from all your hustle and bustle. . . . I can almost see us all together and tell you that everyone of you should come. Oh what a scene. Lord, if it could be so, really" (n.d.).

We know little about Inger Grindeland: twelve letters and some scraps in seven years, awkwardly translated, the original sheets thrown away. But these brief glances are consistent enough to lend a partial portrait of her. She was not altogether confined to housekeeping and childcare, for her efforts at organizing a fund-raising dinner at twenty-five cents a plate for the Lutheran Church in Warren show her considerable public talents, ones that she exercised primarily for her children: "I have thought about going around in the same manner and call on the women so we can get a Ladies Aid if possible. . . . So many of these Norskies here have been away from church worship and have lived so long without it that they don't seem to have any desire to work and do what they should." So, although building a church in Warren ostensibly fulfilled spiritual needs for the community, ensured an acceptable religious education for children, and helped Inger to feel closer ties with her Norwegian family past, the church also provided her with a public alternative to domestic confinement.

Inger Ford Grindeland's strongest ties were with females— mother and sister, infant daughters. Andrew's participation in her immediate life waned over the years. "Andrew has had all he can take care of [in the line of law cases] and believes he will be busy until Christmas at least. . . . At the election he was elected Court Commissioner, so that he will also have some pay for that" (November 20, 1883). She suggests that he gradually withdrew from her companionship— from taking turns reading a housekeeping book aloud together as newlyweds, to playing strenuously with their first child, to absenting himself more and more in the call of his profession.

Inger's center moved from a concentration on him—marveling at his power with infant Louise—to preoccupations with her children and, through them, with public efforts to establish a church. Smallpox, cholera, measles, the diseases that killed people she knew, worried her incessantly lest they descend upon her children too. Inger weakened from work, from pregnancies and worry. What she called rheumatism was one sign, her nervous collapse a more severe one. She accepted the conventions of class and the social mores of her time and also felt anxious about sexual commitments. What she wrote about most to her sister, her closest confidant, was the subject they shared, their children.

Effie Hanson

Between Christmas Day 1917, and April Fools' Day 1923, Effie Hanson wrote over forty letters to her friend Ethel

Buck.[4] Effie lived on a farm near Wing, in central North Dakota, and Ethel farmed near Kent, Minnesota. Effie Hanson wrote about farm work—her husband John Hanson's plowing and threshing and his jobs away from home mining coal. She mentioned the Farmers' Union and the Nonpartisan League, political groups furthering the interests of farmers against railroads and big business. She told of her children growing and going to school, of noisy, "shouting" Methodist gatherings. Her own activities included milking, tending chickens, cooking, and sewing. These and pregnancy, childbirth, infant care, health, and disease were her overwhelming preoccupations: "I have been sewing for that little one. Suppose you knew that when you saw me last fall. But I've felt good most of the time so I can't complain. Ann Erlandson (John's sister) is still waiting for her little one to come. Don't think she has had it yet. Seems like there is quite a few expecting little ones this spring. There are two right in this neighborhood. The children are just crazy for a baby brother. I hope we get a boy too" (March 1918).

Pregnancy—her own and those of her sister, her husband's sister (both named Ann), and friends and neighbors—was a subject nearly always on her mind:

I'll soon have to think about a girl (about the middle of May). But I've felt good most of the time so can't complain [April 1918]. . . . John uses all the horses in the field and I'm so now I can't walk to do any good. I have me a hired girl now. She is a fine one too. I am on my feet yet but don't know just how much longer I will be up. My time is up already. . . . The children are going out to Eva's to stay a few days just about the time I get sick [May–June 1918]. . . . I should have answered the letter long ago but seem like I never get time & baby takes up so much of my time. The stork was here the 10th day of June so you see baby is going on 7 weeks. Brought us another girl baby. Named her Thelma Bessie. I got out of it easy this time. Never had a pain. Mrs. Hanson was with me. She said she never seen anything like it. She didn't see how I ever had the baby. She give me some medicine to make me vomit. That was all that helped me to have it was vomiting. But I wouldn't of vomited if it wasn't for the medicine. I sure was lucky this time. I wouldn't mind having a dozen if I could get out of it that way. . . . Anna is well but her baby is cross these days so my brother John went up there to stay a few days. You must excuse writing as I'm holding baby while I write and she is awfully fussy. [July 1918]

Two years later:

Have been sewing quite a bit lately, and have some more to do too. Sewing for that little one that is coming some time the last part of April or 1st of May. I have not been so very well lately as my back hurts me all the time. Hope we get a boy this time. Anton thinks we have girls enough. Don't know yet who will stay with us. Have been looking for girls but never found any yet. Seems like they are getting married, what few there were. Have wrote to John's sister up by Regan for her oldest daughter but haven't got any answer yet. You know she stayed with Mrs. Hanson when she was so bad, at the last. She sure is a good girl if I do say it for John's niece. So quick to get around. Can harness horses, milk cows or most anything. She is 17 years old. [spring 1920]

John's niece did not materialize and Effie Hanson hired three young women by turn. But the baby was successfully born: "Both baby and me are getting along fine. Baby is so good. Named him Paul Thomas" [June 1920].

Her letters give us an idea of what rural childhood was like in the early twentieth century from a mother's point of view:

My brothers are just over the chicken pox and most every child in Wing has them. . . . My children hasn't had the chicken pox yet and I hope they don't get them this winter either. . . . What did you folks get for Xmas . . . ? John got the girls some beads and [a] rubber ball for Anton, and got some nuts and candy and some apples and put them in their stockings, and they sure was pleased over them. But peanuts he couldn't get a one in town.

I feel awfully good this summer. The children & me took the old team & digger and dug 9 rows of potatoes and carried them in the cellar and had 23 bushel to put in. And we have 50 rows left to dig but John will finish them. . . . My children has bought thrift stamps and 1 war savings stamp with their pennies. They are awfully proud of the books with their stamps [September 29, 1918]. . . . It was nice that day to dig. I had baby along with me to the patch and she was awfully good. She rode along in the wagon all the time. . . . Mrs. Buck, I forgot to tell you that my baby goes all over the floor. She gets on her hands & feet & stands her body up off the floor. Well this is honest. She did this before she was 4 months old, and she gets on her hands and toes & leaps forward. . . . She wasn't more than 3 months old when she started to leap forward. . . . Mrs. Olson didn't believe it until she was down and saw it [late fall 1918]. . . .

The children are learning their abc's now. Anton & Helen knows pretty near all of them but Agnes don't know quite all of them yet. . . . And I made the girls a new dress, dark blue trimmed in velvet, and Anton a suit. Had fine luck with all of them. Sometimes when I sew things don't go right so it takes me quite a while. Have the girls in overalls most of the time. They are lots warmer for them on cold days [late December 1918]. . . . I walked to Mrs. Hanson's and carried the light bread dough and also 1 gal 1/2 cream to churn. And carried the 8 loaves [of bread] back and my butter. I had Thelma to carry part of the way and part of the time [she] rode in the little wagon [summer 1919]. . . .

I churned today and shall scrub & wash windows this p.m. Also gave the children a bath this forenoon. But Anton will get his tonight. He is a little particular about washing before the girls. . . . Made a pair of pants for Anton from some old ones [April 2, 1920]

Anton drives the stacker team. They say he does real well for a small boy. Tomorrow the 26th is Anton's birthday. He is 7 years old and Blanch sent him a silk handkerchief with butterflies on the edge. . . . We would like to take Anton to Bismarck to have him operated for rupture after school is out but don't know if we will or not. Hope we do anyway. . . . Baby walks around the chairs & bed now so suppose he will start out alone one of these days. He gets a good many falls though, but forgets about it again [January 1921]. . . . Agnes goes to school now with Anton & Helen and won't miss a day if she can help it. She likes it fine. Anton & Helen are in Second Reader now. Getting along fine too. Agnes hasn't been going a month yet & can write pretty good for a beginner. She couldn't write a thing when she started [October 1921]. . . . Got some outing [flannel] in Wing to make drawers for the girls to wear over the union suits. The drawers keep the underwear from getting so dirty. Paul is a good boy. He tells me most of the time so it helps lots in the washing. I am so glad I got him broke before cold weather set in [October 30, 1921]. . . .

Our eldest boy is ruptured quite bad. . . . We should of had him operated before but crops hasn't been very good and prices so low that we have neglected doing so. It hasn't bothered him for some time now. But he never will be well until it is tended to. . . . Agnes stayed all night with our teacher Thurs night and she felt good because she was the first one of the children to stay with her. They sure like her fine this year [November 1921]. . . . Children are in school and not any too well satisfied with our teacher. She is so bad to threaten them all the time. Anton takes any thing to heart anyway and he don't seem to be well sometimes. I think it is because of his rupture more than anything else. Every day she tells them she will put them back if they do not do their lessons and she will keep them in next time. The teacher last year was a splendid one. . . . Year before last we had one the same way. Anton's nerves are all unstrung. He got so he would faint away, sometimes. We took him to Dr. and he said that was all that caused it. She was so cross, kept him in so much and pull his ears. It was partly because we are N.P. [Nonpartisan League], and she is IVA [Independent Voters Association]. This teacher now is IVA and the NP children, she has a spite at them [fall 1922]. . . .

Seems like I never get caught up with my sewing. After I was sick [I] made Helen & Agnes 1 dress apiece and Thelma 2, Paul 2 pr overalls from that shirting and me 2 percale dresses so far. But have 2 dresses apiece more for the girls to make, Paul a suit, Anton some light shirts to go with his suit [March 13, 1923]. . . . Have to make the girls 2 more dresses apiece. One navy blue pongee for Sunday. I think I'll trim them in red pongee silk. I see they trim blue pongee in red silk and red buttons. Have a red plaid gingham dress to make for them. Seems like it takes me so long to sew a little this time. [April 1, 1923]

Effie Hanson enjoyed her children; she liked to brag about them, even though she also worried about their colds and their catching the chicken pox and other contagious diseases. She distressed herself over the eldest boy's "rupture," which she did not feel they could afford to have treated. She enjoyed sewing clothes for them, and while cooking, cleaning, and washing took up her time and energy, in her letters to Ethel Buck she did not complain or sound put-upon.

Politics also was important to Effie Hanson, as indicated by the abuse Anton suffered in school from a politically conservative teacher. "We were all to vote. And the Nonpartisans won we hear. What are you folks, or are you afraid to tell us. Well we will tell you the honest fact we that are Nonpartisans and not ashamed to admit it, and everybody around here west & east for a long ways and south" (fall 1922).

But her pregnancies never were long from Effie's attention. In the same letter, she wrote: "Baby is a big boy. He has no teeth yet, and is a good one too. He was 6 mos. the 2nd of Nov. The 4th of Nov. was our wedding day. Was married 8 years. Don't seem that long either." In those eight years, Effie had five births, the two described in these letters and three earlier: Anton in 1913, Helen in 1914, and Agnes in 1915. Some weeks after the anniversary she wrote: "Suppose you know Ed & Ann have a baby boy. 4 boys in all now. I'm wearing glasses now. We went up to see Dr. about my head ache and he said to wear glasses. Which I did and it helped too. We went to Wilton with Eva's father in his auto" (first of the year, 1921).

Effie's account of the doctor's visit is followed by a publisher's note: "At this point in this letter, Effie asks her friend for advice about a personal subject. The paragraph has been deleted." Frances Wold, as editor, apparently omitted something in deference to family feelings; I think it is likely that the inquiry had to do with contraceptive advice. For although Ethel had been married six years longer than Effie, she had only three children. There are other suggestions that Effie confided in Ethel about family planning. That January she had written: "Am cooking beef for supper. You better come up & we will have a social chat." In November: "I do not feel a bit good as my hips & knees just ache and guess it is the rheumatism that bothers me. It isn't anything else."

She also speculated about other women's pregnancies: "Clarence & family are pretty good. Their baby will be 3 yrs in June. Don't think there is anything there yet" (February 7, 1922). And in July: "Clarence & Eva are well. Her baby is past 3 years old. No sign of anything yet."—remarking the absence of births as well as their occurrences. Some births could be harrowing: "Anne E. has another boy, was born the 4 of August. Weighed 8 lbs. They nearly lost him as the 2 women was afraid of him and wouldn't go near him. It was Ed's mother and another woman. They laid him away till the next day & never as much as washed him. So Anna found him soaked in blood. So baby & Anna are getting along fine now." Superstitious fear of an infant who might not live prompts attending women to abandon him in a pool of his own blood. On April 1, 1923, she wrote more about these unhappy in-laws: "Wolds . . . never heard from Anna E. since last Aug. I don't know why they never write. It sure is too bad, way off in Wis. by her self where her relations can't even get a post card from her. . . . She could of died after having her last baby and he wouldn't have brains enough to drop a card about it. A person can guess all kinds of things about what could of happened."

The letters do not directly mention Effie Hanson's last pregnancy, which would have begun the summer of 1922. She became very ill with pneumonia. On March 13, 1922, she wrote: "I am some better but quite weak yet. Can't do my own washing yet or mix light bread. Our neighbor just east has baked bread so far, and washed most of the time. She is a good hearted woman, (a Finlander) but awful good neighbor. Her husband is just as good to help. He can't hardly talk English at all but she can talk it just fine. Am sorry to put off writing to you so long but it couldn't be helped. Hope it won't happen again."

And two weeks later: "We are all pretty well again now. Seems like every body has colds and the flu is up north of

Wing again this spring. I had a bad cough here while ago &
Dr. said it was the flu & settled on my right lung but my
cough is lots better now." Then she explained about sewing
the two pongee dresses. "I will raise what chickens I can any
way. Think I'll get some body to set my incubator as Dr. said
I shouldn't go up the cellar steps for a long time, as I'm not
strong enough for that, or do any carrying for a long time
and chores I don't do at all any more" (April 1, 1923). References to time ("the last days," "this time"); her sewing, which
she also had done a lot of during other pregnancies; and the
general weakness she expects "for a long time" all suggest
pregnancy as well as illness. In any event, two weeks after
this last letter of the series, Frances Wold tells us that Effie
Hanson died "of pneumonia and complications" from the
birth of her sixth child, Andrew Lee, who lived only six
weeks. Hanson sons were shorter lived than the daughters.
Anton died in 1927 of spinal meningitis and Paul in 1939 of a
drowning accident. Helen, Thelma, and Agnes were still living at the time the letters were published, and John Hanson
died in 1957 on the thirty-fourth anniversary of Effie Hanson's death.

If Effie Hanson expressed regrets, they were for being too
far from friends to enjoy frequent "chats" (although the
availability of the telephone kept her in touch with a few).
She had wished also for a larger house: "Don't think I'll
have more than 2 or 3 qts Rhubarb or maybe 4 but not any
more. I'd like to go visit the folks but can't this year. We need
a bigger house but we won't get that either. Well I don't care.
I want to get out of here as soon as we can. It is hard to do it
this year as stock & machinery won't sell for anything" (August 9, 1921). She thought about prices, about national politics, and her family's health and well being, especially Anton, whose "rupture" there was not enough money to treat.
She understood and worried about all aspects of the farming operation. And almost everything (like the size of the
house) was affected by the presence of children. She counted
them equally among her pleasures and her anxieties, and, of

course, had there not been so many of them in such rapid succession, and had she not worked so hard to care for them, she might have lived to die later than her thirty-first year.

As much as Effie Hanson had to say about her children, and as strongly as she concentrated on them, she wrote to Ethyl Buck about other matters as well. The five children were part of a fairly complex life that included farming; politics; in-laws and friends; and her husband, John. The fact that such public services as schools and medicine did not particularly help with childcare made her spend more, not less time thinking about them. In addition, she felt powerless in the face of indifferent and abusive teachers and the prohibitive cost of medical care.

Frances Evelyn Cahoon

Frances Evelyn Cahoon wrote an essay-journal about the birth and first year of her daughter, in which, rather than seeing her child's progress in a context of other events, she tended to explain events, even her husband's death, in a context dominated by the child.[5] She lavished seemingly exhaustive detail upon descriptions of her daughter's first months, beginning with her birth. It is rare to find so exact an account of birth in private writings of the turn of the century. She titled the first section "Her Birthday":

> On the second day of August 1888 in our little house in the village of Carthage, Dakota, was born our little baby—the child of George Clinton Cahoon and Frances Evelyn Cahoon. There was no one with us at the time but Mrs. Cawley, a neighbor, and Dr. J. W. Burchard, the attending physician. The nurse whom we had engaged, Miss Antoinette Foster, a friend of Mrs. Cawley's, had gone out into the country on a visit that week thinking that we should want her the week after. The little one proved too spry for her however, and so when we found the child was coming right along, we sent out into the country for her and Mrs. Cawley agreed to take her place until she arrived. My sister, aged fifteen, Sily Prince, who had been with me for a month before the child was born, I sent out to the neighbor's for the day.
>
> When I awoke at seven or eight in the morning I perceived signs

of the coming event, which grew steadily more conclusive, so that immediately after breakfast my husband went up town, reporting my condition, hastening home to tell me that from the symptoms, the doctor said it was certainly not a false alarm.

From this time until noon, Sily and my husband George were very busy setting the morning work to rights and washing out half a dozen of my night dresses, which being rather dingy I had collected and put ready for the wash the day before—supposing that they would not be required until the next week. I meanwhile did up my work in my room upstairs, carefully attended to all little matters that I thought might be well to see to myself.

At noon George and Sily ate a good dinner of beefsteak and coffee and I ate a little and then Sily cleared away the dishes and went over to Mrs. Cawley's and Mrs. Cawley came over to be with me while Mr. Cahoon went up after the doctor. While he was gone I told Mrs. Cawley where everything necessary might be found, showed her the baby's trunk, laid out the clothes the little one was to wear and then waited the birth which I supposed was coming in almost an hour, as the pains had continued all the morning and were now quite frequent. We were quite interested in some coincidences in this affair. To begin with, a great many things of importance had happened to us on Thursday and a few months before while we were talking of this circumstance George said, "Godfrey, that child'll be born on Thursday, see if it ain't." And surely enough, it was Thursday! Another curious thing was that sometime in the summer I had said to my husband, "What do you want me to give you for a birthday present?" and he answered, "A kid." And when the eventful Thursday came, it was the day before his birthday— his thirtieth birthday.

Well, when the doctor came he blandly told me that I was "not half through yet." And so it was, for the baby was not born until half past five in the afternoon. The day was unmercifully hot, but I could not bear any light so the curtains had to be kept down making it dreadfully trying for my attendants. The time would undoubtedly not have been so long had it not been that I had had cramps. It seemed a little curious to us that my husband and I had never talked over little arrangements until the night before. When he came home from lodge the night before we sat and talked a long time, and when we went upstairs I showed him the baby's trunk all ready for her, told him where the sheets and pillow cases were to be found—my underclothes. After the baby was born I had a nervous chill, but aside from that was feeling tolerably well. When the child was born it had a veil over its face, the first, the doctor said, that he had ever seen out of some hundred cases.

When the child was first born, my husband stood at the head of the bed with his arms around me, I looked up at him and saw every tooth in his head, and his eyes were fixed in perfect delight on the place where he could see the movements of his child. At last when I had been made as comfortable as possible and the little one had been attended to, the doctor turning to my husband said, "Well, Mr. Cahoon, are you satisfied?"

"Godfrey, yes!" he answered—and then added a little regretfully—"but I wish it had been a boy."

I have only to add that Mrs. Cawley's verdict was that I "didn't have a hard time." The doctor put it more kindly by saying that I "faced it better than women usually do with first children," and my husband put it rather ignorantly, "It didn't seem to hurt you as much as I expected, at any rate you didn't howl same as Mrs. Howe did." He had once boarded where a Mrs. Howe was confined.

Until the child was fairly born my husband and Mrs. Cawley both insisted that it was going to be a boy because it was a slow birth, though the doctor contended that it would be a girl—"because girls were contrary and so wouldn't hurry when you wanted them to." Mr. Cahoon, who had hoped for a large child, was a little disappointed to find his daughter weighed only between 6 and 7 pounds. He however spoke of it as 7.

Frances Cahoon appears to have used writing about her daughter's birth as an occasion for expressing more frankly than she might otherwise assessments of her husband's behavior, as well as what she felt and observed during childbirth. The birth heightened her awareness of everything that was going on, including, we may infer, her perceptions of the husband's character: she judged he spoke "rather ignorantly." Her husband, the doctor, and attending neighbor appeared the more crude for what they did not see and did not understand.

The next journal section, "First Two Months," ends, "This was the last period in which we were all happily together," for George Cahoon soon sickened and died. But Frances gave more description to George's behavior with the infant than to the infant's place in the routine of sickbed and death. He is portrayed as a more ardent lover to the child than to his wife:

Her father I think almost worshipped her. He seldom came home for the first six weeks of her life without going to her just as soon as he had kissed me, and throwing himself on his knees by her little bed and laying his head beside hers on the pillow. There he would stay sometimes looking and looking at her in a perfect ecstacy of pride and delight—and he would cover her sleeping face and indeed her whole body with kisses, and then laugh when she would turn and stretch and squint up her little face to get away from his curly beard.

He showed her to every one he could get to look at her, and told of her to every one he could get to listen to him. He took care of her regularly every other night after my nurse left on the ninth day, in order that I might sleep. It was he who washed out her first diaper—why he did it I'm sure I do not know—there certainly was no need of it, but when she was two days old he went off out by the back door and washed the first diapers that were ever washed for her.

It was he who taught her to go to sleep at night in her own little bed—the nurse had accustomed the child to being rocked. I have known him to kneel for two hours in uncomfortable positions by her bed—holding the little nervous hands and laying his forehead against the little rebellious head in order to keep her quiet so that sleep might get the better of her without her being rocked. Sometimes he used to spank her when she cried from temper, and when he did so he would whip her until it was evident she was crying from the smart, and had forgotten to cry from temper. Then he would soothe her by patting her and talking to her, his face against hers and she would tuck her little thumb into her mouth and go to sleep.

It seems to me no man was ever so infinitely patient with a child and yet so absolutely firm. There were many times when because I was still weak from my sickness I would have given up to her for even then she was very persistent but her papa's will was more than her match and he always subdued her. . . .

Her sleeping place was after the first few weeks a little bed made

on her father's black trunk and most of the time this was right at
the foot of Mama's and Papa's bed. Before this I put her in a soft
little nest in the middle drawer of my bureau. . . .

Just before or rather when she was two months old her Papa
went down to Sioux City and while he was gone I remember cud-
dling the tiny little creature up to me and wondering what widowed mothers do whose husbands must stay away forever. . . .

During this period the child delighted her Papa by beginning to
suck beefsteak and show plainly that she liked it as she did also
little pieces of crackers and sugar in hot water. Her father took
great delight in feeding her.

The battle of wills—George besting the infant by "whip-
ping" her hard enough to change her cries from petulance to
pain—intimidates Frances as well even though she continues to describe her husband as an ideal father and husband.

George Cahoon took sick in early November and died on
Christmas Day, although Frances did not say what ailed
him. She described the progress of his illness primarily as it
affected his relationship to little Angie:

Her father's nerves were so weak that he could not bear to hear her
cry and paid less and less attention to her as his disease gained
hold on him. He had always so loved to take care of and play with
her that it was a perfect revelation of his state to me when he said
one day, "Don't leave me alone with the baby again, my dear, I'm
too nervous." During the last two weeks or so of my husband's life,
Sily at her own request, took care of her nights as well as day time.
I had no strength to nurse her, and Sily fed her with milk from
our cow.

In the writing, George's dying is subordinated to Angie's
antics: "Occasionally, I took my husband for a ride and
sometimes Angie went too. When she did so she used to sit
demurely between us like a little woman instead of lying in
my lap. On the day her Father died Sily took her to Mrs.
Coolings and kept her there until her Grandpa came and we
came east. In the morning she used to bring her to me at
Mrs. Cawley's and I dressed her and then at night I used to

undress her." Revelations about her husband come to Frances Cahoon through observations of his interactions with their baby; she mentions him only one more time to say that his funeral occurred the day after their arrival at Syndon, New York.

Frances's father, as she indicated, had come to take her back to the family home, and she also described her father primarily in his relationship to Angie, one that began badly when he said on the journey, "I don't know anything about children." He refused to hold her even long enough to allow Frances to get into a sleigh: "As I couldn't get into the sleigh with her in my arms, I think we should have been standing there until this time if the driver had not taken her." But the man comes around during the train ride east, somewhat to Frances's amusement:

I think he expected her to howl continually, and would much have preferred not having the passengers know he belonged to our family. He spent an immense amount of time in the smoking car at first. Further in the journey when he found himself not positively disgraced by his charges he spent more time with us—and worried for fear the child wouldn't have enough to eat. Toward the last of the trip he showed signs of wanting people to understand that that was his grandchild and took more pains to display her good points to people who were interested in her—as many were, and trotted back and forth between our seat and the stove very contentedly with hot water for her, for she lived during this journey on hot water, crackers and sugar.

Frances Cahoon wrote about her daughter's weight gain, new teeth, efforts at crawling and walking, and her "tricks" —"patty-cakes, waving her hand for bye-bye, point her finger and say sh-h-h." She also described the relationship between Angie and her (Frances's) brother: "While on this visit Angie took a great liking to Uncle Ed. When she first went there she was very much afraid of him he spoke so loud, and used to cower back against Mamma when he spoke to her as if she had been hit. But he was very good to her and trotted and played with her so much and held her a good deal so that she became much attached to him."

Angie was the center of every event her mother described. On a carriage ride

Angie wanted to hold the reins and wanted to stand up a good deal and coming back insisted on standing in my lap her face pressed against mine with my bonnet ties in her hand and thumb and finger in her mouth. She enjoyed the ride very much and pointed out things that pleased her on the way. Although she had had no afternoon nap she didn't go to sleep until we got home—but as soon as we did she went right to bed and never woke up til the breakfast bell rang next morning.

Her mother's observations concentrated closely on details:

Perhaps this is as good a place as any to speak of her sucking her thumb. She had begun it when she was a little tiny thing only a few weeks old and always put her thumb and her forefingers into her mouth leaving the other three fingers free. With these three she always if possible grasped some piece of cloth—a handkerchief, her dress, skirt, my dress trimming or bonnet strings or if she was in bed, the edge of the pillowcase or sheet. This sucking of her thumb always pleased her Papa wonderfully for he said "it was a Cahoon trait."

The journal ends with Angie's first birthday, an event that did not come off as planned. A photograph was taken but not developed and printed, a ring could not be found in the proper size, and a "baby's journal" was out of stock at the bookstore. But the day was not a total loss: "While we waited for the train to come home Grandma went out and bought Angie a scrap book for pieces of her dresses. So that she did have one present just on her birthday."

Frances Cahoon wrote about her infant daughter as though everything were invested in the child. But what she thought about living in South Dakota, her husband's occupation there (which she never names except to say that once he went to Sioux Falls on business), his death, or the move to her family's home—not to mention her thoughts concerning her own future—these topics give way entirely to her daughter's development. Frances's own family apparently was fairly wealthy, with a household of servants, carriages, and expensive gifts. Some of the attention she lavished on the infant appears a way of avoiding such an unpleasantness, for instance, as her husband's undertaking to "whip" the month-old infant to make her go to sleep without being rocked. Such attention to Angie could only have helped the infant's chance of survival; it may also have helped her mother endure a difficult year.

Mrs. Ely's Diary

The writer (who did not use her first name) began a journal on November 25, 1835: "This day I suppose I am 18 years of age." She and her husband, to whom she referred always as "Mr. E.," lived in northern Minnesota as Christian missionaries. People in the missionary group travel to Sandy Lake, Leech Lake, and Mille Lac from time to time. The entries continue, with a few gaps, to February 21, 1839, or a little over three years, during which time young Mrs. Ely bore two daughters: Mary Wright, on May 29, 1836, and Delia Cooke, on January 28, 1838. She was three months pregnant when the diary opens. At eighteen, Mrs. Ely was barely out of childhood herself, and yet as missionary and mother she took on what amounted to double parenting duties. Possibly because she was so young, she thought of both the Indians and her children as her and her husband's responsibility to mold into forms pleasing to the sight of God. That was what she took to be her mission, from which, for the duration of the diary, she never wavered. The diary presents a dedicated young woman, but one whose dedication did not allow her to imagine lives different from her own, or values, standards, and behavior other than hers and Mr. E.'s.[6]

Mrs. Ely worked hard on her missionary duties, and she wrote sternly about the Christian spiritual development of Indians, (Indian women in particular) and her infant daughter, Mary. She also kept track of her own moral progress. Before Mary's birth, Mrs. Ely reported events in the missionary camp; afterwards she concentrated on Mary's discipline. Thus in late November, she reported she "kept school" and "visited an Indian Lodge in which were two women, read to them the word of God. They seemed very much interested, & seemed anxious to be instructed."

She also visited a troublesome family named Cotta: "Went to Mrs. Cotta. Isabella told me that Mrs. Cotta inquired about the 2 Commandment [about "graven images"]. Isabella explained it, Mrs. C. said she never understood so before. She supposed it meant their pictures. Mr. C. was present & said that we made [up] half of it, that it was not so in the Bible. Isabella told him it was just so in the bible. She turned to the place & read it. Mr. Cotta never said a word afterward." On January 4, 1836, there was more trouble in the Cotta household: "Isabella came this morning, requesting permission to stay here untill Mr. Ely arrived & then she would make arrangement with him. She said that she could not stay at home, on account of bad feelings which existed in the family towards her. I told her she might stay untill Mr. E. returns, & then she might settle with him." Two days later "Cotta sent for Isabella to come home he said he did not wish her to go about starving. Isabella has partly made up her mind to go home." Mrs. Ely and her husband apparently extended spiritual instruction to mediating in family disputes.

Much of Mrs. Ely's time was spent with the Indians: "Two Indians came in this evening [Christmas Day], we read the word of God to them, talked to them, they listened attentively." She wrote that a Mrs. La Pointe had "today with her children commenced to attend our family worship morning and evening. Our meeting this afternoon was well attended." On January 4: "This evening we called the children & had prayer meeting, three Indians attended, Mr. La Pointe. Peter told them the subject of the meeting—read a portion of scripture, sung a few hymns—and prayed. The chief's eldest son came in this afternoon. Peter explained the card (Christ feedeth five thousand) to him, talked to him, about half an hour. May the Lord bless the truth which he heard."

The La Pointe family were the object of special efforts:

I had some conversation with Mrs. Lapointe this evening. I inquired into the state of her mind. I asked her how she had felt these days past. She said she felt more the need of a Saviour, than she has formerly, she felt that she was a great sinner, in looking upon her past life, she finds nothing that is good. I asked her if she felt she had ever given her heart to God, she said "No." I told her God knew her heart. God would never cast her away if she came the right way. She must be willing to give up every thing for Christ. I told her God was willing to receive her, if she would only go to him. [January 10, 1836]

Mrs. Ely says very little about what circumstances may have been troubling the people she counseled, but her writing does not indicate that she had any qualms about the advice she gave.

Mrs. Ely mentions her husband, but without suggesting very much about the nature of their relationship in a personal way—she writes of him as a coworker in the mission field. Mr. Ely was ill on December 2 and "took pills." Beginning January 4 he was away for three weeks: "My dear husband left this morning in company with an Indian boy (Kucgetash) for La Pointe. May the Lord go with Him—& bless him." She reported hearing from him again on January 20, when some of the other men, having returned from La Pointe, brought a "letter from my dear Husband. . . . Mr. E. will probably be here this week." And five days later he was. The excursion evidently was successful: "The church at La Pointe are in a very interesting state. God is in the midst of his children there. One soul they trust has been brought out of nature's darkness into God's marvellous light."

Mrs. Ely did not write in a very specific way about herself either, although some of the entries suggest she worried that she was not capable of meeting her own standards. She suffered a toothache, walked "as far as the Women's Portage," wrote letters, several times visited a family named Brabant, and went sleigh riding with Isabella La Pointe. She gave "salts" to one Taw-Rouze who "came this morning to ask me for a little physic. . . . I went to his lodge this afternoon, the medicine had operated well" (January 6, 1836). In general, Mrs. Ely presented herself as useful to the Indian community, having what she thought were their best interests in mind, and rather enjoying her position and way of life. But sometimes she felt troubled and worried about her progress out of darkness into light. On Christmas: "This day we have set apart as a day of fasting & prayer. Resolved that I would pray more & read the word of God with an understanding heart read it carefully & prayer fully." On January 4, the day her husband left and she was in the midst of the Isabella La Pointe crisis: "I have this day endeavored to put my trust in the Lord, to Leave myself in his hands. O may I grow in grace & in the knowledge of our Lord & Saviour Jesus Christ."

With the return of her husband from his missionary efforts at the church in La Pointe, entries ceased until July 1 with the report of Mary's birth on May 29, 1836. From the beginning, the Ely parents were as concerned with their child's being "good" as they were with the Indians' coming into God's marvelous light. They wanted her to be passive and obedient and did what they could to discourage "repulsive conduct," even if that came from intestinal gas. Mrs. Ely's first entries about Mary show how much she and her husband wanted Mary to distinguish herself in rapid physical development and exhibit equally remarkable responses to them as parents:

We think her on the whole a pretty good baby. She does not seem to complain without some reason. She begins to notice those around her & appears pleased when noticed. She is now seven weeks old [July 16,1836]. . . . Usually wairysome at Evening for a little while— last evening particularly so. This morning oppressed by heat, her father spoke to her & she instantly began to cry & struggle, in order to see if it came from peevishness, he spoke to her again— with the same result—but she soon belched wind—unable to decide the cause of her apparently repulsive conduct. A little disquieted in the cradle Miss Cook soothed her a little & she became passive [July 18, 1836]. . . . Sabbath. She has been very quiet, quite playful today. Shows at times quite a disposition to be sociable. Seems to be able to distinguish language from other sounds. She has several times entered into conversation—if we may be allowed the expression—while lying in her cradle—probably wishing to be taken up. Her eyes directed into the face of the individual with whom she would seem to Converse wide open—glistening with energy—a curious & musical articulation of sounds not of a complaining tone—attended with all the variety of Grimaces which one would imagine a child would use in such a frame of mind—the limbs put in most active requisition. Occasionally she would break onto a laugh (silent, for she yet does not laugh audibly). Her whole appearance was interesting in the extreme & altogether irresistible. It would hardly be supposed a Child of her age to be capable of such expression—she is 8 weeks old To-day. [July 24, 1836]

Usually her mother found Mary good natured—"quite loquacious and playful." She enjoyed company and liked to listen to flute music, and sometimes during singing at family worship she made "a mellow smooth sound, significant of gratification & amusement. It would seem that she laboured to join her voice with ours" (August 13, 1836). Mrs. Ely worried lest Mary slept too much or had "pain in the bowels," but she worried even more about what she took to be Mary's sometimes troubling state of mind. On August 4:

Her Mother and Miss C. were both out of her sight, yet in the room. After stretching her eyes in vain at last she rolled her eyes back to look over her head—with anxious look & breathless Silence. [Fear or sorrow] was evidently working in her mind. Miss Cook approached the Cradle, but so deep was her mind affected that she could not prevent her little lip from rolling although the evident cause of anxiety had disappeared. Most of the time she has been extremely pleasant. A placidity rested upon her Countenance. She lay in her cradle hardly to be resisted.

But resisted she should be, her parents thought, and they exerted discipline accordingly:

This afternoon M was determined not to lie in the cradle. She cried & struggled to have me take her. I thought it was not duty to have her indulged. She continued crying I spatted [slapped] her legs and let her see by my countenance & talk that she must lie still. She accordingly dropped to sleep. She has several times showed an unwillingness to lie in her cradle. Her will is beginning to show itself [September 20, 1836]. . . . Her Father knocked off the rockers from the cradle. She had got in the habit of being rocked to sleep & she could not sleep without. We thought it best to have her go to sleep without rocking. The first day she cried very much. She wanted to be rocked. When she saw that it could not be so she finally dropped asleep. The next day she did not cry. She now goes to sleep without being rocked, which is altogether better [October 25, 1836]. . . . She is now six months old & has two teeth. For some days past we have held out our hands to have her come. We thought she was learning a bad habit of going to those only she wanted to. We thought it best, that when ever we wanted to have her come to us to take her right up. This afternoon after I had been washing her sore ears I held out my hands to take her. She would not come. Her will is gaining ascendency [November 29, 1836]. . . . Night before last her father corrected her for crying at night, wanting to be taken up [December 5, 1836]. . . . She has had her hand spatted more than once for taking hold of books when they were in her way. She understands that she must not meddle with them. [January 1837]

At the same time as Mary's "will" was "gaining ascendency" and had to be curbed, the child in her first six months also provided her mother with moments Mrs. Ely could enjoy and brag about: "This evening while getting tea I was speaking to little M. She burst out laughing. This is the first time she had uttered an audible laugh. She has been a good girl today" (September 7, 1836). Mary was "beginning to take hold of things," such as a book held out to her; she could "sit alone in her cradle without any support." Her first tooth appeared on November 22, a day when she had "not cried for 24 hours. She sets up in her cradle all the time most when she is awake." Her parents alternated between admiring Mary and "correcting" her: "Mary is very fond of sucking rabbit bones & bread. She is likewise fond of hasty pudding. Night before last her father corrected her for crying at night, wanting to be taken up" (December 5, 1836), and two days later her mother "had to correct Mary for getting angry." Without pause or comment, Mrs. Ely moved from praise, or at least appreciating Mary's precociousness, to stern strictures.

Mary also exhibited some contradictory behavior: "When M. is told to make patty cake she will spat her hands together. When she is told No, No, in attempting to take anything that she is forbidden she will sometimes obey, if not she is corrected, & she then remembers, for some time. Yesterday I corrected her for crying when put in her cradle to sleep. She had learned to love her bed. When quite young she always had a crying spell when put to bed. Now it is quite the reverse" (February 16, 1837). Her mother marveled how quickly Mary was learning to imitate, but she saw danger: "Mary begins to understand language. She will sometimes imitate. She begins to know & understand more than we are aware of, & watch those around her. She is particularly fond of children. O how carefully we should walk before her, & set her a good example" (February 22, 1837). No wonder, to defend herself against so much "correction" and control, that Mary "learned to love her bed."

Writing about her daughter, Mrs. Ely imitated biblical language as though she were making of Mary another missionary project. Mrs. Ely wrote as unwaveringly about what she expected of her daughter as she had of what she thought Indians ought to learn from Bible lessons. She showed no doubts toward what she was doing. She sometimes switched from praise to blame: "M. has for some time tried to blow her whistle. Today she succeeded to her great gratification & amusement. She repeated it several times. She has been quite uneasy today. This morning I tied her on the rocking chair. She let her piece of bread fall & in bending to take it the chair turned over. She bruised her head sadly. She has sat out on the green grass this morn, for some time amusing herself" (April 22, 1837). Nevertheless, Mrs. Ely did not fail to notice Mary's small achievements. On May 27: "Mary can stand up alone. She began to stand alone a month ago. She also tries to sing when told to."

The diary is silent over the summer, picking up again in late September, when Mrs. Ely was five months pregnant with her next child. Since mid-July of the previous summer she had written only about Mary's development; from September through the following February, when the diary stops, she combined reports about other events with observations about Mary. Thus on September 22, 1837, whe wrote of the Indians taking a sick man to La Pointe to be treated by a medicine man and reported that Mary had begun walking at the end of June and "gabbers but cannot talk yet." Religious training had begun: "We are learning her to fold her hands when the blessing is asked at table & returning thanks. During worship she generally makes out to keep quiet till it is over." The next day she wrote that Mary was "very fond of hearing stories" and listened even though she did not understand them. But the same entry began with a lengthy discussion of disciplinary efforts, Mrs. Ely saying she felt that she yielded too easily in comparison to her more resolute husband:

This afternoon Mary climbed the stairs. I told her to get down but she paid no attention to it. I spatted her leg and told her to get down. She did but immediately got up again & looked at me, to see whether I would say or do any thing to her. Mr. Ely told me not to say anything to her but whip her directly & then added, "She never does so to me. It is because you slack in your government." Alas, I fear it is too true. I frequently speak to her often before she minds. I must begin a different course. I will speak to her once, & if she does not hear, speak to her again, & then correct her if she disobeys. Sometimes when told to do a thing, she is heedless about it & goes rather slowly I do not know what to do in that case, if she understood more it would be very different.

Devoted as Mrs. Ely was to "government," she was not insensitive to Mary's feelings and described empathetically her playing with a younger infant, putting objects in his hand: "She loves to kiss him & try to play with him though she sometimes hurts him. She does not know yet when she hurts & and when she does not" (September 24, 1837). But these understanding moments were fewer than the sterner ones: "I had occasion to correct Mary this morning for disobedience. I requested her to drink some milk she had in a plate, but she would not & screamed. I spatted her leg several times before she obeyed. The rest of the day she has been a good girl" (September 25, 1837). The next day Mary was "pretty good," but the one after that "she climbed on the stair. I told her to get down, which she did. She very soon climbed again. I then went and whipped her & told her that she had been a naughty girl, that she had disobeyed her mother. She then went away from the stairs."

Generally, Mrs. Ely reported a fairly calm routine of outdoor work, religious services, her share of the communal housework, and childcare:

I have been washing today. This is my week for housework. In the afternoon Sister Hester went & helped pick about the hay. Our text for this week we find in Eph. 5,3 [October 2, 1837]. . . . This morning it began to rain, & Mr. E. & myself went to secure the hay, covered it over with boards. It has been raining all day. Mary has learnt to cover her face with her hands while blessing is asked. She is very fond of looking at pictures. She will climb up to reach on the shelf & take down a book & bring to me, to show her the pictures & tell her about them. She begins to say considerable many words. [October 3, 1837]

Mrs. Ely reported another social disturbance among the missionary group: Mrs. Boutwell had gone "to live with Nancy Scoat for a time. She says on account of her children" (October 21, 1837), then a week later Mr. Boutwell arrived from Leech Lake and "Hester returned to this house" (October 28, 1837)—but whether Hester and Mrs. Boutwell are the same person is not clear. Meanwhile disciplinary measures regarding Mary continued: "Mary has left off her screaming in some measure. For the two days past she has been a remarkable good girl. One reason is because she is alone. She plays very quietly. I am learning her to repeat Suffer little children to come unto me. She cannot pronounce the words distinctly, but makes out tolerably well" (November 21, 1837). However, "Friday night she cried bout half an hour for the bag of buttons. She did not have her will" (November 28, 1837).

A little more than a year later Mary was reading "words of three or four letters" and writing "a, b, c, d." And she was memorizing scripture: "She is now learning the 3 chapter of Prov. has learned 14 verses. She has also learned to repeat several hymns, such as Lord in the morning those shalst hear. May God who makes the sun to show. And now another day is gone. Though I am young a little one" (February 21, 1839). Mary was not yet three years old. Her sister Delia, by then a year old, was undergoing the same regimen. Her mother wrote appreciatively of her accomplishments and determinedly that, like Mary, Delia not "have her will": "She is now walking about the house. Understands some things. She has learned to fold up her hands when blessing is asked & when thanks are returned at meals. This morning her father rapped on the table. She was sucking, was not spoken to as usual, but she immediately stopped & folded her hands" (February 1, 1839). Here Mrs. Ely's diary ends.

Women are called "culture carriers." "Like father, like son," we hear. Curses and blessings follow us from "generation to generation." We assume that in the absence of strong rebellion, ideas, habits, and mannerisms of parents will transmit themselves to children almost automatically. When they do not, some call these children rebellious or at least independent. The private writings we have looked at suggest some ways in which language reflects social and economic conditions, for each writer's style explains her, as it were. The year the writing occurred, or even geographical location, have less effect on language—on how each writer demonstrates thinking, what her values are—than her general mode of living. Thus Sarah Pickwell replicates plots of romantic novels about suffering children, followed by wild west stories when she lived in the West. Frances Cahoon reflected upper-middle-class values that isolated children from adults. Effie Hanson, on a farm, included her children in all the other details of agricultural and domestic work. And Mrs. Ely understood child-rearing in the context of missionary duties, watching her infant's moral and spiritual development as closely as she did her learning to sit up, walk, and talk. Mary was expected to be "good." The language of these writers varies, and hence their aspirations for children, but what varies little is their concentration on their children, their focus on minute details of young children's day-to-day lives. Whatever the western movement meant in regard to expanding economic opportunities, new adventure, or breaks with the past, for women, the bearing and caring for children in the West intensified the attention they gave them. It certainly did not release them from children.

It may seem less surprising that women who took care of their children under settlement conditions should have written about such close attachments to children. The examples in these pages remind us that being a parent and responsible for the basic care of infants and children is not made less arduous by an ideology of adventure. For this group of mothers at least, children were all-consuming; the rigors of settlement, even for those who soon abandoned plans, turned the women more fiercely than ever toward their children, to the exclusion of almost everything else. Settlement, with small children, meant more, not less attention to the minutiae and the worry of childcare. How, we might wonder, did their efforts appear to their children? How might the children have remembered those years?

Mrs. Goudreau and Isabella Frazer, with her two boys and somewhat cool attitudes about marriage, both exerted considerable ingenuity on behalf of their children. The reports of them, both third-hand, show them determined and practical, making sure that their children came to the best available opportunities. Inger Ford Grindeland and Frances Cahoon write as women almost neurotically absorbed in their children, fearful of what might happen to them, yet also using their devotion as a way to enhance their own lives indepen-

dent of their children. Inger Ford Grindcland's wanting her
children to know Norwegian culture and language led her to
be a prime mover in founding a local church, an experience
that made her a public figure in the community and gave her
some relief from the exhaustion and anxiety the children
caused (possibly exacerbated by a husband who did not appear to pay much attention). Likewise, at least for one year,
Frances Cahoon's total concentration on her daughter may
have been her saving, when she experienced the initial move
to South Dakota, a difficult birth, the death of her husband,
and the move back to her family in the east. Effie Hanson's
letters evoke a community of parents, living apart from one
another on fairly settled farms and trying to care for children, husbands, farms, and their own health and well-being.
The young Mrs. Ely, thinking she could convert Indians and
train her infant daughters with similar missionary principles, is a disturbing example of one of the consequences of
isolation. Zealous though she and her husband were in their
missionary callings, their enthusiasms for breaking wills
and turning toddlers to Christ might have been restrained a
little had they had more of a community around them of
relatives and friends.

Each of these examples speaks to slightly different circumstances as well as ideas about child-raising, yet all exhibit inordinate care for children on the part of parents and
almost never-ending anxiety. With infants and small children, these writers insist, pioneering at whatever stage was
no adventure. Every day threatened new difficulties, and
merely to put off injury, sickness, and death was an accomplishment. These particular writings are so obsessively centered on the mothers' worries about their children that we
gain little idea about what the experiences meant to the children, how they thought about their lives. These mothers (ex-
cepting now and then Effie Hanson), always with children
on their minds, hardly imagined what their children's own
memories were becoming, so preoccupied were they with
just keeping them alive.

6

Happy Childhoods

The best and worst of times—people have said that their experiences in settlement and pioneering were very difficult, even personally humiliating, and almost equally exhilarating. When they were young, many report, they put up with great physical inconvenience, exhausting labor, loneliness, danger, and shaming poverty, years that in old age they nevertheless remembered happily. Tolstoy is right that "happy" families are not very distinguishable, that tranquil lives tend to uniformity. But under circumstances that promised so little, the relative contentment that some settlers report is worth examining. What were the personal qualities, as well as the social and economic circumstances, most helpful to successful pioneering—if by success we mean that people lived a long time in the place they moved to and claimed relative satisfaction there? For children, what did a "happy" childhood mean?

Such an understanding of "success" does not necessarily depend on wealth and influence: the owner of a grain elevator who served three terms as his town's mayor might think himself a clearer success than the widow whose farm was lost in the depression and who ended her days in a nursing home. And yet, as people speak of their own lives, they mention wealth and influence less often than they do the more private values of good health and contentment. Women especially measure success less by what they and their husbands "did" than what became of their children and the children's children. Families naming doctors, teachers, and other professionals among the second and third generation sound proud of themselves. A woman who went to work in her late teens as chambermaid in a hotel, married her father's hired man, and did not see a third room built onto her farmhouse until six children had been born could brag (a grandchild reported to me in conversation) that one of her daughters helped support the farm during the depression by teaching. To date, all the many children of the grandparents' nine have attended college. That family has valued their children's education as a sign of their collective success. Settlers who reflected on how much they had sacrificed for a fragile living in North Dakota declared themselves satisfied if they could say their children had achieved education and status in farming, business, and the professions. They spoke as if it had been worth it if they felt a degree of personal comfort and contentment in old age, no matter how much hardship had come before.

Clara Bond

The life in North Dakota of Clara Bond gives every indication of having conformed to such quiet satisfaction. Her parents moved about a good deal, worked hard, and while they did not particularly acquire fame or fortune, they paid attention to their children. It would appear that thanks to such attention, especially from her mother, Clara achieved professional recognition. Clara's son is an insurance executive, and her daughter, Jean Guy, who recounts her mother's story, served a term on the state board of higher education and is married to a man who has been state governor. Clara's grandchildren and their spouses represent the occupations of lawyer, college professor, farmer, nurse, personnel director, social worker, and contractor.

The account of her life in these pages is based on a biographical essay written by Clara's sister, Ruth, and on a telephone interview and other conversations I have had with Jean Guy (summer 1983).[1] Although she grew up and was educated in Iowa, Clara Bond came to live in North Dakota when public welfare was growing as a profession for women. Like teaching and nursing, public welfare was seen as a "natural" extension of women's nurturing family role; it was safely low paying and not likely to lead to positions of power. On the other hand, more than a few women were able to carve influential and creative careers for themselves within such traditional occupations, even those that served children. That was the path Clara Bond took and found rewarding. She and her children remained in the area. Her parents farmed, but she did so only briefly, preferring, with others in the family, professional and business careers.

Her parents were among late farmer settlers in west-central North Dakota, and Clara Bond achieved the position of juvenile commissioner in Fargo after a long career in secretarial and administrative positions. Her growing up was untroubled, Jean Guy says, in large part because she always had received careful attention from her parents. Clara Bond worked and earned her living all her life, but when she was young, her work appears to have been selected more for her benefit than the family's. Her mother had a good deal to do with making those choices and in seeing to it that decisions regarding the family's farming in the West (decisions for the most part made by her husband, William Bond), interfered as little as possible with their children's education and professional training.

The Bond family was of Welsh and English descent. They arrived in West Virginia before the Revolution, and later moved to southern Minnesota, near New Ulm, where William Wallace Bond, Clara's father, was born. That generation came into a very large family. Wallace and his sister Alice were the eldest of four pairs of twins and four single children (one other pair of twins and one other child died). When Wallace was sixteen, his father died, and his mother, Martha Sperry Bond, supported her twelve children by nursing, even though she had had no formal nurse's training. She was in high demand, and the family moved several times through southern Minnesota, living in Spicer and Willmar as well as New Ulm.

Clara's mother was Elise Grott, whose parents were prosperous farmers in Schlesvig Holstein. Elise had a twin sister, Emma, and one other brother. At age seventeen or eighteen she traveled to Chicago with a friend, Christina Juhl (whose brother Mads was married to Emma Grott), and in Chicago married a man named Lund, who died not long after the birth of Elizabeth. By 1892 Elise owned a laundry in Webster City and that year married Wallace Bond, who helped her operate the laundry. About 1894 the Bonds sold the laundry and bought a farm at Kamrar, Iowa, and six years later sold it. Wallace then managed a succession of creameries—at Highland, Trumball Lake, and Grettinger, so the family moved often, always living on the edge of towns. His salary was $50 a month and all the cream, butter, and milk the family could use. In Grettinger good cream was not available for butter, and there was a fuss with the director, so Bond quit in spite of good pay and returned to Webster City to work in a dairy, then to Belmond as bulk man for Standard Oil. Last, Wallace Bond ran a gravel business for the Great Western Railroad. Elise, meanwhile, gave piano lessons, traveling several days at a time by buggy to earn enough money for a piano. She intended Elizabeth to train to be a music teacher. When it came time to move to the farm in North Dakota, the land was bought with money from Elise's piano lessons. Clara was born May 30, 1893, in Webster City; Ruth in 1897 on a farm in Kamrar, and Edwin in 1900 in Cylinder.

According to family lore, Clara was a strong-willed child, sometimes considered a "problem" because of her quick energy and ambition. She reportedly wanted always to be in the forefront of whatever was going on, to be leading things, Jean Guy reports. She had parts in school productions, gave declamations, and played basketball. After graduating from high school at age sixteen, she attended Highland Park College in Des Moines from 1909 to 1910, where in nine months she completed a one-year secretarial course.

Clara was four years older than Ruth, and Ruth three years older than Edwin. The children divided themselves into two groups, Elizabeth and Clara having a rather similar experience in the family and somewhat different from that of Ruth and Edwin, for the two older girls had pretty much left home by the time the two youngest in the family were well in school. Or such is the impression that Ruth Bond has given in a reminiscent essay she wrote in June 1984 at age eighty-seven. Elizabeth and Clara appear as rather distant older sisters who did not take part in the family and school life that Ruth remembered with Edwin. Ruth begins her narrative in 1905, the year the family moved from Webster City to Belmond and the year she says she felt new possibilities. She an Edwin were being paid attention to in a new way. "We were very happy with the change," she wrote of the move, "because I did not do well in school in Webster City. After enrolling in the 3rd grade in Belmond my troubles went away, and I loved my teacher Madge Jackson." Her siblings also appeared to have had few troubles:

My sister Clara had been in the eighth grade in Webster City for one half year, so she wanted to go into high school instead of taking the eighth grade over again. She always had very good grades, so the Supt. Mr. Nevlin allowed her to do so. Edwin was not old enough for school as he was only 5 years old. Elizabeth did not finish high school because of her health, and because my mother wanted her to be a music teacher. She had taken piano lessons when we lived in Grettinger from the sisters at the Catholic convent in Emmetsburg, and also from a professor Bultick in Webster City. Not long after we came to Belmond she started to give lessons.

Elise Bond's urging upon Elizabeth an early career as music teacher assured her the beginning of economic independence and likely a better education through her instruction in music than the general programs of the local schools would have provided. At any rate, her mother kept in mind the future of her eldest daughter. According to Ruth, Belmond also offered Wallace Bond improved opportunities in his work for Standard Oil: "His job was to deliver gasoline and kerosene to Belmond and about 5 or 6 other towns close by. . . . The first thing my father needed to do was to buy two horses, which he did. I remember they were two beautiful black horses to pull the tank wagon. Not long after we had them they both died because the load seemed too heavy and they needed to be fed very well. They both developed colic and died. After that Dad bought mules as they were able to stand the hard work."

The house the Bond family lived in evoked the place Ruth lived at the time she said her troubles disappeared:

I remember the price was $2500 and that was a real bargain because it was a large two story square house with a porch across the front. Of course it was not modern but very few houses were in Belmond. One fourth of a block of land went with the house, and it had a nice barn on the back of the lot to house the mules.

My mother knew she could get teachers to board and room with us in a nice house like that and of course Dad had the job with Standard Oil Co. which was considered very good. We were all delighted with this new home which was by far the best home we had ever lived in.

It had a large hall through the middle of the first and second floor with an open stairway. There were two parlors on one side, and the dining room and kitchen on the other side down stairs, and four bedrooms upstairs, all without closets. There was a large closet at the front of the hallway upstairs with a stairway that led up to the attic. Handy to the kitchen was a platform outside the back door, and a pump for water supply for all the house. No electricity of any kind.

It was not long before my mother had two school teachers boarding and rooming with us. It was while we lived here that Elizabeth started to give music lessons. She must have been eighteen years old when she started giving lessons [making her year of birth 1889].

There is a relish for details in Ruth Bond's account of the house and the activity that emanated from it; it was the anchor of her grade school years.

It did not take long before Elizabeth and Clara were getting acquainted around town:

Elizabeth became acquainted with two young women who started a milliner store in town. Their home was out in the country and they drove in to town each morning. They would like to get their dinner in town so they came to my mother and of course she was eager to add two more paying guests. They were Mary and Nell Barry who later became very dear friends of our family. They made such lovely hats for Elizabeth that looked so nice along with her curly hair. . . .

Edwin started to school while we lived in this house, and his first teacher was Miss Pursell who stayed with us. She was a very pretty girl and had several boy friends while in town. Elizabeth also had a boy friend who was John Rule, who later became her husband. He was employed in the First National Bank in Belmond. There was also another young man who was interested, but Elizabeth was not interested in him.

The house in Belmond held particularly good possibilities for Ruth herself:

I remember making friends at school and also girls who lived in our neighborhood. We lived about five blocks from school and this one friend and I usually went together. I remember putting on plays in our barn during summer vacation. We sold tickets for a few pennies to those who did not belong to the caste. Those were happy days. Dad bought Edwin and me a scooter that we propelled with our feet, so when Mother needed something at the store we could get on our scooter and go get it. We could also buy smashed chocolates at this store, and get quite a bit for a few pennies.

The Bonds belonged to the Christian Church and then attended the Methodist Church, where the children went to Sunday school and Elizabeth played the piano. But piety did not dampen their exuberance: "My father did not want any of our family to play cards or dance, but Clara wanted to go to dances. Finally he had to give in, and both my sisters were going to dances." Unfortunately from the children's point of view the four-bedroom house only five blocks from school that boarded favorite teachers lasted only four years, for then the family exchanged houses with the aging parents of Bernard Minenga, who lived on the edge of town. Ruth wrote of this second house:

It was really a good move for my folks as there was about twenty acres of land along with a good house with furnace heat which we did not have where we were. There was also a good barn and other out buildings. There was a large garden space, an asparagus bed and several kinds of small fruit and several pie cherry trees. There was also a large lawn and shade trees. . . . [My father was in] the business of selling sand and gravel soon after we moved there. We hired a man to load the sand onto a wagon and hauled to be loaded into box cars which could be set on a siding of the Great Western railroad which ran right near our place. In fact the Rock Island railroad and the Great Western crossed right in front of our house. Edwin and I were very happy about the trains going by and we used to wave to the men in the engines and they would wave back.

This more rural setting meant that children had a longer walk to school and fewer nearby friends to play with; the family bought a one-seat buggy "for transportation to town." Wallace Bond prospered enough with the sale of sand and gravel to stop delivering oil. Land on the edge of town also made possible a small dairy operation, into which the two younger children were recruited, with little enthusiasm on their part, as Ruth implies in her passive verbs:

The folks had several cows, so they decided to sell milk. It was decided that Edwin and I were to deliver the milk. We had a small delivery wagon, and one horse to pull this wagon. Edwin rather thought this was fine, but I was getting to the age when I didn't care for the job. But those days one did what your parents thought was best and of course we could use the money. The milk was in bottles and rather heavy to handle. I think we just delivered the milk about 3 days a week, after we got home from school. If the weather was bad Dad took over. . . . Edwin and I were to help Dad and Mother with the chores around home. One of the big jobs we had in the summer was to mow the large lawn that we had. It rained a lot in Iowa, so the grass was heavy. By the time we finished doing it all, it was time to start over again. There was no such thing as a power mower, so it was really work. We had seven cherry trees, so when they were ripe we had to pick cherries. Mother also had some of Edwin's friends come to help. Some of the cherries were sold at the grocery stores down town and Mother canned a lot for cherry pies and other desserts. She also sold raspberries and currants, and asparagus. Besides taking care of the fruit, Mother always had a big garden. My mother was a very thrifty person and a hard worker. She baked all the bread we used, and at one time she entered a contest sponsored by Gold Medal flour and won a kitchen cabinet. We were all very proud of her.

Edwin and I had a lot of fun playing in a pond of water which was in the gravel pit on our land. The gravel had been taken out down to the water level and formed a pond of nice clean water which was no more than two feet deep. Dad got us a flat bottom boat and we would row around in this pond. Usually we had some of our friends come, and usually someone would be hanging on the boat and floating along.

But what Clara and Elizabeth were doing looked to Ruth more glamorous than hauling wagons full of milk bottles. Clara was working at the MBA Insurance Company in Mason City, Iowa, and Elizabeth taught music to a large number of students. "I remember how I used to envy them," Ruth wrote, "because they bought nice clothes, and Elizabeth and some of her friends used to go to Mason City and go to shows and do their shopping." Clara's secretarial training, like Elizabeth's in music, assured her employment: she "had to take dictation in short hand from the different men in the company and then type the letters from notes. Some of the men were not easy to work for," partly because the women in the office were more adept at taking dictation than the men were at giving it. Elizabeth became engaged to John Rule, who with his brother undertook a three-year dental program at Marquette University in Milwaukee, and Clara broke an engagement to a doctor.

The year 1912—when Clara was nineteen, Ruth fifteen, and Edwin twelve years old—brought great changes to the Bond family. Wallace Bond left Belmond with a boxcar full of horses, furniture, and the dog for a farm in North Dakota he had bought the year before. The move did not meet with unanimous enthusiasm. According to Ruth, "Mother did not like the idea as she never liked a new country, and also because Grandpa and Grandma Damgaard came to Belmond to live because we could look after them. It was then decided that we could move back into town, and Dad could go to Dakota in the spring in time to put in the crop, and Mother and Edwin and I would go up after school was out and spend the summer there." The land was bought in partnership with Elise's brother, Theodore Grott—he was to buy a tractor, and Wallace would pay for the land and do the work. The arrangements Elise made in Belmond with her children suited them very well—a return to the pleasures and conveniences of town living:

> Soon after Dad left, Mother sold the place [in the country with the dairy herd] and purchased a house just one block from school and about 3 blocks from where Grandpa and Grandma lived. It was a very good location. An addition was built on the back of the house upstairs and downstairs. A nice large kitchen downstairs and a screened in back porch, and a large bedroom and a screened in sleeping porch upstairs. The house was made modern and we now had our first bathroom. We soon had two teachers boarding and rooming with us and two more who came for meals.
> One thing I still remember is that we had no electricity as my job after school was to clean, fill and trim all the lamps for the house.
> The next three years were happy ones for me. I went into the eighth grade when we moved into the house in town. It was nice to be right in town and easy to get places. The one teacher who roomed with us was my eighth grade teacher Miss Fitzgerald. She was willing to help me with my arithmetic when I had trouble.

Elise was seeing to it that her two youngest children went on with their education and lived as comfortably as possible. She also provided income by boarding teachers. Clara had gone to the farm in Almont, south of Bismarck, with her father to keep house. Wallace's building priorities were the reverse of Elise's: "The first building on the farm," Ruth wrote, "was a large machine shed to house the tractor and other machinery and a lean to was built on one side for living quarters. It was built just for summer use as we were to return to Belmond in the winter. Dad planted flax on the land he broke and harvested around 1600 bushels." After his first year, Wallace returned to Belmond for Christmas, bringing a fur coat to Elizabeth as a wedding present, and neck pieces and muffs for Elise and Ruth: "He had trapped the beavers in the Muddy Creek which flowed through our land. Everyone was delighted with these unexpected gifts. Dad had stopped in Saint Paul and taken the pelts to Albrecht Fur Company and had them made up there. Elizabeth wore that coat every year for many winters after she and John were married and lived in New Salem."

Differences between the house in Belmond and the farm in Almont marked very different ways of living, and Eliza Bond did all she could to ease the transition for her children, principally by seeing to it that their education was interrupted as little as possible. In the spring of 1913 she and Edwin left for North Dakota before school was out, but Ruth remained with Elizabeth to finish the term. Ruth described the adventure of traveling alone:

I went to St. Paul with some friends who put me on the Northern Pacific train, and I rode all day, arriving in New Salem about 10 o'clock. Dad had told Mr. Neas who owned a hotel to meet me, which he did, and we walked about 3 blocks to his hotel with him pushing a two wheeled cart with my suitcase. I was a tired girl and pretty lonely that night. The next day I was to take the train to Almont, but Mr. Neas said he was going to drive with horse and buggy to Almont on business, and maybe I would like to ride down with him. So that is what we did. It was about 12 miles up and down hills, but we finally arrived in Almont just as Dad was going to drive to the depot. Needless to say, I was very happy to see him. I climbed up in the seat on the lumber wagon, and we started for an eight mile drive to the farm where Mother and Edwin were waiting for us.

The summer, she wrote, "was all a new experience for me. Mother and I had a two wheeled cart with one horse which we used to travel around the country side. The roads were only trails and many times we would take the wrong turn and get lost. We also went to town and bought the groceries, and usually had dinners at Sherwoods who had a sort of hotel. The Sherwoods were folks from Iowa, so we felt sort of closer to them for that reason. In fact several of the business- men in Almont were folks from Iowa." Commuting between Iowa and North Dakota continued. That fall of 1913 Ruth and Edwin returned in early September for school, and their parents followed after harvest, but that was their last winter in Belmond. The next summer Ruth was accompanied to North Dakota by her friend Clare Snyder, who hoped the drier climate would alleviate her hay fever ("which it did"), and the family did not return to Iowa. The Bonds had bought a farm of 320 acres for $5,000 and built an addition to the house: "a good sized living room, 3 upstairs bedrooms and a screened in porch on the front of the house. The location was good because of some trees near the house, and close to the valley road which led to town. The improvements on the section of land we owned was on the wrong side of the creek and in order to get to the road we had to ford the creek which was sometimes very high in the spring." These ex- pansions meant a stronger commitent to farming, and from Ruth they drew a reluctant reaction:

The folks decided that to make farming pay they needed to get cattle and stay in Dakota the year around. That meant that Edwin and I would not go back to school in Belmond. I don't think Edwin minded too much, but this was a blow to me. I would miss the last two years in high school. I was to go up to New Salem and go to high school. Mother and I went up to New Salem to find a place where I could work for my board. The place I found turned out to be very unsatisfactory, so I returned home.

Edwin rode horseback to Almont to finish his schooling in the seventh and eighth grades. For the younger children, the move from Iowa to North Dakota brought a stop to their education, at least the kind of education that had brought Elizabeth and Clara into professions.

Then real disaster struck in the form of a late July hail- storm that destroyed an exceptionally fine crop, just when the family was thinking of building a new granary to store it.

"Mother wanted to leave and go back to Iowa," Ruth writes, but since the house in Belmond had been sold to pay for the farm, there was not much to go back to, and "of course that meant losing everything they had." They bought groceries with what they earned from selling milk and got by, as did many others in the path of the storm. The loss of the year's crop and her own inability to finish high school led Ruth to begin teaching. She tells of that professional beginning also as something of an adventure:

There was a school being built east of us several miles, and friends encouraged me to take examinations at Mandan and apply for the school. Amanda Nelson, my best friend, decided to do the same thing, so we did a lot of studying and took the exams. She passed the first time but I had to take the exams over again. I think maybe she answered questions about North Dakota that I was weak on. Anyway I passed the second time and applied for the school and was hired. I was 18 years old in August when I started to teach in October. The school house was not finished until October, so the 9 month term lasted into June the next spring. My first year salary was $45 a month. I kept one month's salary and gave the rest to the folks to buy seed to plant the crop the next spring. They had already borrowed all they could at the bank, so it was very necessary to have this money. I spent time doing some plowing under a rye crop that was ready to harvest when the hail hit. It made a good crop the next year.

I rode horseback up through a sort of prairie road to the home of an older couple, the Dinharts, and unsaddled the horse and put him in the barn and then walked up hill a mile to the school. Then I had to build a fire in the stove so the school would be warm when the children came. Some days were very cold and I did not dare to miss getting to school because 3 of the children walked about 3 miles and needed to get in where it was warm. They usually had frozen spots on their faces in severe cold weather, and we thawed them out with snow.

Ruth Bond's teaching venture in a rural school typified the experience of many women at age eighteen, but it departs from what her two older sisters were doing at the same age.

Ruth was earning her living, to be sure, and in addition contributing to the operation of the farm, but she had curtailed her own education to do so. Instead of the family's arranging itself around children's schooling, as they had until they all left Belmond, Ruth now was adjusting her affairs to fit the needs of the family, specifically the farm.

Elizabeth, Clara, and Elizabeth's fiancé, John Rule, joined the Bonds in North Dakota, but they were less directly involved in maintaining the farm than the rest of the family. Clara had come with her father during the summer of 1912, partly for her own health. A doctor in Mason City had told her she was overworked and anemic, presumably because of the secretarial job for the Modern Woodman Brotherhood of America Insurance Company and the strain of her engagement to the Roman Catholic doctor Steve O'Brien. Her family liked the fact that he "moved in the nicest circles" but otherwise preferred she not marry him, and Clara herself decided that, although he did not insist that she convert to his church, she nevertheless could not bring up any children as Catholics. Clara returned from that first summer on the Almont farm to the insurance job, and she broke her engagement.

John Rule planned to begin a dental practice in New Salem, North Dakota, a thriving town on the railroad that had only a single elderly dentist. He and Elizabeth were married in 1916. Elizabeth and Clara had come to North Dakota just before Christmas of 1915 and began, Ruth reports,

to work up some dancing classes. Clara had taken lessons in Des Moines, and Elizabeth was to furnish the music on the piano. The two dances I remember were the tango and the rumba. This venture turned out to be very enjoyable and rewarding, especially for Elizabeth. Two of the towns where they had classes were New Salem and Glen Ullin. They met a lot of nice people, and usually were invited into the homes of their pupils for lovely dinners while they were in town. The New Salem folk were very happy to know they were to have a music teacher for their children, and also a new dentist.

She added, "When the girls were conducting their dancing classes, a young man, William Behrbaum, was one of the pupils. He and Clara started going together and later on became engaged. He was employed at the First National Bank in New Salem." (They did not marry.)

Ruth's leaving Belmond, Iowa, had not meant that she had lost contact with her school friends there, and in the summer of 1917, after her second year of teaching, she returned to Belmond to see her friends graduate from high school. It was a happy return:

Two of my best friends were teaching country school. If they went to summer school in June they could teach in town, so I planned my trip to go to Webster City first and later to go to Belmond. Howard was working for the Belmond Tel. Co. that summer, so he and I were together on a great many dates, along with Susan Morse and Hazel Snyder and their boy friends. There were six of my best girl friends at home that summer and we really had a wonderful time. We had picnics and slumber parties and all sorts of get togethers. The last part of August I was to start for home. I went to Mason City where I visited my relatives for a few days, and Aunt Emma came the day appointed on the train, and I joined her at Mason City. She was going home with me and was to take Grandma Damgaard back to Iowa [this was Elise's mother, who had been living with the Bonds since the death of Elise's father in the spring of 1916]. . . . When I got home I had two surprises waiting for me. Mother told me that Elizabeth was expecting a baby in September and the bad news was that the school board had hired someone else to teach my school. I certainly felt badly about that but knew it was my own fault for not signing my contract before leaving on my vacation.

Elizabeth's baby arrived while Elizabeth was at the farm visiting with her Aunt Emma, but the delivery went well. However, soon after, the infant developed serious digestive difficulties; he was put to nurse with a woman in New Salem, who had just had a child of her own. "But some one of our family had to be at her home to take care of J.W. He cried a lot as he was always hungry." Elise, Elizabeth, and John took turns caring for the infant at the nurse's home, and Ruth wrote, "It was up to me to take care of Dad and Edwin out at the farm." The child recovered by Christmas, and Ruth's autobiographical reminiscence ended.

Jean Guy's account of her mother continues, however. Clara had secured a secretarial position in Bismarck with T. R. Atkinson, city engineer, and lived in a boarding house. Although people thought it unusual that a young woman should work alone in an office with a man, Clara became very successful in her profession. She worked also in the Morton County Courthouse and as secretary for the state senate, an appointed office, for which she took minutes and kept official records. She was energetic and resourceful. In 1918 she rented a section of land on the Standing Rock Indian Reservation (when Indian lands were being taken by settlers). In early April she put in a crop with her father, who provided the machinery. It was just before this journey that Clara had met Sidney Mason, whose family also was succeeding in North Dakota.

Sidney Mason was born in Buffalo, North Dakota, and both his parents had grown up in the region—his mother as one of seven children whose parents farmed near Dickey, and his father an only child born in Minnesota. His mother, Nettie, had taught country school at age seventeen, and his father, Leon, was depot agent first at Dickey for the Northern Pacific Railroad, then at Buffalo for fifty years. Also an only child, Sidney attended Macalester College in St. Paul for one year, then joined a volunteer ambulance unit in France in 1914–15, returning to Bismarck for a commission in the U.S. Army that found him in small towns showing propaganda movies to counter pro-German feelings.

At a dance in April in Bismarck he and Clara met; they were married August 26. Sidney was not yet twenty-one and he had not finished college; Clara was twenty-five. The couple had no money and no savings, and there was a war on. Their honeymoon consisted of going to Clara's farm to harvest the crop. She told of driving down to the farm, seventy-five miles in a heavy, crude lumber wagon, with a canary in a bird cage. They stayed in the shack while they harvested. That winter they continued working in Bismarck, went back the next spring to put in a crop, and stayed on the farm for several years. One of the ways Clara tried to earn money while they were farming on the reservation was by baking bread, but once, when it froze on their way to town, people would not buy it.

Certainly there is no way of knowing what constitutes a "good" or "happy" childhood, or even whether such childhoods lead to especially productive adult lives. However, it is possible to identify individual lives that appear to include both, and Clara Bond, her husband, and her mother and sisters, by their own accounts and the testimony of those who knew them, sound like products of such experiences. None was particularly famous, yet they exemplify varied lives, particularly for women at that time.

Clara, for instance, had two children; one of her grandmothers, widowed early, had borne fourteen, ten of them twins. Clara involved herself aggressively in high school dramatics and sports and took a year of secretarial training, both giving her a considerable edge over women and most men (Sidney had had a year at Macalester College). Elizabeth took enough music lessons to teach piano and dancing, an artistic occupation with social as well as economic opportunities. Ruth's education was curtailed by the move to North Dakota, but she had a good start in Iowa and continued professional and intellectual interests through teaching and, after 1918, as a writer for the *New Salem Journal*. She gave all but the first month's teaching salary to the family farm, but soon saved enough money for a Model T Ford. Their mother, Elise, was careful with her children. She saw to music lessons for Elizabeth and secretarial school for Clara, guaranteeing the income for education through music lessons, boarders, and her chicken and butter enterprises. She was reluctant to move to North Dakota and did not do so until the education of her children was well in hand.

Clara entered an opportune profession at her mother's

urging, and she made useful contacts by being secretary to North Dakota's first state engineer and as appointed secretary to the state senate. By farming briefly before marriage and establishing herself professionally as a secretary, she was able to provide major family income after marriage. She chose fortuitously in her husband, by all accounts a generous and sanguine man, not jealous of her achievements, and himself a well-regarded insurance salesman. Bad health troubled her—she nearly died of asthma in the 1940s—and she made what may have been an important negative decision, not to marry the successful doctor in Mason City.

The Bond women were inventive, taking advantage of whatever opportunity came along, from teaching the bunny hop in farming towns to enlarging child welfare services, as Clara did when appointed juvenile commissioner in Fargo. They were not typical. Few women came to North Dakota as children with their settler parents and stayed to find productive careers of their own (other than teaching or nursing). For that matter, Sidney Mason was not entirely typical either, especially in being married to a woman whose career was more publicly visible than his. Nevertheless, the Mason and Bond families probably came as close as anyone to the promise of western settlement: that by answering the homestead call, parents might provide a better future for their children and descendants and at the same time adhere to the optimistic relationships with children that middle-class urban families were aspiring to.

The Historical Data Project

The Works Progress Administration (WPA) in the late 1920s and early 1930s sponsored the nationwide Historical Data Project, which employed interviewers to record biographical information about local residents. In North Dakota, several thousand of those interviews are in the archives at the State Historical Society (not all states preserved them). The surveys record many expressions of contentment in old age and of relatively "happy" childhoods, as well as many less happy life stories. The quality of the documents varies: some interviewers were barely literate, others betrayed frustration with the aging people they talked to. Some of the "pioneers" had little to say or resented being asked. A subject qualified by having lived in North Dakota since 1889, the year of statehood. Questionnaires are in two parts. The first part is a form for names, birth dates, and other facts about belongings people brought with them, the size of their houses, and lists of neighbors and businesses. The second part is an anecdotal biographical essay of a page or more, some written by the pioneers themselves.

The project records the stories of survivors—those who neither died nor gave up and moved away from North Dakota. However sketchy the accounts, they express the unremarkable, the ordinary dailiness people coped with. The essays tell best of the small things that were important at the time, and they glance at what the days were like for children. Like the sources for Clara Bond's life—her daughter's conversations and her sister's essay—these WPA interviews hardly approach intimacy with their subjects. Some interviewers expressed disapproval of the person they were interviewing, or they did not understand what that person was saying. They were constrained by time and the formality of the interview form. Nevertheless, if we keep in mind such limitations, I think that every now and then we can hear something close to a voice touching on genuine experience, and that little is better than no contact at all.[2]

Melissa Thompkins

Melissa and William Thompkins moved in 1883 from Wisconsin to a homestead near Jamestown (Melissa's father was Seaman Richards Randolph, born in 1820 "on water," according to the "Family Data" chart). "Coming to the Territory without any money, was pretty much up hill work," the essay about her begins, and it continues with sometimes odd specificity—often the way people remember the most important things. The Thompkinses shared a boxcar with another family, transporting their furniture, a cow, three pigs, and two cats: "While the car was standing in the yards in Minneapolis, the door was opened and the cats escaped and were lost." It cost them a loan of $7 to "get their goods off the car," and Williams earned money "feeding a separator" for a neighbor farmer—a walk of nine miles to work. Random details accumulated in these interviews give a convincing portrait of actual living.

"Hardships—we went through all kinds of hardships—we came here without a cent. Three children were born in Wisconsin, the youngest being only five weeks old when we arrived in Jamestown," said Mrs. Thompkins (who was interviewed in 1938, William having died in 1937). "We built a house or shanty about 12 × 14, and mind you it only had the siding on it. The dish cloth would freeze on the oven door of the cook stove." (While not being used it was not always kept burning.) "Oh it was awful." To reinforce and make the building more comfortable, Mr. Thompkins would "cut the snow in large chunks and bank high against the house, then throw water over it, then all froze, and would make a thick coating of snow, which kept the winds out. Necessity was the mother of invention in this case." When asked what was the nature of the fuel to keep warm, and do the cooking for the family, Mrs. Thompkins replied, "Everything that would burn—we burned buffalo chips, gathered buffalo bones for fuel, burned sheep manure, hay, anything. Those were hard times."

A cellar kept vegetables and milk from freezing, and frequently it was necessary to cover the vegetables over to keep them from freezing when it was extremely cold. During the first few years, when the family had no means of transportation, William would walk to Jamestown, carrying a basket of eggs, and he would receive as little as eight cents per dozen in trade, carrying groceries home twelve miles from town. In the beginning they saw "lots of Indians, but they were no worry, they never bothered us. We had lots of water and wells, but water was not very good, it was salty, we grew to like it. One day we went to visit my sister, a terrible blizzard came up and we could not get home and the pig froze."

Melissa Thompkins concluded, "Those pioneer days were pleasant ones to look back at, even though they were hard ones." At the time of the initial interview, the Thompkinses lived in Jamestown and were to celebrate their sixtieth wedding anniversary on New Year's Day, 1937, at a tea given by the Pioneer Daughters. Yet for all Melissa Thompkins's expressive detail, the interviewer, Foster Dartt, wrote that he had not been able to "get any more information because her memory is poor." Melissa Thompkins evidently was not interested in schools, churches, or wells. Under "Describe furnishings and heating of the church" is typed: "Let some one [else] describe it, I don't remember," and after a request for "relics," it says, "Never interested in any." The interviewer may have felt used as an audience on a long day. Nevertheless, we get a glimpse of Melissa Thompkins' life and her feelings about it.

Margaret Gates

Margaret Gates drew even worse scorn from her field worker, Cecil R. Baker, who wrote: "Mrs. Gates has such a poor memory that it is almost unbelievable the things she just cannot give any information on, including dates and family data." His hostility may have escaped her, for the biographical essay ends, "Mrs. Gates explains that her seventy-six years have been ones of happiness. She has had no hardships, if she had her way she would love to go back and live it all over again. She had gone through cold weather, storms in the winter, droughts in the summer but as a final word she insists 'you do not have to go to California to get sunshine, we have it in abundance right here at home.'"

She was born in 1862 in Scranton, Pennsylvania, one of four children of Irish immigrant parents, John and Mary Flannigan. Her father worked in the Scranton mines. When Margaret was eleven years old and in the fourth grade, her mother died, and Margaret "was left in charge of all the household duties besides the care of her three younger brothers." Four years later, in 1877, John Flannigan moved the family by train to Jamestown, where he was hired as section foreman on the Northern Pacific Railway, which was being extended to Bismarck, a hundred miles to the west of Jamestown. In 1877 Jamestown "was just a Fort and a town of a few tents." The Flannigans were housed "in a section house provided for them by the railroad" for a year until John Flannigan became section foreman at Crystal Springs, thirty-five miles west of Jamestown, where the family remained for five years. "All this time," the biography tells us,

the Flannigan family had to go without schooling and church services. For recreation and past time all the children had to do was to meet the trains and talk to every train crew that came through Crystal Springs. The train crews would bring the family a daily supply of food and any clothes they might need from Jamestown. As Mrs. Gates explains it, "The snowstorms and blizzards were their biggest amusement, watching the storms play havoc with things about them." The children would have their recreation playing in the snow; the boys would hunt and fish for wild game as wild game such as antelope and buffalo were plentiful. Fresh meat was in abundance at all times in the Flannigan home.

Worried that "Crystal Springs was too much isolated and too lonely for his children," John Flannigan arranged for a transfer to Terry, Montana, where, upon their arrival in 1883, the family found that

there were no buildings, just the section house. The people around Terry were a wild lot, but very friendly, most of the people were either Indians or cowboys. Everyone that came to Terry would camp around the section house. The Flannigan family were never molested or had any trouble with any of the people out west. Mrs. Gates recalls she could go to the door and see large herds of buffalo going by all the time. Buffalo meat was their source of fresh meat which the boys and Mr. Flannigan could shoot at a minute's notice.

The sociability of Terry lasted three years. In 1887 the family returned to Jamestown, where Margaret met and in 1888 married one George Gates, "a young man from Wyoming, Minnesota, who had come West for adventure" in

1880. He found it as teamster on a mail route between Bismarck and the Black Hills, then as fireman on the railroad. Except to mention two sets of twins, "one set dying in infancy," and six children altogether, the biography says nothing more about Margaret Flannigan Gates's adult life. It concludes with the fact that she visited her grown children a week at a time and said, "This is my life traveling, I enjoy it more than anyone can imagine."

How did she become such a happy woman?—orphaned, denied schooling, an eleven-year-old mother to her siblings, keeping house in railway section houses? These circumstances promise a pathetic story, but she did not tell it. Instead it is the biography of someone who was too interested in noticing everything around her—trains, snow, wind, animals—to feel sorry for herself. On the Montana trip father and children stopped in Glendive, "a small western town with no sidewalks, just yellow clay which played havoc with everyone's shoes." She reported no further calamities after her mother's death. Her father evidently supported the children adequately; there was plenty of game for meat; company housing; and, in Terry, much sociability. No one is reported seriously ill; no other children died. And for all the lack of schooling, churchgoing, or other cultural amenities, Margaret and her brothers evidently found enough to interest and occupy them. Even though work took John Flannigan away from the household, he paid attention to his children, going so far as to change section jobs so they might enjoy more companionship. This "biography" is, of course, the merest sketch, written by an impatient "field agent"; nevertheless, Margaret Flannigan Gates's verve comes through, fostered in a hard-working, but not deprived childhood.

Theresa Mutz

Theresa Mutz was eighty years old when she was interviewed for the Historical Data Project. Field worker Cecil Baker said that she owned "one of the most modern farms in this part of the country, it has all the most modern improvements of the day" and that she was "in fine health today,

never having been sick a day in her long life." But homesteading in the 1890s was not easy. She had moved to Jamestown
from the farm in 1917 after her husband died, a move she
had made "entirely with her horse and buggy." Baker wrote,
"In the year 1896 Mrs. Mutz was in quarantine with scarlet
fever with her children. At that time Mrs. Mutz had two children dead in one room and four near death in another room.
This to our pioneer was the hardest part of her pioneer days
to lose her loved ones like this with not a chance in the world
of saving them from this dreaded disease."

Like Margaret Gates, Theresa Mutz came to the Jamestown area when she was first married after a childhood of
hard work and limited education. Until she was ten years
old, Margaret and her family—her father, Peter Wojeck, was
German, and her mother, Caroline Killian, French—farmed
in Germany, where Margaret and her four younger brothers
and sisters worked hard: "All five of the children as soon as
they were old enough to do any work at all had to help with
any type of work that was there to be done. So the entire
family were always busily engaged in making the living.
Peter Wojeck did not believe in allowing his children any
time off from work to get an education, hence the entire
family of five were deprived of any type of education." In
1867 the Wojecks moved to Wisconsin to join other German
Catholic settler farmers, and in 1875 Theresa married Martin Mutz "in the Catholic church at Arcadia, Wisconsin."

The habit of being "busily engaged in making the living"
stayed with her and launched Theresa into the new adventure that came with marriage: "As soon as Martin Mutz and
his new bride were married they left at once on a freight
train for Jamestown, North Dakota. In this freight car they
brought with them a wagon, cook stove, yoke of oxen, seven
chickens, beds, couch and a small amount of food. The Mutz's
shared this freight car with another family coming out to
Dakota also." They arrived on Good Friday, 1879, with impressions similar to those of Margaret Gates: "'There was
not one bit of snow on the ground but a terrific wind was
blowing,' states our pioneer, wind was something the people

from Wisconsin were not used to." They had $75 to start with: "A well was dug and thirty five acres of land broken on their quarter and a small garden planted the first year"—one that in 1937 still produced. While Martin cultivated wheat fields and built a barn and house, Theresa Mutz actively contributed to family income as well:

In 1885 an addition was made to their claim shanty, this gave Mrs. Mutz enough room to board and room the school teacher who was David Stauffer in 1885. The life on the Mutz farm was one of hard work for all. Mrs. Mutz did more than her share of the farm work to help make the living. She had her little chickens and made butter which she sold in Jamestown, North Dakota, for ten pounds for one dollar. Mrs. Mutz kept a small amount of butter for their family use as they had no lard to cook with. For a little pin money Mrs. Mutz made aprons out of gunny sacks to pick up buffalo chips which the people used for fuel in those early days. The Mutz family would make trips to Spiritwood Lake a short distance north of their farm to get wood to burn.

There is too little information in Theresa Mutz's biography to judge what the homestead farm near Jamestown offered her children, but Theresa herself spoke as though she did not feel victimized either by the hard work of her adult "pioneering" nor by her strict, work-focused upbringing. One of the attractions of leaving Wisconsin may, of course, have been getting away from family discipline. Nevertheless, she spoke as though she had grown up expecting to take care of herself, to carry an active share in providing family income—witness her taking in boarders and selling butter and eggs and gunny-sack bone-gathering aprons. In addition, the hard work organized by her father and then her husband evidently paid off, for both families had enough to eat and decent housing. Apart from the bad scarlet fever outbreak, the Mutz's did not report suffering major calamities.

Isabel Blades

A spirit of adventure also blessed Isabel Blades, who, in her mid-seventies, the project interviewer found "apparently in

the best of health." Her relatively content longevity out-
lasted several sad happenings, and she had in common with
Margaret Gates and Theresa Mutz at least one very careful
parent. Her German father and mother were farming in
Ingersoll, Canada, when Isabel was born in 1862. In 1884
they moved to Chicago, and then to Clinton, Iowa, where
began what might have been written as another pathetic
abandoned-waifs romance: "The only remembrance Isabel
had of her father was upon their arrival in Clinton [she was
three and a half years old], he took his whole family of seven
children and his wife to the Iowa fair. He left the family at
once and never has been heard from since." What despair
drove him?—seven children, perhaps, no work in Chicago,
and bafflement at how to earn a living in Clinton—Isabel did
not say and possibly could not know. At any rate, the more
resilient Elizabeth was now in charge: "This left the raising
of the large family to Isabel's mother, she through her tire-
less efforts was able to educate her children and provide for
them until they could go out and make their own living." It
was not easy for her: "Isabel's mother was handicapped because she had no education, so all the work she could get
was hard labor. Isabel's mother was unable to go to school
because she came from a large family, she was the oldest of
ten children in the Holman family. What knowledge she did
receive came by studying with her children while they were
attending school," a resourcefulness not lost on her daughter.
Isabel herself managed schooling as far as the first three
months of high school, when she stopped because the eldest
child, Fred, had died in a drowning accident. Her mother decided to move back to Chicago—"the home was broken
up" and sold, marking an end to that period in the family's
history.

    By the time these changes were taking place in 1880, Eliza-
beth Parkhouse had succeeded in readying her daughter to
"go out and make [her] own living, which she commenced
to do in Chicago" by signing on in the household of one
Captain Gilbert, "who was in charge of Fort Buford, D.T.
[Dakota Territory]." Isabel was twenty years old. To reach

her new employment on the army post, which straddled the Montana-Dakota border, Isabel traveled by train to Glendive, Montana, where the Gilbert family met her. She told of the eighty-seven-mile journey to the fort as though it were a western adventure. "The first thrill," as she called it, was crossing the Yellowstone River by yawl, "a flat-bottomed boat manned by four oarsmen, and four guards. The oarsmen said they would not take any screaming women across the river because it was dangerous enough trying to avoid large ice cakes which were as large as a block twelve by fourteen feet square and larger. It was a tremendous task to take the boat across without a smash-up because the weight and force of the ice cakes would totally demolish a boat in no time at all."

After the party crossed the Yellowstone River, they were met by a United States ambulance drawn by four mules. They were only able to make twenty-five miles the first day of travel. The party tied up at a settler's home for the night, and with the two Gilbert children, Isabel and Mrs. Gilbert stayed in the house for the night. The four guards and Captain Gilbert slept in the hay in the barn. During the night all the harnesses for the mules and two mules were stolen. While the Gilbert party was eating breakfast, the four guards were sent out to find the harnesses and the mules, which they did in a short time. For breakfast they had eggs, fried venison, and coffee. The second day the party was able to make better time, and they reached Fort Buford. In order to cross the Missouri river to Fort Buford they were forced to walk on planks placed on ice cakes on the Missouri.

The fourteen months Isabel Parkhouse waited tables and did housework for the Gilbert family left her with vivid memories: "The soldiers of the fort were more of the undesirable class of soldiers that were sent from other forts, and as Isabel states it was indeed a tough place," according to her interviewer. But except for a few cattle stolen by Indians, "all was peace and quiet most of the time." Temperatures during the winter of 1884 were fearfully cold, down to sixty-seven degrees below zero in January. She remembered that if "the soldiers marched back and forth on the parade grounds in one complete round of the parade grounds their faces would be frozen. The only relief the men could get would be to put a lot of snow on their faces at the end of every round on the parade grounds. With such extreme temperatures the days were very quiet and bright."

In the spring of 1884 Isabel married Jim Blades, one of the soldiers at the fort and a native of Maryland. Her life took a strange repetitive turn, and, although the interviewer interpolated in parentheses, "(for personal reasons Mrs. Blades wishes no mention of her husband)," he included more than brief mention of him. A year and a half after the marriage, their daughter was born in Bismarck, and that spring, 1886, they moved to Jamestown, "where Jim Blades became very dissatisfied with working conditions . . . in 1889 Jim went west to secure work. He remained in the west just a few months, coming home and started a livery stable on Sixth Avenue North, where the North American Creamery Company is now located. He ran this livery business until 1902 when he disappeared and has never been heard from since." After eighteen years of marriage, James Blades, like Isabel's father, James Parkhouse, vanished without a trace. Their only child, Mattie, had died in 1898, when she was twelve years old, so Isabel was left with no children (compared to Elizabeth's supporting seven).

Isabel was resourceful and joined forces with her mother: "Mrs. Blades had to make the living for her small daughter and herself by taking in washing and doing dressmaking. She secured a house on the east edge of Jamestown which cost her $3 per month rent. In 1900 Mrs. Blades' mother came to visit her, her mother lived with her daughter Isabel until 1904 when she passed away at the age of eighty-two years." Without her mother, her daughter, or her husband, Isabel was alone after 1904, when she was forty-two years old, but again she found a way to see her through:

The Blades were always Methodist people at heart but in the year of 1902 when Jim Blades left his wife she had the misfortune of falling and breaking her ankle. While she was ill with her broken ankle she was informed she would always have to be on crutches the rest of her life, this brought her into the Christian Science faith of which she is a staunch believer in today. Several times since 1902 Isabel Blades has had the misfortune of falling and breaking her bones and through the healing power of Christian Science she has always been cured.

Isabel was in her seventies at the time of the interview. "The only motive she has in life is her religion, she told me 'there is nothing else to live for.'" Again, a more astute interviewer might help us to understand what Isabel Blades meant by her last remark; it may not have been meant as despairing but sounds as if she felt her religion was a strength in her life rather than merely a last resort.

Adelaide Pettey

"Adelaide's ninety-one years of learning how to overcome obstacles" evoked admiration and personal memories in Field Worker Cecil Baker. She had been a part of his childhood in Jamestown—"a mother to all the boys in town," he wrote. "A group of ten boys that lived around her neighborhood had a certain type gang whistle in order to call the groups together. To this day she recalls that call and says she misses that more than anything else because her boys, as she called us, have all gone away and have homes of their own." Baker named her "a grand old lady" and quoted her as saying, "I am strong in body and mind and enjoy living."

Adelaide Pettey's difficulties began at age four, when her parents placed her in a Chicago orphanage and soon after died of yellow fever. She was adopted by a family named Martin. Three years later Mrs. Martin died, and six months after that so did the foster sister who was caring for Adelaide, "so Adelaide was forced to go back to her foster-father, Mr. Martin." He was a contractor by trade and traveled around the state of Illinois; he died in 1859, when Adelaide was fourteen. Fortunately, she had learned to sew when she joined the Martin household. When Adelaide lived with Mr. Martin she "had taken such an interest in sewing and had become so efficient with the needle that by the time she was eighteen years old she was a full-fledged seamstress. Adelaide Martin was following up the art of sewing, covering the states of Ohio, Illinois, and Iowa."

Adelaide was ambitious about her education. It began in the Martin household "with character training rather than book knowledge" and proceeded rather fitfully because of Martin's frequent moves. Nevertheless, "with the aid of her sewing" she graduated from high school in Lyon, Illinois, when she was sixteen, two years after Martin's death. The next year a college was started in Lyon, and she hoped to attend, but at the last moment decided she did not have enough money and "had to go back to her trade, that of sewing." At the outbreak of the Civil War she "landed," Cecil Baker writes, in Fulton, Illinois, where she rather anticipated Rosie the Riveter of World War II:

At this time all the men of the day were called to War, thus leaving most of the work turned over to the women. Adelaide Martin's part in the Civil War was replacing a printer in the Fulton Gazette, in Fulton, Illinois. She was just as efficient as a printer in the Gazette as she had been through life as a seamstress. In one of my interviews with Mrs. Pettey she told me, "she could still set type with the best of them." At the close of the Civil War Adelaide Martin went to Vicksburg, the scene of one of the heaviest battles of the Civil War. Adelaide stayed here just a few months, then she returned to Boscoville, Wisconsin, to visit some friends.

Adelaide Martin's biography does not describe her foster family or her relationship with them. Nevertheless, in spite of the deaths of both parents, her foster mother, the sister who was to care for her, and, when she was fourteen years old, her foster father, Adelaide did not appear to have been left uncared for or feeling personally abandoned—at least her interviewer recorded nothing to give that impression. Speaking of Adelaide Martin's career in church work, Baker wrote, "In her younger days she always managed to get into a home where good Christian folk lived," and at sixteen she was baptized "in the Mississippi River at Fulton, Illinois," a sign, possibly, that family and community were looking after her. In addition, the sewing she learned from Mrs. Martin and the independence she evidently acquired traveling about with Mr. Martin prepared her well to take advantage of expanding job opportunities during the war. The sequence of dates is not always clear, but when Adelaide was visiting in Wisconsin, she met an engineer in the lumber mills, a widower with three sons named M. F. Pettey, and she married him in 1868, when she was twenty-three years old.

Adelaide's choice in a husband was hardly less fortuitous than her portion of parents and foster parents. M. F. Pettey suffered so badly from the malarial damps of Wisconsin that in April 1882 he traveled to Jamestown in search of a drier climate and free land (his eldest son, Charles, having preceded him). He left the rest of his family in Boscoville, numbering now an additional six children—including two sets of twins, of which one twin died during his absence. (In Jamestown Adelaide bore twin boys, who also died.) A misadventure in a blizzard dissuaded Pettey, however, from country living, so that when Adelaide arrived in 1883, the family lived in Jamestown, where Pettey worked as engineer in the mill. In Jamestown Adelaide was not idle. She "helped to bring in the living for her family by her splendid sewing"; she nursed the sick and did undertaking work; she was anesthetist to a doctor; she hung paper and made soap, all for "pin money," her biographer writes, "to help the family along in the years when help was needed by doing all these different things for other people. 'There is nothing one cannot do if he really puts his whole heart and mind into the thing' are the exact words she has told me many times," he wrote. This resourcefulness and independence she expressed in admiration for the technology of the sewing machine:

In 1865 Mrs. Pettey saw the first sewing machine. The people of the time were actually amazed to see a machine that would make the needle go up and down so fast and still sew perfect stitches. This make of sewing machine was the Florence—Mrs. Pettey bought the Florence sewing machine as her first machine, in 1865. This machine made a lot of money for our pioneer, with it she had sewed for many people following up her trade. Mrs. Pettey kept the Florence for about ten years when she traded it off for a Wheeler and Wilson machine in 1875. This machine did not prove to be very efficient so Mrs. Pettey traded this machine off for the well known Singer machine—this machine is still in use by our pioneer after forty-four years of continual sewing it runs perfectly. Mrs. Pettey told me, "If I were forced to sell all my household equipment I would keep my Singer because even at my age I would soon be able to make all the money back to buy my furniture again in short order."

Mary J. Towley

Mary J. Towley wrote her own biographical essay for the Historical Data Project. She was born in Canadice, New York, in 1853. Her parents were farmers, and in 1858 they moved to Jackson, Michigan, again to farm. Mary attended school for nine years, then "helped my mother at home until July 5, 1876, when I married Rescam Sanford Towley," the beginning of six peripatetic years. The couple opened a dry goods store in Beloit, Wisconsin, in 1877; two years later Rescam clerked in Manston, Wisconsin; a year later they bought a store in Elroy and a year and a half after that in Galesburn, Illinois. That store did not prosper either, and a year later the couple moved to Chicago, where Towley worked as a salesman for two years before another move back to Beloit, Wisconsin, and another try at running a dry goods store. "This one proved a success," she writes.

Mary Towley's next venture was to scout the Jamestown area of Dakota Territory for land:

In the spring of 1882 my brother Herb Winfield wanted to come to North Dakota to live, but did not want to come out alone, so my husband and I decided that it be best if I go with him, and at the same time look over the country out in the Dakotas. Early in March we put out for the west and arrived at Jamestown on a cold day about 5:00 P.M. We stayed at Jamestown over night then hired a man, wagon, and team to take us to where Ypsilanti is now. After arriving there we pitched the tent and I stayed here until in May when the two children and I went back to Beloit leaving Herb on his homestead about 4 miles from Ypsilanti. When I arrived home and told my husband about the country and the opportunities here he became all worked up so in April 1886 we moved out to Ypsilanti.

The children she had with her were two-and-a-half years and three months old. As "worked up" as her husband was over the prospects of Dakota, no move was made for four years. Understatement guides Mary Towley's writing: "Life here was not so pleasant the first few years. We had no farm machinery so had to buy as far as our money went and borrow the rest. Crops were as a rule very poor due mostly to hail and dry weather. Our food and fuel was purchased at Ypsilanti and Jamestown. The clothing was all home made with the exception of shoes and probably a few other items."

But conditions did improve. In 1902 they built an eight-room house, "a large barn and a two story buggy shed." Three years later, her husband died, "leaving me with one daughter and 3 sons. The children were pretty well grown up so we managed to get along fairly well as Rescam had left enough insurance to keep us a couple of years." In 1905 the eldest, a daughter, was twenty-six, and the youngest, born in Ypsilanti, eighteen years old. One or another of the children and their families continued farming, although at the time of writing, Mary Towley said the farm had not been paying well. She herself sounded satisfied with her arrangement. She was staying with each child by turn for six months ("Essie lives in Minneapolis, I am making my home with her at the present time"). She also received $50 a month from one son and $25 from another. Her children appeared to have prospered: one son was an electrical engineer, another supervised an experiment station in Sheridan, Wyoming, and the third owned a lumber business in Verona, North Dakota. Three children were married, one not.

These brief life stories, all, it happens, from the Jamestown area, reveal no famous personages. They happen to be by and about women who outlived their husbands. All the women and most of the husbands reported themselves on the whole satisfied with their lives, even though several also chronicled early deaths of one or both parents, few if any years of schooling, and hard work. Several of the subjects took the place in the family of the mother who had died, or they became partners with their mother in keeping the family going after a father had died. These biographies also include some elements in common that are lacking in the lives of children who suffered irreparably. The Jamestown settlers mentioned no serious health problems—they evidently were physically strong. They also escaped destitution. While none claimed wealth, and most admitted to impoverished years, the writers nevertheless grew up in and continued to maintain households with stable family incomes. Perhaps most critically, each "pioneer" recounted episodes from her childhood that indicated that she had been the object of attention from her parents. Each was paid attention to by someone—enough to tide her over vicissitudes and to give her the security, self confidence, and independence she needed when the time came to set out on her own.

7

Martha and Ole Lima

People report widely differing qualities of experience during the settlement of the American West. "Pioneering" for some was an adventure, for others a time of terrible hardship, depending, often as we have seen, on how much knowledge and money they had to start with, the region where they settled, even the price of wheat and other crops. Another consideration affecting how people felt about coming to the new lands had to do with the period in their lives when they attempted the venture. For young people who were not married, or at least did not have children, and for people in middle age, staking out a homestead or starting a business in a frontier town could be full of excitement and fun. But for families with young children, western settlement sometimes turned into a dangerous and sorrowful experience.

Children's first years are precarious; they die more easily if conditions are not right, and so can their mothers, infant mortality and deaths in childbirth being notoriously high in the late nineteenth and early twentieth centuries in the western states. Fathers often married again, and sometimes second and third wives died in childbirth, along with additional infants. But not all men whose wives and infants died on settlement farms married again or found an unmarried female relative to take care of their household. Single fathers are not an invention of our day.

The Lima family were happy together. They worked hard, and they should have thrived as a family, but they did not, for first an infant daughter, then the mother, and a few years later a second child all died. The father brought up a son and a daughter, and he himself lived into his seventies. The experience of most of his adult life was to be a parent to three children and to live by himself. The story of this family, moving through losses, suggests how much rural settlement depended upon an intact family group to maintain reasonable comfort. In their letters, it is the parents we hear, but even so we gain some idea of what difference it made to the children that their mother died.[1]

Martha and Ole Lima were high school classmates in Norway. They arrived together with other friends in Cooperstown, North Dakota, on May 25, 1893, and married six months later, on December 31. In less than six years, Martha bore four children; one died at age two. Martha died of tuberculosis in 1900 at age thirty-two, leaving Ole to care for three children. One of them died at age nine. We know about Martha and Ole Lima from letters they wrote to Ole's parents and to his sister in Norway. The letters were returned, a few at a time, between 1939 and 1974 to their daughter Ruth McMahon, who translated them into English—thirteen from Martha, and many more between 1886 and 1927 from Ole. There also is an autobiographical essay Ole wrote in 1928. Ruth McMahon has written that the letters were "gathered up in the old home at Lima by my Aunt Ane Vatne, who with her husband had recently moved back to Norway. She persuaded Per Lima, the Cooperstown blacksmith, somewhat against his own judgment, to bring them back to me when he returned from a visit in 1939. 'Why carry such useless stuff?' Later my Aunt Malena at Lima and her daughter Guda found additional letters, which they mailed to me." Fortunately, Ruth McMahon did not think them "useless." The series is not complete, and there are no letters received by Martha and Ole.

Martha was born in December 20, 1868, near Sttavanger, on the southwest coast of Norway. She attended a folk high school at Sandnes and worked as parlor maid in London for two years, where she learned some English, and then was interpreter in a tourist hotel near Roldal, Norway. She and Ole were not related but shared the same last name because ancestors of both families had lived in Lima. Ole Lima was born February 23, 1860, at Lima, and died near Cooperstown at age 71 on April 23, 1931. He had made an earlier trip to America, from 1886 to 1890, to help work off debts for his father's *gaard*, or landholding in Norway, which he was to inherit. When Ole returned in 1890, he took over the gaard for two years and then sold it to Malena and Torgar Gjesdal, his sister and her husband, before traveling again to North Dakota in the group with Martha. Martha and Ole had met on his first return while they both attended the same high school at Sandnes. Earlier, Ole had learned shoemaking; that and farming were his primary skills.

Martha's letters have a gentle way of keeping the person the letter is meant for very much in mind: "Torger! you forgot to tell me if there are many berries in the garden? Apples? I rested after dinner today, slept, and dreamed that I was in the garden at Lima, eating currants with all my might. When I woke up I was very thirsty" (1893). Martha writes whimsically about herself:

Imagine! we are now about to get married. On the 23rd of this month I will quit work here [she had been employed since her arrival in 1893 at the elegant Palace Hotel in Cooperstown, evidence of the wealth produced by the vogue for large-scale mechanized "bonanza" farming, which temporarily thrived in the region] and then we had wished to have a little wedding on Christmas Eve, but something interfered, so we will likely have to postpone until New Year's. I suppose I can just as well whisper to you what it was that interfered: you see, I wanted a new dress for the occasion but it was impossible to get it sewed before Christmas. [December 10, 1893]

Ole and Martha might be said to have collaborated on a "gendered" principle of letter writing: "Ole reminds me that it is only appropriate for women to relate details and 'trivialities'—and thus leaves that chapter to me. I wanted him to tell you what we grow in our garden, how many cows and chickens we have, etc., as I assume that you are interested in such things." She described planting trees and a garden of cabbages, carrots, kohlrabi, onions, melons, and cucumbers. "And I must tell you, Mother, that I have made juice, preserves, and something that is now turning into wine, from chokecherries and plums"—this after their first summer on the farm near Cooperstown, which they had bought from Ole's sister and brother-in-law, Ane and Andreas Vatne (August 26, 1894). As to the wedding, Martha realized that what was relegated to women's writing was what her in-laws most wanted to know: "Perhaps you and Mother might be interested in hearing a little more of 'childish' talk about our wedding, and now I shall tell you"—of Ane Vatne's baking and other preparations (January 3, 1894). Martha regretted the absence of their families: "It was a beautiful day, but a sense of loneliness was felt even then, in the midst of our joy: we missed our dear ones who remain in Norway. How glad would we not have been to see you all about us that day, and how pleasant it would be if you could visit us in the future when we have our own little home!"

"As for the bridal couple, I think they were quite nearly got up," Martha wrote to Ole's sister, Malena. "Myself, I could not see too well, but I thought Ole was so handsome and young in the dark blue suit and white collar and white silk tie which I myself had crocheted for him, and a flower in his coat lapel." Ole was thirty-three years old, Martha twenty-eight. Her brown dress, made by Ane Vatne, was "trimmed with the crocheted rings you have seen." It was others she thought of, her letters insist, and repeatedly she praised Ole to his sister and parents, usually describing their joint activities as though she were only an observer:

Ole is doing a little of everything. He has sheep and cows, and he and Andreas work together at looking after them. Other than that, he is a "carpenter"; he has begun to make a loom and other things having to do with weaving. Furthermore, he intends quite soon to select a place where we can "set foot under our own table." What more shall I tell about him? He is president of the young people's society which was recently organized here. If I should say more, it would be that I whispered: he is so good, and so kind and dear, I pray God bless him and help me be as I should towards him. [April 1, 1894]

In April 1897, Martha wrote to Ole's grandmother on the occasion of her sixtieth birthday, reporting warmly about their lives and concentrating on Ole:

Now the spring thaw has really set in, though there is still much snow, several feet deep in some places. Ole has been at the Ballatin schoolhouse today to hear Edwards preach. It was hard enough to get anywhere on foot, and driving was out of the question, as there is so much water over the prairie. He had boots on, and had to wade only in the shallowest places to avoid getting wet. . . . Besides, I shall tell you about a few things, Grandmother. Ole has completely worn out the brown large-checked suit; it looks horribly ragged, but now I intend to use the trousers for patches on the coat—so it can serve as a barn-jacket.

Martha described the mended condition of a "best blue suit" and a green checked one. A hat Ole had bought in Sttavanger "the last summer he was home" was so worn that she thought "it is the dirt that holds it together!" Then she added, "I still have my good black dress material which I brought along—lying un-sewed" (March 20, 1897).

Often these letters home to Lima came in pairs, one each from Ole and Martha, and not more than a few days apart, dividing up subject matter according to whether it was more appropriate for Martha or for Ole to report. On June 6, 1896, Ole said that the sheep wintered well, tree seedlings were growing, he was building a house, the water level in the well had risen, a neighbor's son was herding their sheep, and two Norwegian Lutheran congregations had joined under the name "Ebenezer." His letters often had much to say about local church politics—this one remarked that a week-long synod meeting in South Dakota intended "to try to make an end of the bitter doctrinal battle between Pastor Neland and Professor Bergsland." Martha's companion letter of June 3 corroborated his ("Ole is busy"), adding that the hens were reluctant to incubate—"Last year there was an everlasting clucking at this season." But the event that took up two long paragraphs was one Ole did not mention:

Now you shall hear some joyful news: On May 20 we had a well-formed and healthy daughter. She is quite good, and is strong and plump—has dark brown eyes, too, and her hair is coal black. I think she resembles her father most. I am much stronger and better now than after David was born. [David had been born 15 months earlier, but there are no letters for that year.] I hope that this time I shall escape the long and painful abscess of the breast which I had when David was new-born. Anna Njaa is here this time also, and she takes the very best care of both me and the children.

It was characteristic of Martha, who repeatedly mended her husband's suits but had not yet made herself a dress, to refer to earlier illnesses as retrospective good news when the ailment was not repeated.

At fifteen months, David was jealous of the baby, and Martha described this scene, in which she shows how much she understood the child's feelings:

David is troublesome—but yet dear. He finds it hard to be left so much to his own entertainment. His little sister he does not seem to be very fond of; we can by no means get him to kiss her or pat her nicely. Rather, he gives her a real fast slap on the head, or strikes at her face with his finger-nails. I feel a little sorry for him: he may come in, hot and tired from outdoors, expecting me to take him, and when he gets to the living room door and sees me with the baby in my lap he looks so disappointed and angry and begins to whimper and cry. His papa he dearly loves to be with; he clings tightly about papa's knees when he notices that he is about to leave him.

Martha appears to judge herself more strictly in regard to the child than she does the anxieties Ole evidently causes him.

Martha's next letter, on November 22, 1896, to Ole's sister Malena, more than hints at strenuous days with two small children: "It is especially the children who are the reason for its being so difficult to undertake letter-writing. They are both small, you know, and need much care. And when they are not on my hands, there is cooking, baking, cleaning, washing and ironing; and besides I wish so awfully much to sew and knit a little, and then I need to read something once in a while—and where is there time for letter-writing?"

Hired help hardly lessened Martha's domestic work; people would not stay, and often the "girls" were children themselves. Even when for a short period someone was hired, much of the person's time went to the men: "This summer I had an eleven-year-old little girl to help me, especially in bringing coffee out to the field to the hard-working menfolk. Now we have no girl, but a young man, Ole Rasmussen Madlan. He works a little around the barn and cattle; he works for his board now in the winter months. Ole has various things to go after, and the roads are long and the days short, so he is greatly in need of help. He is always busy, himself too." An eleven-year-old fetching coffee and a young man expecting board probably meant more rather than less work for Martha.

Martha wrote more to Malena a month later about the infant: "Gunhild Mathilda—yes she is truly exceedingly lovely, sweet and good—and you need not think it is exaggerated because I say it. She resembles her father and his sisters; but when I soap her hair so that it is white, then she marvelously resembles her far-far [grandfather]. David talks a little bit, especially "no." This word he uses at all times, right or wrong."

Ole's companion letter for December 20 reported on the previous fall's crops and a two-day snowstorm, "the violence of which I think most of the people here have never seen the like." He told how he poured hot water through the snow and ice to get water for the cattle. A new pastor was to preach that day, and "in November our county was visited by a Swede named Franzon, who had traveled around the world and had visited almost all mission fields and had much to tell. He was also an interpreter of Scripture, spoke of Christ's return, and seemed to propound a teaching very similar to Dimleby's." Ole did not write of Martha or the children.

Martha, like Ole, wrote about religious matters, but she expressed devotion in a more personal manner than did her husband. She did not report engaging in church politics, as he did. Writing to Ole's parents, she mentioned a religious event in Norway, apparently trying to make connections with her own family:

We hear that there is a revival in Gjesdal and that people are seeking and finding their Savior. This is really the best news. There is something I want to talk to you about. I hear only most rarely from my sister and other relatives at Oltedal. Feeling sad and troubled, I ask: is there none of them who might wake up and seek God? Grandfather mentioned in a letter the places where people have been awakened, but Oltedal was not among them. Do any of you ever go there? My dear ones, will not one of you, or both, if it is not too inconvenient, go in there to visit Per and Lisa, and also go to Udslaataa. And then when you write, tell us you have been there, and how you found them, if they are well, and whether the children are thriving, etc. You can just as well tell them, if you wish, that I asked you to do this, and greet them from us.

Subsequent letters do not say whether this visit was made.

Without doubting that Martha was concerned about her family's spiritual state, we can see that what she really wanted was any word at all. "Feeling sad and troubled" was her primary reason for writing, and whether or not someone were "thriving" her main concern.

Martha and Ole's third child, Edith Ruth (the compiler and translator of the letters), was born November 3, 1897, eighteen months after Gunhild Mathilda. Ole wrote to his parents four days before the birth, and Martha wrote four days afterwards. Ole began apologizing that "constant hindrances" had kept him from writing earlier. He did not say the impending birth was one of them, but that harvest had not been as bountiful as he had hoped: "I, who was not one of the most unfortunate, reaped hardly 10 bushels of wheat to the acre, threshed almost 1200 and received less than 900 on my share. The price is, however, almost twice as high as 2 years ago, so that I can reduce my debt by half, I think. For beginners like me there are always so many extra expenses for buildings and machinery and for breaking new land."

Church affairs also preoccupied him, including a complicated disagreement among various factions, about which feelings, including his own, ran high: "Since that time there has been considerable expression of opinion in the congregation, some rejoicing that Edwards has been brought to right; others think the whole difficulty comes from a power-greedy priesthood, which cannot tolerate a bit more of congregational freedom here than what existed in the Norwegian State Church." He also reported on the other two children—that Gunhild was at his sister's (but not that she was there because of the expected birth) and that she was teething. He also described David's antics, appreciating a certain infant aggressiveness: "David is right in my hands now as I am writing. He shakes the table and wishes, by all means, to take possession of the inkwell. He has been given the pencil, and with this he scribbles wherever he can reach. He talks without let-up, makes up many yarns. Most of the time he uses a very rolling "r." Then he wants to get hold of all the tools he knows about or sees, and has a great interest in all sorts of machinery." The letter does not mention Martha.

Martha began her companion pages eight days later with a humorous appreciation of the males in the household: "It is Sunday today, and still beautiful weather. It is very still in the house, too. Ole is at home. He has gone upstairs with David, undoubtedly with the intention of getting himself a midday nap, but it will apparently be a short rest! For I hear David using every art and industry to keep Papa's attention directed to his own little broad person. 'You must hold open with your eyes, Papa,' I hear every once in a while. . . . Our beautiful little Gunhild is with Aunt Ave."

After this reassuring scene of domestic tranquillity, Martha reaches the major event in her life just then, the birth of Ruth: "I am, for the time being, in bed. We have a big healthy daughter, born last Wednesday morning, 3rd November. I am well and strong, and am also watchfully cared for and waited upon. We have B. Herigstad's 17-year-old daughter Karen with us for a while."

The winter of 1898 went well, Ole reported: "We have the finest winter weather in the world: a little frost, much clear sunshine, and no snow; and it is exceedingly pleasant to be outdoors" (January 2, 1898). In March he reported: "We are already at the end of winter and have had no real snowstorm all season. O what splendid winter weather. We have been spared from any serious illness. David and Gunhild have, however, had their cross times over teeth. The smallest one, Edith Ruth, is quite cross and crying; now and then we have a wakeful hour at night on her account. Otherwise, they grow and thrive, all three. During the winter we have had as nurse-girl one or another daughter of Tonnes Vatne. The last two weeks we have not had a girl" (March 23, 1898).

In June he wrote that "we have all most of the time been well. The little ones, however, have each had a spell of a little cold and other indisposition. Now David has a stubborn cough, possibly whooping cough" (June 26, 1898). They had had good rains, he bought more land, and a prairie fire destroyed tree plantings. In church matters, the installation of a new pastor was "regarded by us as a great victory and forward step for congregational and church freedom; for here it is confirmed that the congregation is really in authority to ordain and install its minister. Hereby the minister is also released from many hindering bonds which hamper most of the synodical ministers. Hauge's Synod is now said to have risen so high in churchliness that they think of uniting with the Norwegian Synod and the United Church."

Ole Lima liked to generalize; much of his writing is fairly abstract. In the fall of 1893, a little more than six months before his wedding and six months after his return to North Dakota, he was optimistic about prospects for settlement:

"Is it advisable for more people to come?" you ask next. In answer to this I say that for one who has little or no prospect of making a living in Norway by his own endeavor, he will find conditions here in America different in this respect. And if your question aims at finding out whether this place is soon filled up, then I can inform you that there will still for a long time be found millions of acres of tillable land, so that the country still has room for many people. The cities, however, are probably full, especially of tramps!

This letter lacks salutation, but presumably was to his sister Malena and her husband, for Ole takes up the on-going worry about his relationship with their parents:

And what do I think of coming back? Yes, that I will tell you: in case that you, for one reason or another, should find that you have to leave Lima, while Father and Mother are still living, then I should earnestly wish to find myself in such an economic position that I could take your place. I have not yet discovered any especially remunerative way of making a living; but it is of course true that the so-called luck strikes now one and then another. And since I know that Father and Mother make so much of having one of their children in the house, I will apply myself to doing whatever may be in my power that it may be so.

Ole lacked Martha's humor and good nature; he often sounded morose, even a week before his wedding day:

You ask how I am faring. As for my health, I am well. But one finds a lot of things to be disgruntled about. The times are poor, people are ill-natured and look only to their own advantage, so that he who does not use beak and claws to grab things for himself has to satisfy himself with—nothing. And a fool is he who places any confidence in a spoken promise. It is indeed remarkable that it can do even for a "Christian" to behave himself in this manner. But a degraded Christianity it appears to be. It is sometimes so painful that I hardly know which way I shall turn. [November 25, 1893]

A week before his thirty-fourth birthday Ole wrote gloomily: "Well, so I have attained still another birthday, God be thanked. Would that my life be not entirely in vain, useless, as the unfruitful tree that was threatened with destruction.

It appears to me, certainly, that so far I have been quite useless, and this because God's will was not my wish, and my life therefore was one of self-love. O, that it might once in all reality become otherwise. Pray for us. Forgive me" (February 18, 1894).

He viewed national and local politics as dourly as he did his personal shortcomings:

The political and economic life in this country looks strange, as you surely know through the newspapers. The nation, like a body, writhes on a bed of suffering. Things appeared quite critical to many when all the railroads stopped. Of the army of workers on the Capital you probably know. Conditions here in Dakota are however not of the very worst, it seems to me. The daily wage, as in part of last year, is 1 1/2 dollars per day, and that is not too bad. Threshing has already begun; fall work will be finished early this year. [August 26, 1894]

Ole could turn good news into bad:

Little David is a good boy, 1/2 years old, and gives us a great deal of trouble, day and night. And then we have innumerable lot of flies. And although thousands daily drink themselves to death on poison, the number alive still remains great. On the other hand, we are free from all kinds of lice. Fleas are to be found hereabouts, but rarely. We have extra good water, "healthy air and general peace." The flock of lambs grazes 1/2 Norwegian mile from here, and when we wish for meat we butcher a wether. [August 25, 1895]

He sent the letter a month later, when he added, "David continues to thrive, and grows and is very gay and full of laughter, so much that it borders on the immoderate" (September 22, 1895). Apparently Ole could not bear too much joy, even from his infant son.

For their first five years in and near Cooperstown and the first four-and-a-half years of their marriage, Martha and Ole Lima's lives continued fairly sanguinely. Their letters home give a plausible sense of daily living in this family, how each parent looked at the world and at their children. Both worked hard—Ole broke land, built a house, planted trees, cared for sheep, and engaged in church affairs. Martha, after some months at the Palace Hotel, kept house under rather restricted conditions and bore and cared for three infants. But in the summer of 1898 came a sadder change. Martha wrote to her "Dear parents-in-law":

Our dear Gunhild Mathilda is dead and buried. She died Friday, 22nd July, and was buried Saturday the 23rd.

I need hardly describe our feelings, for you will surely understand us. You, too, have experience. We know that God has done this, and that it is his love, and we thank him—while our heart bleeds from the wound.

Our little Gunhild had whooping cough, and seemed to be quite ill. She had mostly sat or lain in the baby-buggy on cradle the last eight or nine days. She certainly ate very little, mostly drank water, but she was not worse than that she played with David a little now and then. The last day and night before, she coughed less, and I hoped the worst was over. She always wanted to be in Papa's lap when he ate his supper, and she looked no worse the last night than she had before. We went to bed, and Gunhild lay by my side. We went to sleep for a short while; then I was wakened by a strange sound that came from Gunhild—she was then in convulsion. I became so confused, called to Ole, "Gunhild is choking to death!" He flew up instantly and took her off my arms, and we thought she would die at once; but not so.

She struggled all night without a breath—the poor, beloved child. The cramps became worse and worse. As we understood it, she was also unconscious, so she must not have felt it as terribly as it looked to us. A half hour before she died the battle was fought out, the cramp left her, and her face became still and marvelously beautiful and happy. Oh, you should have seen her then! She looked as if she already beheld Jesus in his glory. She looked at us, and Papa asked, "Does Gunhild want to go to Jesus now?" She answered, "Yes." Then he asked, "Can Gunhild see Mama?" To this she also answered, "Yes!" and turned her eyes to me. Then she became still and resting.

Was she not fortunate after all? She has reached the goal, and

we continue here in the world of strife, liable to sorrow and pain.
But God be praised who gives us victory through Jesus Christ!

Many people came here for the funeral—and many flowers.
Gunhild was 2 years, 2 months, and 2 days old. She had only cut
the four front teeth above and below. I rather think the convulsions
came from teething trouble.

Ole is very busy getting the hay in. David and Ruth are still
coughing, but seem quite lively.

Greet relatives and friends, and all in the house, from both of us,
by Martha. She died between five and six in the morning.

In the nineteenth and early twentieth centuries, any death,
and especially the death of a child, was an event calling
for vocal public expressions of grief. It was important to
die "well" and to write expressively about death (a more
permissible subject than sexuality, especially for women).
These were the years of the cemetery movement, when
cemeteries turned into parks, and undertaking burgeoned
into lucrative business. In private writings, deaths typically
were described as dramatic events, the details treasured and
elaborated upon. Thus Gunhild's parents admired her saying "yes" when asked whether she wanted to "go to Jesus
now," and her mother had the satisfaction of reporting that
it was to her the child turned her eyes the last time. Sentimental religious language—"was she not fortunate after
all"—contrasts to the practical "Ole is very busy getting the
hay in." Martha tried to put the best face on things—she did
not call attention to the bleak landscape, primitive housing,
exhaustion and overwork, and Ole's possible emotional distance from her—and she took many opportunities, as we
have seen, to emphasize how family members in Norway
continued to be important to her and Ole. She let them
understand that thinking of them helped assuage her loneliness. Martha never asked for sympathy, but once subjected
to such acute sorrow, she expressed confidence that sympathy would be forthcoming.

Her letter evidently crossed with one from the Lima parents, for Ole's next, of October 20, 1898, gave nearly the

same recital, with the addition of a few details about David: "This event has at times seemed to us hard beyond measure, and even little David sometimes wakes up at night in bitter weeping because we no longer have Gunhild. She was in truth a beautiful and lovable child. One of the last days she lived she sat in the cradle with a little bottle, and sang to David. Afterward she asked, 'Dave, did you like that?'" (October 20, 1898).

There are no letters for the year 1899, when, in September, the Limas' fourth child was born and named Gunhild Mathilda (following the practice of Norwegians and other Europeans to name infants for older siblings who had died). This birth came nearly two years after Ruth's and fourteen months after the first Gunhild's death. The next pair of letters from Martha and Ole, dated February 7, 1900, contain Ole's report that "the doctor has recently declared that Martha is suffering from consumption." Between his description of their wedding in January 1894 and of Gunhild's death in October 1896, Ole had not mentioned Martha by name, although she, as we have seen, described at length what he had been doing and praised him to his relations. Now Ole gave clinical details about her diagnosis:

She has coughed and spit a great deal, which began late in fall and has grown worse as time went on [late fall was just after the birth of the child in September] until in the last weeks she has been weak and tired. The doctors in Cooperstown we had no confidence in. Dr. Platou, who formerly lived in Cooperstown, has now for several years lived in Valley City, but comes to Cooperstown once a month to care for patients. He was trained in Kristiania University and is regarded here as a competent doctor. To him we wished to turn. He came to Cooperstown January 25th, and we went there and he examined her, but could say nothing definite about the illness. He wished to take sputum for examination under the microscope, and would then write to us about the result. This proved to be that he had observed a great many tuberculosis bacteria in the sputum. He sent us at the same time two prescriptions, for which on Saturday I went to Cooperstown and procured medicine.

The previous Sunday Martha had been well enough to attend church, and, Ole remarked, "I definitely believe it is fruitful to listen to this simple, direct presentation of the word of God." They had a young woman working in the house, but, Ole wrote, "It is extremely difficult to get servant girls even if one pays them 2 to 3 1/2 dollars a week." He reported on the other children: "David is healthy, and wild and noisy, so that it is often very trying to Mama's nerves [David was five years old]. Edith Ruth is at times exceptionally happy and full of fun; then again so unhappy and cross that she is impossible. She still has some rash on her hands which bothers her with its itching. Little Gunhild Mathilda no. 2 is now weaned, 5 months old. No 1 greatly resembled Malli Th. Edland; no 2 considerable resembles Gurina Th. Edland."

The letter that Martha wrote on the same day as Ole's was her last. She addressed it to Malena, and like her other letters to this sister-in-law, it is less formal and more intimate than her letters to the senior Limas:

Dear Aunt Malena!
You know it is too bad I have put it off so long writing to you and thanking you for the letters I have received from you. However, it is better late than never: therefore thanks, dear Malena, because you have been faithful and good, and have sent me some words now and again.

Well, how are you managing alone with the house and children? I can understand and feel for those who are exhausted. If only the little ones would be content and good, the half would be well.

It is fine when one can by some means help oneself; but then it is just as fine to be helped, when one no longer can. Ole has told you in his letter to Grandmother how it is with me. Yet he has not told you how good he and other people are to me. He stops at nothing when he can bring me nourishing food and drink, and fruit. And friends and relatives have visited me and brought with them whatever they could think I might eat.

Everything is so undeserved. The great God and Father be praised and thanked for all his grace and mercy toward me. Disobedient and stubborn I have been toward him all my days. And when I regard my life in the years that I have sought the Lord's face, then I see that my face should be covered with shame—I am an unfruitful branch. But still I throw myself on Jesus' mercy. He must be faithful and save even the most perverted, through mercy.

Beautiful word! Greetings from Martha.

Typical of her manner and style, Martha begins with her feeling for "those who are exhausted," praises Ole, and berates herself as an "unfruitful branch"—presumably because she was dying. One hesitates to make an armchair diagnosis, but it is hardly surprising that Martha should suffer tuberculosis, a disease that throve on exhaustion. She had born four children in four years and nursed the last one during her own illness. She had only occasional domestic help, and, if Ole's writing style was indicative of his personality, received less emotional support from him than she had returned. To be sure, she was among acquaintances from her home area in Norway—the family of another of Ole's sisters lived nearby—but she wrote as though she were estranged from her own parents. She expended a lot of energy on others, Ole most of all, but she reported few emotional returns. Martha Lima was a young woman of considerable ability: she spoke English, had worked in several hotels, and managed a household under fairly rudimentary conditions. Her quick feeling "for those who are exhausted" explains her condition all too well.

The next letter, from Ole, was dated four months later, June 17, 1900. Martha, he thought, was a little better and had been able to do some sewing. She and Ruth had been at his sister's, and Gunhild was with another family (and never again lived with her parents). "David and I are home alone," Ole reported, angry that he had not been able to hire anyone to help with housework:

Yes, we are busy, that is sure. It looks as though as long as people are poor they can help each other endlessly; but if they get so much of earthly goods that they can be called "self-helped," then no thank you, they help only themselves. It has been painful, yes, revolting, to observe these things the last months. No matter how high the wages they may be promised, it helps nothing. And that we as Christian people have any duties or responsibilities does not seem to occur to them. "I need no help; let others help themselves as best they can" seems to be the language of the heart translated into action. Well, everything has its time and its limits.

Dry spring weather had destroyed his wheat crop and forced him to haul water for the cattle. And, he concluded, "I am unusually tired in the daytime and have a little toothache on the left side, as well as an aching in the left half of the head"—with housekeeping as well as outdoor work falling to him, Ole was feeling the exhaustion that Martha had known all along.

By the time of Ole's next letter (October 14, 1900), Martha was very weak but at home. The baby was still cared for by the Lunde family, and a "hired girl" had been with them for a while. However, Ole confessed that he himself had "entered a sort of desolation which destroys all ambition, so that one week goes after another, yes months, without anything being done." Martha sometimes could sit up in a rocking chair but had stopped taking medicine and ate very little. He wrote,

It is as if life is destroyed inch by inch; it is lost and "yet," says the apostle, "it is renewed inwardly day by day." The body, it is true, is like the wheat, to fall in the ground and die; but on the resurrection morn we will be clothed in a new, indestructible, glorified body, which will be able to enjoy the unending beatitude. There are many things that are better to flesh and blood, and thus death too is no welcome guest. But it falls to everyone's lot, and the question is only to place oneself in the right position to it, so that the physical death becomes an entrance to life.

Ole Lima was angry that domestic work should be so hard to do, now that he was the one doing it, and the ravaging process of Martha's disease appalled him. Nothing had prepared him to cope with both housework and death. His language suggests that dissonance: he described housework in harsh, everyday words and used abstract literary language for personal sorrow—bodies falling like wheat.

Martha lived only two weeks after this letter was written. Ole writes in formal language to his parents of her dying:

> Thanks for your last letter.
>
> It has now already become my heavy lot to report that my dear Martha has gone away. Her illness overcame her and ended in her death on 2nd November, at 3 o'clock in the morning. Monday, the 5th of the same, her earthly remains were brought, amid great participation, to her last resting-place on the graveyard near Ole Westley's house.
>
> It is already two weeks ago tomorrow, and yet I have still not managed to send any letter to you. You must excuse. I first sent word to Lisa [Martha's sister], then to Martin Edland [a relative], and then I have gotten no further.
>
> I do not find myself able, for the moment at any rate, to give any detailed description of Martha's last days and blessed dying. This much, however, you shall know, that as far as we could understand, she embraced, with all her heart, Christ's redemption, and consoled herself with a complete forgiveness of sins without any merit of her own. This is truly a powerful comfort, and an easing of the bitter pain of sorrow and loss.
>
> And yet it is often as if I am overwhelmed here in my loneliness. No one who lacks experience can put himself in my position. Now I go about here alone with David and Ruth, and must do, as well as I can, the very most necessary things in the house, as well as care for the cattle. Little Mathilda is still with Sven and Justine.
>
> Will you greet Torger and Malena as well as Ole Starevald. Erik was here and saw Martha the day before she died. Greetings, Ole Lima. [November 18, 1900]

After 1900 Ole's letters home every few months showed how drastically Martha's death had changed his life, but it did not greatly change his basic outlook. He wrote increasingly detailed accounts of church affairs and disagreements among factions; about the progress of his farming; a course he took at the Bible college in Wahpeton (partly to help improve his English). He also wrote more about the children than he had before. Over the years he tried a number of

living arrangements, boarding them with one or another
relative or friend so they could be taken care of and go to
school. Sometimes David, Ruth, or both were with him for a
while, but Gunhild Mathilda seems never to have lived at
home after her mother grew ill. While Ole became more involved with and aware of his children, he wrote as though
he thought of them primarily in relation to himself and did
not imagine their inner lives to the extent that Martha had,
for example, when she described David angry to find her lap
occupied by another baby.

Ole never found anything to take the place of Martha's
emotional support, the cheering on she conveyed to his parents. He was alert in a dour sort of way to local religious
conflicts and given to using pious language to meet emotional crises. When they were with him, Ole got the children
off to school, saw that they were fed and clothed and put to
bed, and provided for their religious training at a Norwegian
school, but he did not appear curious about their individual
selves. He wrote of them as burdens and reminders of his
sorrow, even though they had to have been a primary help
toward what recovery he made: "But often I am attacked by
desolation and hopelessness so that all ambition is gone.
I am fairly well after my illness, and have now for a week
also done the chores. My sole companions from morning till
night are David and Ruth, but they are quite entertaining.
I have to tell stories—now it is about Norway and grandparents and aunts and cousins, then about Abraham, Isaac,
Jacob, and Joseph—that one they want to hear over and
over" (November 18, 1900).

Six months after Martha died, Ole began boarding the
children: "When it became impossible for me to search out
any feminine help, then I procured a place for Ruth with Ane
[his sister], and David with Anna Njaa, married to Baard
Pederson Herigstad. My food preparation has also been
accordingly. I have gotten Mrs. Sven Edland, who lives a
5-minute walk from here, to wash clothes and bake bread.
I myself have been cooking coffee and eggs in the morning;

noon and evening—milk and bread and butter" (June 4, 1901).

At the end of 1902 he reported that the previous winter the children had been sick, Gunhild Mathilda with pneumonia in February—"Lively as she was before, she is now so weak that she cannot walk without help." However, by the end of the year all were better:

They are thriving well, so that is a joy. Mathilda is no doubt the one who does not quite keep up with the others in growth and weight; but Ruth is so rosy and fat, and besides so wild that she means to erupt. She is still with Baard and Anna. Mathilda is still at Lunde's. David is at home and provides my only company; that is to say when he is not in school. He has so far been at the English school most of the days since it started in the middle of November. Some days it has been so cold that I have not dared to send him off. It seems to be easy for him to learn; and between us we converse as well in English as in Norwegian. In arithmetic I think he is talented. He will be eight years old the 27th of February. [December 14, 1902]

Once, Ole tentatively suggested to his parents that he might alleviate his domestic difficulties by marrying again:

But ugh! to be alone and alone without end. And when I look at the children and think of their future, what results it may have to thus throw them from pillar to post, then it happens that I have of late thought as follows: perhaps after all a stepmother might be better for them than no one at all. But where is she to be found? is of course the question on which everything founders. And if the future should ever unloose that knot, it would not be against your wishes either, would it? [n.d.]

He did not mention the idea again, and he did not marry. By the spring of 1904, the family, scattered as it was, appeared fairly settled, and Ole reported to his parents:

David is now at home, and has just been repeating "Father, we will go to Norway; father we will go to Norway." Then he took out the photographs of Lima, and wanted me to explain who lived in each of the houses. Both he and Ruth have all winter been permitted to stay with Ane and Andreas Vatne and have gone to English school to Anna C. Westley, who says they have made good progress. Ruth remained there to go to Norwegian religious school, if possible. David is in his 10th, Ruth in her 7th, and Mathilda in her 5th year. This last one is so inately delightful that it is a great self-denial not to have her at home. Justine says that she grows more like her mother; I think she is even more like her aunt Ellen. They have much fun and satisfaction from her. She can sing several songs in English and is very quick in thought and talk. She now seems to grow and thrive as well as anyone. [April 22, 1904]

As the children got older, Ole found them more interesting, commenting especially on David's intellectual development:

David and Ruth learn easily and make good progress in school. They are so eager about reading and numbers that as soon as they have come home and eaten, they take their book or pencil and paper again, and I must act as teacher. David knows big figures. Thus I can dictate thousands, millions, billions, and whatever big figures I wish, in any order, and he sets them up in an orderly addition problem and finishes it without help. They cannot read Norwegian as they can English. But then they have had almost no Norwegian school. David will be 10 years the 27th of February; Ruth was 7 the 3rd of November. Mathilda is at the same place where she has been. I have not been able to take her home yet. This is my little world.

Ole was alert to the fate of other children. He reported the death from typhoid of the daughter of a railway worker: "It is the third daughter they must bury, and that is hard. Inga was an especially gifted girl, and therefore the father had paid for her schooling for several years until she was almost far enough along to continue her studies at the university" (June 25, 1905). Misfortunes came to many, and of all ages: "Two weeks ago Ola Vatne, brother to Kristian Vatne in Sandness died, in the faith of his Savior, and was buried two days later. The youngest daughter of Sven Lunde died 3–4 weeks ago, of consumption. Margit, daughter of Betual

Herigstad, has lost her mind, and had to be taken to the insane asylum at Jamestown" (February 2, 1908).

But a closer death disturbed Ole's "little world." Gunhild Mathilda had never been very strong. On August 11, 1907, Ole wrote to his parents that "Mathilda has ailed a little since early this spring; however she looks fairly well now." Eight years old, she was doing well in school and had learned to read both English and Norwegian—"in the latter language she has had no instruction she must have received it as a birth-gift." But, he added, "I fear she will hardly live long. God's will be done. She is a sweet, lovable child, with more than average development for her age. It is often hard to think that I, as her father, cannot be able to have her at home and care for her, though I suppose she is well off where she is, for that matter." Two months later, Mathilda was taking medicine and staying home from school, but looking "very alert and lively, as if nothing were wrong with her." Ole had ordered a sewing machine for her from Chicago—"I thought it might bring her pleasure" (October 12, 1907). In late February Ole thought "Mathilda can not remain long in this sinful world because two doctors have declared that she suffers from tuberculosis of the lungs. I think I can say, not only with resignation, but with true joy, 'God's will be done'" (February 23, 1908).

Over a year later Ole wrote about Mathilda again:

Sunday I went to Cooperstown, where the Lundes had moved with Mathilda to see her. Poor thing, she could no longer do things for herself. I went back to Vatne, and to church to listen to Andre in the evening. On April 1st. I received word that I must come to town to help watch over and care for Mathilda. I went the next day, and was there until she slept away on Holy Thursday morning at 6:30. As we surely hope, she celebrated that Easter with her mama in heaven. O, what a splendid hope! Saturday we followed her earthly house to its last resting-place, close to her mother's grave with its white marble monument.

As he had when describing Martha's dying, Ole combined factual details—Mathilda, he wrote, suffered most from bedsores—with pious language: "There is nothing to live for in this world unless we can be permitted to do our Lord some service in his small disciples—the poor, the hungry." A year earlier, when he had for some months not expected Mathilda to live long, he wrote at length about sin in regard to children:

Afternoon; I am now home from church, where Pastor Broen had service for the children. He spoke of the dangers of which this world is full, especially for children; that the kingdom of darkness was busy, and had placed its snares in many places, including the public school, in order to catch the little ones while they were young, and make them slaves of sin and Satan. One need only think of that Satan's den on the opposite side of the street—the opera house. And where is there a place on this earth which is not dangerous for the child's soul? One must fear and ask in alarm: Is it possible for the child to get by all snares without being caught? O yes, by God's grace it is possible. If the parents are in the right relation to God, and to the child, then it can be done; but Oh, how careful one must be. [May 10, 1908]

Ole had had little contact with Mathilda and, like other parents of his time, wrote as though children were not necessarily expected to live. And when he thought about members of his family who had died, his own feelings, not the personality of his wife or child, were the main focus of his mourning. Remembering Martha's birthday, he meditated on his loss. He wrote that Martha would have been

today 40 years old if she had lived. Yes, many things would have been otherwise had she still lived. But silence! God does all things well. If he has taken her out of the strife, home to his glory, he has also, I must admit, heard her last prayer on earth, and held his father-hand over the lonely and the motherless; and we have endlessly much to thank him for. And I am sure that "once will be solved each earthly puzzle, and answered every wherefore I pondered on." The author of this song went through the waters of sorrow when in early life he lost his mate. He had two boys who gave him much encouragement, but there was still a constant and deep sadness upon him the 36 years he lived as a widower. It was W. A. Wexels. [December 20, 1908]

Ole frequently reported and moralized about deaths of people he knew. Richard Brosten had died suddenly of inflamed intestines: "Left a widow and 6 children under 11 years, had just sold the farm and was going to move to Canada. Poor people! He had made no serious effort to find God in the days of health. . . . Might we who live in health and still have time, take heed and warning from these many sudden deaths we read and hear about" (August 2, 1910). A few months later came the sudden death of Mary P. Lunde, the woman who seems to have taken care of Mathilda. Ole went to the funeral: "O, how much spiritual poverty and misery exist. May the Lord have mercy on our Norwegian people. Our minister is completing his work among us; may we get a better one instead" (January 8, 1911). In the same letter he dreaded his own aging (he was fifty-one years old): "When I am feeling as I do now, I am strongly reminded that my time of departure is near, and that one must be ready at all times. If I am still to remain on earth for a time, and if God wills, it is surely not impossible that I may see the dear fatherland once more"—this in answer to a query whether he would be traveling soon to Norway.

After Mathilda's death, the lives of the rest of the Lima family—Ole, David, and Ruth—continued without major misfortunes. On February 2, 1911, Ole wrote that he and David were "out traveling" and visiting his sister's family and Ruth in Osakis, Minnesota, where Ruth had been attending school. By April 1911, David, now sixteen, was working at another farm for $25 a month. Two years later Ole reported from the farm in Hannaford that "both David and Ruth have come home. Therefore it is now something of a 'home.' Both are very competent and willing" (August 10, 1913). The following year, however, Ole felt deprived because the children had left: "David again began high school in Cooperstown two weeks ago. He is home again today. Ruth aims to go to bible school, which begins Oct. 21. Judging by all signs, I must be content to be alone on the farm this coming winter. This is indeed lonely and sad to look forward to, but it looks as if it is to be so. Something unpleasant each of us must have a share of either in one way or another, in body or in mind, sometimes both. But it will not always be so" (September 27, 1914).

Speaking about the children as they grew up led their father to reflect about them allegorically. When they were sixteen and thirteen years old, Ole had concluded: "May God, for the sake of Christ bring us all through the world's desert which often is so dark and clouded that one knows not where to turn, and into the safe haven of peace. May no one be missing then!" (April 10, 1911). During the winter of 1915 David again attended the Cooperstown high school and Ruth the Wahpeton Bible school ("and she writes that it goes well"), the same school Ole had attended some years earlier. Their father lamented his loss: "And I sit here alone day after day, week after week, month after month, and must try to supply the necessary money. I have left some wheat and flax from the last crop, and hauled out 4 loads after New year. The price had been high lately—chiefly because of the war around Germany" (January 3, 1915). Good fortune continually seemed difficult for Ole to accept.

Four years later, in spite of the intervening First World War, the Limas still enjoyed more good than bad fortune. David was not drafted but studied engineering at the University of North Dakota. Ruth finished both high school and Bible school in Wahpeton and enrolled at St. Olaf College in Northfield, Minnesota. None of the family, Ole wrote, had suffered the Spanish influenza, "and that is great." But he was far from cheerful, and he felt his age: "I am in my sixtieth year." He wanted to stop farming but worried about the expense of educating his children, and he never was able to shake off desolating loneliness: "I am beginning to be tired of it all, and wishing for a quiet corner to live in. On the farm there is too much that needs doing, and when I am alone about it, both outside the house and inside, it is too much of a good thing. David will not be any farmer, and I think of selling. He came home from school the 1st of June, and the 20th he continued westward to the silver mines of Idaho, 1,000 miles.

Since Ruth finished school this year in May, she has been at Ogsakis, Minn., with Vatnes" (July 13, 1919).

In 1925 Ole made another trip to Norway with Ruth, who returned separately, on her way back visiting in Washington and Minneapolis, where David was living. But, Ole wrote, "In the fall she is coming to Hannaford to teach in the high school there. And when she is as near as one Norwegian mile from here, I will surely now and then be able to see her at home." Two years later he wrote again of his loneliness: "It is often lonesome here on the farm, and I think, if I could sell it, I would not have to be alone so much. . . . In a week I expect Ruth home, and that makes it more homelike. She has promised to continue at the same place next year also. It is a 4-hour drive by car from there to here. She sold her car last fall, and now takes the train back and forth" (April 22, 1927).

In 1927, when his letters home ceased, Ole was sixty-seven years old, David thirty-two, and Ruth thirty. He lived four more years. "He died," according to Ruth McMahon's introduction to her translations of the letters, not "while residing on his own farm, twelve miles southeast of Cooperstown, North Dakota, but while making a visit to relatives at Edmore, North Dakota, on April 23, 1931."

What can Martha and Ole Lima's family tell us about families in the settlement years, particularly the lives of children? What, to use Martha's word, makes them "thrive"? In America, Ole kept connections with his sister's family by living nearby for many years and, when she moved to Minnesota, by visiting her; the Vatnes' taking Ruth from time to time further kept the two families in touch. Ole always showed that he felt responsible for his children's physical well being, education, and moral and religious instruction. If he could not manage them in his household, he found others able and willing to do so, and he made it possible for David and Ruth to attend college.

Emotional connections among this family were more ambiguous. As long as Martha Lima was alive, she provided emotional sustenance and encouragement to her husband

and children; she entered quickly and generously into their imaginations; she thought of them as individuals apart from herself. When Martha died, Ole was deprived of her shoring up and felt himself unable to provide that kind of support to anyone else. Instead he sought it from others and in his last years came as close as ever to finding in Ruth a substitute for Martha, when she arranged teaching positions to be near him. He never ceased to mourn his loss. That yearning, as much as anything, may be the force that kept him writing home, worrying about his children's proclivities toward "sin," and, however morosely, keeping intact a strong sense of a family whose members were rather tenuously connected. David's refusal to farm and his defection to Idaho sounds like a severe blow to the system that so long kept Ole in charge of those around him. Ruth's willingness to come "home" to teach, on the other hand, he may well have seen as his reward, his due in old age.

The correspondence of course reveals almost nothing directly about the children. All we know depends upon one or the other parent's point of view. We hear of the children only from their father and then primarily as they did or did not live up to his expectations. He reported on their state of health, occasionally their moral character, and their progress in school. But what their thoughts might be, even whether they too sorrowed for their mother, Ole never said. We can wonder whether Mathilda's dying when she was nine years old might have been forestalled by warmer contact with her father and siblings, but we cannot know.

8

Over Fool's Hill

Children in Three Families

It has become a point of pride to be able to claim that one's family "pioneered." Ever since the national bicentennial of 1976, rural communities in the Midwest that were settled as late as the 1880s have increased their enthusiasm for centennials. Farms owned by a single family for a hundred years are proclaimed "centennial" farms; families, churches, and towns compose commemorative histories of themselves; historical societies and museums burgeon in the smallest communities. Yet all this activity transpires in the midst of what is being described as a farm "crisis" so severe as to change forever the complexion of the rural social landscape and almost to eliminate altogether family-focused agricultural operations and town centers. While this memorializing—in a manner so apparently disengaged from present events—may be a sign of little more than romanticism, wishful denial, or stubborn resistance, the process may well also reveal the ways in which second and later generations have assimilated that past their settler parents brought them to.

For all the enthusiasm in gathering "histories," there are stories one does not tell, subjects not spoken of, although few deny that such events occurred. The fact of abortion, for instance, makes celebrating difficult; others also appear so taboo as hardly to apply to the idea of history at all: alcoholism, petty crime, mental illness, retardation. Such a misfortune as abortion is assumed to happen only in cities—rife with crime and excesses of every sort—but not in the whole-

some, fecund countryside. A daughter tells of knowing about
her mother's difficult labor with a child who "came double
breech." The mother had helped this daughter in her pregnancy: "I didn't dilate when Cal was born, and the doctor
said, 'I can't save them.' Ma got hysterical. She said, 'Well,
it's not so bad about the baby, we haven't seen him or loved
him.'" Both mother and child survived, but some time later
the mother asked this daughter whether she were pregnant
again: "I said no, and she said, 'Are you sure?' and I said,
'No, can't be.' Cal was almost two. She had a fit and said,
'You're going right to the doctor to Minot,' and the doctor
swore, and she was terribly mad. So I had surgery, was
there for two weeks, and then I never got pregnant again. In
those days you never talked about these things with people"
(S 19).[1] Yet it is subjects not talked about—those even sur-
geons swear at—that cannot help coloring the memories of
people who have lived long enough to realize the past. Details easy to approve of—and rhyme into state songs or
dramatize in village pageants—rub against what is not approved of and bring forth sometimes dissonant versions of a
past. Yet people bringing this more difficult information deserve a hearing.

The context in which people view their past may vary: accounts might be set as a journey of immigration from one
country or area to another or from one stage of life to another. Life stories can be told around an important event,
such as a war or memorable adventure; or set in narrators'
sense of community—their feelings of belonging to a city,
neighborhood, ethnic group, or, in the case of the discussion
in this chapter, the particular towns they lived in during
their first years of settlement development. Rural America
and its bucolic small towns contain complicated individual people, who, as well as they have accommodated to a
more collective and watched-over social landscape than city
folks are used to, nevertheless are not anesthetized by the
fresh country air. Popular impressions of small-town life are
fraught with contradiction. We want to believe that virtue
and health repose in all those little towns that time forgot,

that small towns do indeed breathe the moral air of their rural settings. Opportunities may be limited, but that is a small price to pay for everyone's looking out for everyone else; if the gossip impedes adventure, it also attests to "caring." Norman Rockwell has not lost his power to make good and simple living appear the norm. Grant Wood may paint a stiff farm couple imprisoned behind pitchfork tines, but we would expect that anyone living there, in Grant Wood country, would not see things that way. It is the outsiders who are the nay-sayers: writers like Sherwood Anderson presenting a peculiar Winesburg, Ohio; Mary Wilkes Freeman spying on eccentric maiden ladies in depopulated New England villages; Willa Cather exposing strange people on the Plains. Southern writers like William Faulkner, Eudora Welty, and Flannery O'Connor have not been alone among major writers to observe strange and wonderful behavior in sparsely populated communities. And yet, it could be argued, writers made outsiders of themselves by virtue of their education, their social and physical mobility, and merely by being artists and writers. But if "outsiders" indeed are the only ones to discover (presumably out of their imaginings) a rural life that falls short of the wholesome and bucolic, what do we make of the trip to the surgeon in Minot, told so matter-of-factly?

The teller of that tale is a member of one of three families who immigrated in the 1880s from South Russia to homestead farms and townsites in North Dakota and are the subject of this chapter. They intermarried, and in the early 1980s one of their granddaughters interviewed as many people as she could find of her parents' generation about their parents and what they remembered of the pioneer experience. Her intention was to produce three "family histories" based on those interviews and on photographs. The fact that Florence Clifford, a professional musician and lifelong resident of the state, conceived of and carried out the project in itself attests to the success of the immigrant venture for these particular families. Not every member can have achieved equal "success," however it is measured, and yet Florence herself symbolizes the accomplishment of the original venture. For all the pain and frequent regrets, her dislocated ancestors could say it was worth it. The third generation is indisputably "American," never more so than in this attempt to retrieve its past.

When Florence Clifford asked relatives in her parents' generation about their parents, she was told about childhoods. These children described what their parents had done to them, but they did not often imagine their mothers and fathers as adults independent of children (who, at the time of the interviews, were in their seventies and eighties). Some of these children had been born in Russia and remembered a little about extended families in agricultural villages. Those born in North Dakota, because the families had many children, came at widely varying stages in the families' evolution. First children were born in sod or wooden claim shacks, last children in comfortable, even luxurious frame or brick houses in prospering towns. The depression of the 1930s was hard on all of North Dakota, but before that, these particular families prospered—with a farm, a store, and a hotel.

Interviews reflect generational differences. The children think of themselves as "modern": they went to school, learned English (and taught it to their parents), married by choice rather than by marriage broker, eventually drove cars, wore fashionable clothes, and were less obsessed with the idea of work than their parents had been. Family albums contain snapshots of children on tricycles; of young women friends, arms about each other, in silly poses and wearing men's suits and ties. There are pictures of young men and women in automobiles; of children and adults sitting in a row on running boards; of picnics and country outings. The second generation evidently saw their parents (and the grandparents who came as well) as clinging to old ways that appeared increasingly odd, if not perverse. While these children worked hard to help support the family enterprises, they also strained to loose themselves from family ties. Attitudes vary, and most reflect ambivalences. Some people spoke angrily about their fathers' overbearing ways and the severe beatings they received as boys. Children pitied mothers for constant pregnancies and never-ending anxieties about children. They spoke bemusedly of parents' mannerisms, special foods, eccentric habits. In the view of some of these children, growing up in settlement times was a strange experience; they remembered one bizarre anecdote after another. These family accounts everywhere assert the "normal"—work, churchgoing, sociability, sickness and health, and increasing prosperity. But they also weave in something else—mixed with irony and detachment—that makes us think the brave experiment barely escaped going askew.

Rosina Hirsh and Johann Schmidt traveled from Russia to the United States on the same ship, but five years apart. They met and married in Eureka, South Dakota, in 1894, the year of Rosina's arrival. Johann was nineteen years old when he came with his parents and a brother from Guedendorf, on the Black Sea, another brother and his wife having made the trip earlier. Rosina was born in Rosenfeld. She came at age eighteen with a younger sister, the daughter of her mother's third husband, who wanted to join her older brother, a lawyer, in Eureka. Rosina worked in this stepbrother's household and had not intended to stay in America. Rosina and Johann had six children (the eldest, Waldemar, was Florence Clifford's father), and they ran a hotel in Anamoose.

Florence's mother's parents, Katharina Morlock and Johann Lippert (the second family), grew up and married in Neudorf, South Russia. They emigrated in 1884 to Ashley, North Dakota, where they owned a general store. They had eleven children: two infant boys died in Russia, and three daughters died of diphtheria in Ashley. Florence's mother was the youngest.

The third family is that of Josephine and Johann Howitz, whose eldest daughter is the mother of Florence Clifford's husband, Thomas J. Clifford. Josephine grew up in Kalisz,

and Johann in Dolins, towns in the Austrian province of
Galicia. They were married in 1885 and had nine children,
the first three dying in infancy. The Howitzes farmed near
Langdon, North Dakota, arriving there by way of Russia,
then Landanbery, Canada, where they had tried unsuccess-
fully to settle. Josephine's parents, Peter and Magdalena
Delvo, came as well, as did a sister and her family. The
Howitzes were Roman Catholic, the Lipperts and Schmidts,
Baptist.

In addition to being joined through marriages in the third
generation, these families shared similar ethnic backgrounds
and large families, and they engaged in comparably successful occupations—farming, banking, running a store and
hotel. As reported by their children, their interests and attitudes about themselves did not vary much. They could almost be described as a blend of a single family, noting differences and variations as they occur.

If the children of immigrants sometimes had reservations
about the childhoods their parents brought them to in the
New World, immigrants themselves often left home with
ambivalent feelings. It was not an easy departure for any of
the three families. Rosina Schmidt said, "I can still see my
mother running along the train when I left, crying and crying, and saying, 'She'll never come back again.'" That was
the last time Rosina saw her mother (S 3). Rosina Gimbel
Hirsh, the mother, was married three times, Rosina's father,
the first husband, having died when Rosina was eleven years
old. Mrs. Hirsh died in Siberia: "They took her to Siberia to
work them to death, to freeze them to death, for slaves. Most
of them froze to death in the cars; they didn't have any heat,
and most of them couldn't take it" (S 37).

Yet Rosina also had memories of prosperity and comfort
in Russia before these oppressions:

Mother said they would go down to the Black Sea and spear sun-
fish. They would walk into the water up to their waist, and the sun-
fish would lie on the bottom—she said big fellows—take a spear

and stick it down through him. And then they had a point on it, and pick him out. She said you could see them lying down there in the bottom. The Black Sea was fresh water. She said they hauled them out to the fields, put them into the furrow, and plowed them shut to fertilize the field. They put the fish into the furrow, and the horse was always slipping around on them. After about an hour, they changed horses because it was awfully hard on them. [S 37]

Rosina's family was wealthy enough, with scattered tracts of land around Groszliebental, to afford a coachman and other hired help. Family lore included a gruesome story: "Ma said that their hired man slept in the barn up above the horses on a sort of bench up there, and one night he heard something, and he got up, and there was someone trying to get into the barn, and the fellow stuck his finger in the hole and tried to lift the latch, and the hired man took his knife and whupppt, the finger was off" (S 2).

When Rosina tried to work to support herself as a cook's helper in a nobleman's family, conditions were not easy: "She said she got so hungry for meat (they weren't given any) that she snitched a small piece of chops frying in a pan for the nobleman's dinner. She was caught and beaten" (S 3). The distant Russian past, back where they had never been, becomes, for the children of immigrants, a terrible place of Siberian exile and death.

Rosina Hirsh's feelings about leaving Russia were mixed. The opportunity came when her stepsister wanted to join the brother in South Dakota and needed an older person to go with her. Going gave Rosina the chance to escape the abuses in the nobleman's kitchen (and possibly death with her mother in Siberia). And yet she could not forget that her mother "came running behind on the track, and threw up her arms and said, 'Ach Godd, Ach Godd, my kinder, my kinder'" (S 4). Johann Schmidt, the man Rosina married in Eureka, had left with similar feelings of hope and regret: "Dad often says if they would have had a good government over there, they would never have left the country in Russia.

They had a beautiful country where they were, but the government was no good, in fact the Czars were oppressing the people, and that's what brought on the revolution" (S 4).

Florence Clifford's mother's parents, Johann Lippert and Katharina Morlock, grew up and married in the village of Neudorf in South Russia. Two of their eleven children were born and died before the Lipperts left Neudorf in 1884. Johann's father had died when Johann was eleven years old, and he was brought up by an uncle who trained him as a cabinetmaker, a trade Johann continued in the Dakotas. Katharina's parents farmed; her father was *burgermeister* (mayor) in Neudorf. She worked in the fields with her father and continued to do so after her marriage, returning two days after childbirths. Katharina had a beautiful singing voice, and took lessons in Russia, but in the Dakotas she was no longer able to study voice. Her children remembered her singing around the house, "and during her last illness she sang a song in bed—a hymn—shortly before she died" (L 2). In addition to the two infant boys who died in Russia, three daughters died of diphtheria in Ashley.

For Katharina, the Dakota venture mainly held regrets. She so missed her family in Russia, that had she known that she would never see them again, she would not have come: "In her loneliness Katharina used to be so homesick she would go out in the fields and just roll in them and scream out her anguish." When the little girls died, "this was another of the times that she went into the wheat field, hiding herself in the high grain and she would lie there and cry her heart out. This was the way she dealt with tragedies" (L 5). She "was so grief stricken that sometimes she would milk the cows until the pail ran over" (L 25).

Katharina had happier associations with Russia. Florence wrote of her grandmother's cooking bread dough balls on top of the oven and making a Russian turnover "filled with a pumpkin mixture of salt, a bit of sugar, onions and pepper. Some of this mixture was spooned onto a circle of dough. The circle was then folded in half and the open edges pinched together, forming a semicircle. It was baked standing upright on the flat end, and served as the main dish" (L 31). Florence associated her grandmother with nasturtiums and other flowers she grew, and said, "In her late seventies, she would look out of the window a lot to see what was going on in the neighborhood, or she just sat and listened to me practice the piano" (L 31), perhaps a reminder of the singing lessons she had given up in Russia.

Josephine and Johann Howitz's life on the Russian-Austrian border was not a happy one. They journeyed to North America, settling first in Canada, to avoid conscription into the Russian army. Johann had lost five sisters to diphtheria, and a brother of his died by falling into the vat in the sugar factory: "They didn't have any advantages in the old country, just work, work, work. . . . They were all anxious to get away because there was no future for them, men or women, and they wanted to have a better life," according to the children (H 4).

Life was harsh for children as well. The strain that mothers felt could be too much for children: "In Europe they had a little boy named William that they doted on very much, and they had a baby named Joseph too, and one day Josephine went someplace, and when she came back, little Willie had gotten into the lard and smeared the baby just full of lard, head and all. When she came home and saw this, she was so angry she gave him a sound thrashing. Shortly after this, he got sick and then died. And this bothered her terribly that she had beat him so badly" (H 4).

Joseph came down with scarlet fever on board ship, and his mother had to stay with him "for weeks" of quarantine on Ellis Island: "She said she cried buckets of tears, saying it was the most horrible time in her life." Joseph died later in Canada, and Josephine "thought Johann would lose his mind grieving over the two children that died. He was a more loving father than she was a mother, seemed to have more time for it" (H 4).

There were some details of their parents' Russian origins, however, that the children associated with pleasurable comforts. Their mothers' head scarves, foods, habits of praying—these they described as quaint or mildly eccentric. Josephine Howitz "liked tea very much because they lived in Russia for a short time where she learned to drink tea. They had a samovar there, and she would drink it in a tall glass and add milk and sugar to it. When the children were sick, this was a special treat that they got" (H 5). Josephine wore switches and a "transformation"—"hair on a strip, meant to be combed into your own hair with some of your own hair over it, but her hair was so thin that when she put it on there was nothing to comb through. They used to laugh at her" (H 16). She had broken her wrist, leaving her hand crooked, and to cut bread "she would hold it in her hand and cut it toward her. She had a large stomach and would always rest her arm on this stomach. She held the bread against her stomach" (H 18).

Josephine wore stylish, if old-fashioned clothes:

I remember her getting ready to go to church. She had a frilly little thing on her front to make her bosom bigger and then she had a padded bustle and that she tied around her waist and it lay in the back and gave her more of a seat because she was built like Babe, not much of a rump, and it made these dresses look better on her. She did have quite a bit of bosom but at the same time it was fashionable to have quite a bit there and they had those leg-o'-mutton sleeves. I was fascinated watching her put on all of this gear because most of the time at home she never wore that. This was for dress-up. [H 5]

Rosina Schmidt's children also commented on her clothes: "Grandma had a tight garment when she was pregnant, and she was working at the homestead, and all of a sudden she felt a mouse in there. She had a wrapper on with a tight bra, and it was connected somehow. She got so scared she took ahold of it, and grabbed it, and when she let go, the mouse fell down dead" (S 18). The aprons she wore made her children think of earlier generations: "Usually she had an apron on. All those old people used to. They would kind of hide behind the apron. My mother was different. She had the apron on, or sometimes [would] take it off to make it more convenient, or she'd put it aside and go ahead and do the work, but not the old grandmas. They thought they were pretty well dressed if they had on an apron. They always wore one" —. Johann Schmidt's mother, Anna Marie, who lived across the street in Anamoose, knit angora "pussy bonnets" for the granddaughters and neighbor girls. She made a special occasion of the marriage of one of the granddaughters: "She never opened her living room, and she had beautiful walnut furniture in there, caned seats, lovely, but nobody ever went in there, and she didn't heat it in the winter either. The door was shut. But when Al and I were married, one time we came over there and she opened the front room door and said, 'Come on in here,' that we were company. And I said, 'Come on, Grandma, we're not company.' But she said, 'Ya, come on in here.'" (S 8).

Katharina Lippert "was always dressed in dark clothes as most of the ladies in those days were. They wore usually blouses and skirts," and at home "percale small prints, never anything splashy. She got a shawl from the old country, and it had big red roses on it and embroidered all around the whole thing. She picked all of that embroidery off. It was sent to her from Russia. She thought it was too colorful" (L 18). Katharina too wore scarves, or *tiechles*, from Russia. Candy and scents also had associations with Russia: "Grandma liked peppermint candy or memonen troppe (lemon drops) and that was really their mouthwash in those days. When they went away they always put one of those in their mouth." The women also liked sprays of mint: "They would run them through their hands and squeeze them and then swish them under their nose and have a nice handkerchief all crocheted and folded up in their belts, very proud of that. Once in a while they carried a sweet pea. They liked sweet peas" (L 18).

Russian was the language associated with older people: "The old men would tell jokes about Russia, that they had heard in Russia. They all could talk Russian—not much, but they did it. Grandpa understood Russian" (L 9). Old men came around to the Lipperts' store in Ashley to pass the time and "chew sunny seeds (keife Kerne). They would have more fun telling stories. Once in a while they would laugh, and I think they were telling jokes in Russian" (L 10). "Grandpa could speak Russian quite well years ago, but he forgot it all. He could understand even in later years. Uncle Phillip could rattle that off just like a bullet. He was the oldest" (S 4). German, however, was the language spoken at home, and English only after children started school and then taught their parents, although Johann Schmidt had learned some English in night school in Eureka.

Alien as they may have felt in comparison to United States-born settlers, these families quickly realized that they were less foreign than anyone who came from Russia later than they did, and like many others, they made it a point to help newly arrived settlers from the same country. Johann Schmidt was known as "Honest John" not only because he did not cheat anyone, but also because he helped others start in business. A minister told of Johann's offering to help him once when he was feeling low: "Of course I didn't want to tell him [my troubles] because he helped so many people and he used to help every preacher's family" (S 12). Johann Lippert's children were impressed by their father's generosity. He was "very compassionate. When people came from Europe they had nothing to live on, and he would extend credit to them. He would buy a cow and give it to someone who had children but not milk, and they were supposed to give him a calf. Or if a cow had two calves, they would keep one and give him one. But sometimes people would say they were very sorry, 'but your calf died'" (L 6). Once Johann practiced charity inadvertently. He and his son disagreed about buying surplus World War I army jackets to sell in the store. Johann insisted they would sell, and when they did not, "one day he got a big box and he packed all those old jackets into this wooden box, and then he added a couple of shoes and some gloves and some wool shirts, and sent them over to Russia to his brothers" (L 10). His generosity went so far as to take new settlers into his house— twenty on one occasion: "They spread grass on the floor for people to lie on. Everyone lay in a row, and the last one in closed the door" (L 3).

Religion was a comfort, but it was apt to bring on homesickness as much as it brought comfort. For the young, religion further emphasized their separation from their parents' past. Church and prayer were vital to the older people but could alienate their children:

Grandpa knew his Bible. The minister was there only every third Sunday, so the brethren or deacons would give the sermon, and when Grandpa was up there, we kids were pretty quiet. I didn't even swing my legs. They were very faithful to their church and to their religion. Faithful to God too, because times were so hard and everything. Every disaster was God's will, that's the only way they could cope. Each had their own characteristic trait but here was also a common bond between them, so that if anything happened, like if somebody's barn burned, they would all get together and help them build the barn, or if somebody got sick during harvest time, the neighbors would all get together and they would harvest for them. They had to do that, stick together.

After church, when the service was over, all had to kneel down and pray. And they all prayed at once. And sometimes the kid that was in the bench in back of you would grab onto your legs and hang on. I wasn't listening. I was bored and sometimes would not understand the sermons as a kid. I would work my arithmetic lessons or something because the prayers lasted pretty long. Sometimes after the sermon the preacher would say that whoever felt like adding anything, could. One old guy always felt led to add to the sermon every Sunday morning. We would cross our fingers, we would hope he didn't feel "led." [L 14]

These services could become emotional occasions: "They all had such a hard life, and all cried very easily. If they were in church services, and a minister told of some disaster, the whole church would be sniffling. The women were all crying. I always heard Grandma, she always was crying the hardest and loudest. I couldn't understand her, but she was sincere" (L 17).

Katharina and Johann Lippert were devout people. "God wants only refined gold," Johann said, and his children supposed he thought death came to him only after he had been refined. For Katharina, the deaths from diphtheria of her three daughters in a single week brought on a crisis. Lydia, the eldest, said before she died that she wanted her mother "to get right with God" because Katharina "had struggled for many years trying to believe that God would forgive her for her sins. She had trouble believing, and Lydia knew that, and that's why she told her to make her peace with God" (L 5). Katharina was considered even more religious than most women, partly because she disapproved of dancing and card playing: "The stundebruder were a group of people that got together to worship and read the scriptures and pray—they wanted to have this in addition to church, sort of like a prayer group, in Neudorf, Russia. My mother didn't go, but they used to call her 'studebruder' because they went dancing and she didn't like to dance" (L 20). Younger people also attended church, but with rather different purposes. They went church-hopping:

We went to church a lot. They had different meetings at various churches. We went to the Seventh Day Adventist—my friend and I—and the Methodist. We visited all the churches. I had a friend who lived across the street, a daughter of the pastor of the Evangelical Church. We just wanted to check it out and hear the programs. It was someplace to go, and there was always a lot of singing and special numbers. We just liked to listen to those things. That was a form of entertainment available to us. There wasn't much else. [L 20]

Schmidt children also were impressed by their parents' religious devotion:

Dad most of the time made up his own prayers at the table. Seldom that it was a set prayer. The good Lord was very very dear to him. I can still hear my mother pray sometimes for us kids at bedtime. She'd kneel down beside the bed when us kids crawled into bed, and she would pray a lingo; I tell you, sometimes it made you think what she was praying. There were four of us sleeping in the same room. Sometimes she mentioned one of us, that the Lord would take care of us and she hoped that we'd stay well or if we were sick, then she was there, that was all there was to it. It was always in German. Dad too. I never heard him pray in English. [S 15]

The eldest Schmidt daughter described the daily family ceremony called "family altar," which, while it derived from practice in German-Russian European communities, for her symbolized strong ties she felt with her family. A brother, however, thought his father "too strict a Baptist" and described the scene with some annoyance: "My dad ruled with an iron hand in his family affairs. When he read the Bible there was no discussion, no argument, or anything like that. That was it, and everybody had to sit there and wait until he got through reading the Bible." Sunday meant the family gathering and two sessions of Sunday school, which this son thought "too much" (S 21). But the sister gave a more appreciative view. This disagreement between a brother and sister may reflect gender differences in men's and women's response to religious observance. Men used Bible readings and leading services to enforce their authority, while women found religious observance one of the few sources of comfort and emotional expression—the "crying" described among older Lippert women. For one daughter, "family altar" was a tie to family:

As long as I can remember not one of us kids got out of staying for the family altar in the morning. My dad had a system. We got up punctually at a certain time, and Mom would have breakfast ready and then we had each, if we could read, we had a German Bible, and in the dining room there were windows all along the south side, and there was a long low radiator right in the middle below the windows and the Bibles were all piled on there. One of the boys would go and pass them round. We each had our own and the ones that were too young didn't have to read. But Pa would read, and we would all read around the table. Ma, and Pa—I always sat on Ma's side and we'd kneel down by our chairs. Pa would pray first, then Mother, then Walt, and I and all the way down. Those kids just said a short prayer. And one time Walt said, "I haven't got my homework done. I have to go to school." Pa said, "You sit right there.

Tomorrow you do your homework in the evening, then it will all be done." So we knew we weren't going to get out of it.

And you know that when I got married, when I left and came back from Minneapolis, we had our own little house there. And in the morning Al and I were all alone. One morning I was so lonesome just to be with the family, so when Al went to work as soon as he was gone, I snuck off and walked from way out east of town where we lived in a little house over the winter, and when I got there they were just sitting around the table. I stood there and I could have just cried, and Pa saw it, and he said, "You sit down and eat with us." And I said, "No, I don't want anything to eat, I ate." But he knew I was just lonesome. And then I stayed for family altar and then I felt better. I went home after a little while. But it was just the group I missed. Al and I had devotions too, but there wasn't anybody around. I think of that so many times. No matter who was there, it was the same thing, always the devotions. [S 20]

Ideas about health and medicine reflected folk knowledge acquired in Russia, partly, of course, because none other was available in rural areas, and many were suspicious of modern methods, often with good reason. Herbs, poultices, and incantations sometimes worked and sometimes did not. Ephraim, the eldest Lippert son, contracted typhoid fever, and whereas the rest of the family had been inoculated, he "didn't believe in it," and died (L 22). Some folk remedies, while evidently effective, struck second-generation settlers as odd, if not disquieting. When Peter Delvo was partially paralyzed from a stroke and spent much time in bed, fried angleworms were applied to soothe his bedsores. The worms were dug up in cow manure, and, a granddaughter said, "All I saw was those worms hopping around in that pan, and that was enough for me" (L 16). Josephine Howitz relieved her headaches by placing a heated saucer on top of her head and kept it in place with a shawl (H 25). According to her daughter, she practiced faith healing:

When a child would not do well and was losing weight they would bring it to Mother. She would measure the child with a string and then measure the child's foot, and use that foot as a measure. If it didn't come out a certain way it meant the child wasn't doing well, and she would say a prayer over the string and give the mother some prayers to say and the mother would have to say these prayers once or twice a day, and Josephine would also do this. Then the mother would bring the child back in a week and they would go through the process again. It never failed. Pretty soon they would be blooming little kids. [H 6–7]

For colic, Josephine Howitz placed coals from the fire into cold water, "read them some way," and said prayers. "Many little scrawny kids, weepy crying kids, and the mother would come and plead with Mother and Mother would think nothing about it. She would use the coals sometimes when an animal was sick too" (H 6–7).

In the Schmidt family also, herbal and other home remedies and folk healing continued European traditions. They used leeches:

Mother used to bring those blood suckers and I used to go to the drug store and get them and take them back for her later on. They put those blood suckers on my grandmother and you could see how red they would get. It was supposed to be good for their body. The druggist would sell them, and then take them back and somebody else would use them. John Miller, when he killed cattle in the slaughter house, he would cut the jugular vein, and he had a cup and he would hold the cup under there and get a glass full of blood and used to drink that. He was the butcher. At that time there were no doctors. [S 31]

Garlic was recommended during the influenza epidemic of 1918: "You could smell garlic everywhere you went. Everybody had garlic. I got so sick of smelling people with garlic breath. Garlic is an old method for high blood pressure too. Grandma chewed it. She had heart trouble" (S 31). Another odd treatment was tried when one of the boys fell down the cellar stairs: "For a long time his head went to one side, and then he had to take electric treatments for a long time. My dad had bought a machine of some kind and it gradually straightened him out" (S 31). Patent medicines appeared as compromises between the old and the newly commercial: "They had Alpenkreuter for a woman when she gets her period. They didn't know that it was mostly alcohol. Some of the women in the neighborhood talked about Alpenkreuter" (S 31).

Relations of parents among each other, as far as their children could observe, seemed distant, and their intimacies were kept from children. They evidently saw some, but not a great deal of open affection, yet they could see that their parents understood each other:

They didn't show openly their affection for each other. My dad, when he first came home at noon time, my mother would be at the stove or someplace, he'd come over and kiss my mother. She never refused it. Dad left most of the decisions in the house to her. She nearly always got what she wanted. She wanted that room in the dining room where she kept the flowers in the south side of the dining room. I don't know whether he gave her money to spend as she wanted to, but she always had money. How she got it or when I don't know. Dad always had something on his mind, always had business on his mind. Never saw him, very seldom saw him in an argument. They wouldn't argue around the kids. If there was something serious or something came in, they would go in the front room, lock the door so nobody could go in, and we never heard anything about it. We weren't allowed to hear anything about it, but they had it out. [S 45]

During the depression this father lost a great deal of money from bad loans, but he "never discussed business with anyone. That's where he made a mistake. Never discussed it. Never with my mother. I don't think my mother ever knew it. She was a woman. I don't think he ever told Mother anything. He saw it coming but didn't want to worry her. But we never knew it. That was really something. Ma used to say, 'Don't know what's wrong with Pa. He hollers in the night.' He had regular nightmares. He kept her awake and didn't even know what he was doing" (S 15).

When these children thought about their own relations to their parents, they tell anecdotes about momentary intimacy, playing with the beards of otherwise gruff fathers, but day-to-day connections between parents and children appear distant. The children "were all held on the lap by the parents, when they were babies. Never told us that they loved us, but we knew they did. They would come to school programs. Don't remember Dad coming, but Mother did. When we graduated from high school, Mother took us all out and bought us ice cream, to Glosback's drug store. But my dad, he wasn't sociable with his family" (S 21). One thing this father did do with his children, at least the boys, was supervise their boxing: "He liked boxing. He would put us kids in the ring, would push the table back in that big dining room 16 feet by 20 feet. He had boxing gloves. If it got a little too rough, shuppt, that's enough. He would sit and referee" (S 23).

The same father also appears to have treated sons and daughters rather differently. He had an "iron hand," one son said. Meals were not sociable: "At the table we weren't supposed to talk. It was always 'Ess, ess!' That was a waste of time to visit. Very strict, very strict" (S 13). The iron hand was applied in beatings: "I was seventeen years old when he gave us a licking." Three boys were having a fight. "Dad came in with a rope that he had put into water and he whaled it to us. I had welts on my seater, I couldn't sit down. They were just like a finger from that rope. He separated us. He was mad that night" (S 13).

The one daughter felt she had a special place in the family: "Pa had me spoiled. I was the only girl—and six boys they had—and Grandpa never had a sister. There were just Uncle Phillip and my dad and Uncle Andrew, three boys, so I was special." She could wheedle money from her father for dresses and other luxuries that her mother would not give her. "I never got punished by my dad, not once. But I was good too, I minded him. He spent more time with me than Mom did. She was so busy always with the whole family and the company Dad dragged home at noon." The daughter was given a bicycle, which the boys took from her as often as they could learn to ride: "None of the rest of us ever got one." A brother agreed that she "was kind of [their father's] angel because she was the only girl. They say that every time another boy was born he would cry." But it also was reported that their mother once said "she'd rather have six boys than one girl—honest, that's what she said. It was easier to dress boys and they weren't so much trouble" (S 12–13). An expression of their mother, Rosina Schmidt, fits the mixture of affection and harshness between parents and children in this family: "If I can just get them over fool's hill," she said, "I'll be all right" (S 18). The relative distance between children and parents may partly have been a family habit. Anna Marie Schmidt, Johann's mother, who lived nearby, liked to have her grandchildren visit, but never for long, they said. She would give them one piece of peppermint candy and tell them to go home and help their mother. She had acquired the habit in Russia of sending children off: "She always sent her own children—where they grew up they lived in homes and farms were back—and so they would go out into the field, and she always sent the three boys, John, Phillip, and Andrew to their grandparents. Their grandparents raised them and they would stay until evening and then they would go home" (S 5).

There was distance also in the Lippert family. Josephine appeared to dominate Johann, but only superficially: "She out-talked him, but if he was going to do something, he would do it whether she liked it or not. It didn't happen often, but once in a while it did. Mother flew off the handle fast, but it didn't faze him one speck."

There was some disagreement as to whether or not their father was hard of hearing:

Mother accused him of having a hearing problem, but I think that sometimes he just tuned her out. She would yell at him and he just wouldn't answer. One of Dad's outstanding characteristics was that he was very calm and let things go over his head, and patient. He would just let her rave on, and he was very, very generous too. I never knew him to say no to Mother either. Mother always had all the money she wanted. She they got along well in that respect. She handled all the household money and I can't ever remember him telling her not to. Mother would devil him sometimes and he just let it run off. He was boss of his domain, but Mother was bossier, much bossier. She would scold the kids, and they would have arguments sometimes, but he ran the outside and she the inside of the house. But the boys did what he said. [H 9]

A daughter described how she saw the family getting along:

She was quick with her punishment if you didn't do it right. [It was Josephine's first child who had died after she punished him.] You couldn't blame her—she had a big load to carry and got pretty tired sometimes. In a big family if you had a problem you went to your older sister or brother. You discussed it and did whatever was necessary. You didn't go to Mother because she was busy and had a lot and was quick with punishment too. She had a temper, but for a reason usually. Got over it and never carried a grudge.

Parents discussed their problems together but Mother was the dominant figure and ruled the roost. Father was much more lenient to the children too. Not openly affectionate. I saw my father put his arm around her, but that was about it. After my father wasn't there, my mother would lament, "If he were only here," and I said, "Yes, so you could give him hell again." He was very patient and maybe he didn't do everything the way she wanted but she really missed him when he was gone. [H 8]

Another daughter said that she and her younger sister "were not wanted very badly. The only thing that saved Babe and me was that we were girls" (H 9). Nevertheless, they remembered their father fondly in his black leather chair: "He would sit and rock and smoke his pipe and lots of times after dark with the lights out we'd come in and open the door, and he'd say, 'Good evening.' Kind of scare you." She agreed that her father would put his arm around her mother, "but they weren't lovey-dovey. He would always have the baby on his lap and would feed it at the table. When a new baby came he would hold the next youngest one and feed it. Babe sat on his lap until she was practically grown up" (H 9). The eldest daughter observed that her parents "weren't too demonstrative, but they were very loving," and she felt that she was special to her father: "He favored me, I know. I was a little special because I was the only girl for quite a while. He would take me by the hand and we would go for a walk or he would sing a little song for me, or maybe he had some candy for me" (H 12). Nevertheless, the children did not think they were the center of much attention, except on birthdays: "When it was your birthday everybody would beat up on you. It was kind of fun, because you were singled out. I was the youngest so got a lot of whacks and the hard ones too. You kind of enjoyed it though because you got extra attention on that day. It wasn't often that you were special except on your birthday" (H 10).

These children's reminiscences about what their parents thought of them bring to mind ambivalent questions. Were boys preferred over girls, or girls over boys? In these large families did parents regret having so many children, or any at all? Did parents and children feel allied, or in opposition to each other? In different years, in differing states of mind, each of those questions draws both affirmative and negative answers from someone in each family. A Lippert daughter remembered sitting on her father's lap—she said he was a "softie"—and combing his mustache until he fell asleep. But, thinking about her father, she also said, "They never told you in those days that you were pretty. He told me once that the prettier the girls were, the greater temptation there was," and he warned against the beauty of her own daughters. A granddaughter told of sitting on her Grandfather Lippert's lap: "His stomach was so big there wasn't much lap to sit on, and I was always glad when I could go. I don't think he cared much about children" (L 16). Few men of that generation, she thought, showed affection to children. "If you didn't behave, you got one" (L 14).

By choosing their children's partners, parents are known to have used marriage as a way of keeping children under control, while younger generations have declared independence by means of marriage (often unwisely, according to the elders) and escaping parental control. Some German-Russians who married in Russia came together through arrangements made by their parents or a commercial *Kuppleman* (matchmaker). But not all—these three particular families had romantic courtship stories to tell. Both traditions came with them to North Dakota. In Russia, Katharina Morlock and Johann Lippert lived in Neudorf, but Johann had to cross a footbridge to reach Katharina's part of the village. Local boys did not want anyone else taking out the girls in their neighborhood, and one night they waited for Johann on the bridge, threw rocks, and beat him up, breaking his arm. Katharina told the story to one of her daughters, who used it against her father when he scolded her for being out late: "You were out too when you were young. You went out to see Mother, and they threw rocks at you" (L 2). Her own experience "about boyfriends" both repeated and vied with the experience and authority of her parents:

There was a young man who came from Ellendale to see me. He was a nice spoken and looking character, came on a motorcycle, wore white pants. The local boys didn't like to have him around, so they threw mud at him as he rode by on his motorcycle. Old man Steinwand took my father aside and asked him if his son could have a chance of marrying me. Then there was Henry who asked me to marry him, and he said, "The world is coming to an end anyway." I wonder what he meant by that. [L 27]

Yet the same Johann Lippert who had braved stoning to further his courtship, when he was a grandfather tried to make a match between a granddaughter and one of his friends who had come from Russia. The granddaughter gave an amusing account:

They lived around Streeter, about fifty miles, and he was telling me that he was the only son they had, and that they were a wealthy family, and they had lots of cattle, and how many acres of land they had, and that someday it would all be ours. So he went into the bedroom, and got a photograph of this boy and showed it to me. And here was this guy sitting in the middle of the picture on a chair and had his hair parted in the middle and sort of clipped on each side, and it must have been an old picture because he had button shoes on, and I started to giggle, and Grandpa shook his finger at me and said, "You're going to be sorry one of these days." [L 14]

That was the last she heard of the suitor.

But one of Johann's sons, who became a Baptist preacher, succeeded in arranging a marriage for another brother, who was described in the family as "a little bit slow" and whose story tells us something about how developmentally disabled people were taken care of before the widespread existence of public institutions. The "slow" son once tried to steal candy from the family store to treat children at school, where he finished sixth grade: "It was surprising the letters he would write as limited as he was." The family grew to be grateful to him, however, during their father's illness before he died, for it was this brother who took most of the care of him. But it sounds also as though he was subject to physical abuse: "Grandpa was rough. I won't say he hit him, but maybe he had to be firm with him. I often think he was born that way, but how handy he came in for Grandpa in his last days when he was sick" (L 20). The "slow" son's arranged marriage turned out well:

Aunt Maggie was a wonderful woman, [he] was lucky to get her. She never complained. She took care of him as if he were a little boy. Hadn't met him before the wedding. She was a widow and Uncle arranged the marriage. She said, "I didn't have any children, and this was my child." Reverend was out there preaching some place and built up a real reputation. So he arranged for them to meet each other, and she thought, "Well, a Lippert," and so she married him, just like that. Then she told me a couple of times, "I can't have children, and that's my baby." So she just resigned herself to taking care of him. She had a dignity about her. [L 24]

Social customs like arranged marriages were part of a strong heritage that German-Russians brought with them and that strongly affected their American-born children, for while a young woman could fairly easily dismiss her grandfather's choice of a husband, the effects of small details stuck harder. Food, for instance, lastingly connected all generations to ways of living in Russian *dorfs* (villages), particularly foods associated with holidays: "Christmas was a time of good food" in the Howitz family. "Lots of oranges, bananas, nuts, peanuts, candy. Hard candy, gobs of it. Christmas Eve was a very special occasion with lots of German dishes, and fish, a white fish of some sort. There would be potato dumplings, cheese dumplings, and kraut dumplings, and some fancy kind of soup and something made of wheat." Hand-picked kernels of wheat were soaked overnight and boiled, then mixed with honey and poppy seeds, a dessert called *Gutya*. This dish had additional superstitious powers: "Dad would toss it to the ceiling and if it stuck it meant a good year, and if it didn't it meant a bad year. It was said that at midnight on Christmas Eve the animals spoke, and this struck fear into the hearts of the children. They were terribly frightened of ghosts anyway, because grownups would tell ghost stories and scare the devil out of them. Nobody was in a hurry to clean the spot off the ceiling" (H 2).

Children remembered the ghost stories: "They were supposed to be true. People over there were very superstitious, they believed in a lot of that stuff. It was interesting, but it was awfully scary." One of these stories suggests ways in which immigrants tried to accommodate themselves to the new surroundings:

There was a house where John Wolfe and his wife lived, about a mile from Jerome's, and it was haunted. When the couple went to bed, they'd hardly get upstairs before they would hear noises downstairs, footsteps going up the stairs, rockers rocking, the sewing machine running, and all these noises and they were frightened. The Wolfes had bought second-hand furniture from Fritz Klein, and they bought the bed that his wife died in while giving birth to her final child. Fritz Klein didn't keep that child, he gave it up for adoption. Wolfes had a spiritualist out there, and a priest blessing everything, trying to eradicate the ghost. Finally they got rid of the bed, and the ghost disappeared. They felt that the mother could not rest for some reason, maybe because they gave that child away. That was the theory. But after they got rid of the bed, they had no more problems. The Kleins had five or six children, and she died, and this baby, they just couldn't keep it, and this couple wanted a child, and so they took it and he was raised as a Klein. The bed caused the unrest in the poor soul, according to the story. [H 2–3]

"The whole countryside was nervous about the bed," this daughter said, insisting several times, "we were just scared to death"—enough that once when she and her sister were sitting at the kitchen table, they were so startled by their mother coming in when they thought she was in the garden, that they ran out of the house: "We never stopped running, and Mom yelled at us, and we ran a half mile to where Dad was bringing in the cattle, in the fall of the year. Mother said she yelled and yelled, but we just keep right on running" (H 3). The daughter claimed that all because of the ghost stories and the neighborhood haunted bed, "I don't know how many times they had the priest there." The solution to this disturbance, interestingly, was neither prayer nor an ability to "eradicate the ghost"; rather, the ghost obligingly disappeared when they "got rid of the bed." No one blamed the family for putting the infant out to adoption, or priests and spiritualists for failing in their efforts. The solution to community disturbance was to "get rid of" the source, as though a group that has had to assimilate so drastically could endure only so much.

There were other odd and disturbing "ghost" stories: twins thought to have been buried alive; someone dug up after burial who had "turned over in his grave." People were buried the day after they died. A daughter said, "Mother thought an aunt of mine that died and was buried quickly probably wasn't dead. It seemed that she never got pale. Her cheeks were rosy, she always had red cheeks, but that may not have been. It was probably just the pigment in their skin" (H 3).

Not all of the behavior that these children found odd in their parents was attributable to superstitions about ghosts or talking animals or dough-prints on the ceiling. Some of what they observed their elders doing they reported as

merely eccentric or grotesque, such as the Schmidt grandmother eating sparrows—a practical if unusual habit. There
were women in the community with an ingenious turn
of mind:

One time they ran out of milk. They had a restaurant there and I
knew they were out of milk, and a guy wanted some milk for his
coffee. The old lady had a small child, so she went in the back
room, and put some milk in the cup and do you know where she got
the milk? Out of her breast, and she gave it to the guy for his coffee.
That guy never knew, he never found out that he drank milk out of
her breast. I could see it from where I was standing. I could see into
that back room and she didn't have enough sense to look back and
notice that I could see what she was doing. I never told my mother
about it. [S 44]

Sons and daughters remarked on the wide separation
between men and women among older immigrants. Men
would leave their wives at the store, where children were
put to sleep on the floor or on top of merchandise while the
men went about their business elsewhere, and the mothers
waited. There were stories about men sometimes forgetting
their families and having to come back for them after starting for home. To a young woman, the habits of some old
men could appear crude: "Then there was Nagel who came
only about to my chin, a little skinny man. The first time he
was drunk in the store he came up to me and said, 'Aye, aber
du bist a shoenes maedle' ('Oh, but you are a pretty girl'). He
sprayed me. I was right by the candy counter, which was at
the end so he could get in front of me. After that I stayed behind the counter so he couldn't get close to me. His wife was
right there and heard him. He didn't care. Every time he
came he told me what a nice girl I was" (L 11).

But it was not only older people who exhibited strange behavior, for the second generation told odd stories about
themselves. One son said he and a brother dug graves as a
summer job to earn money for university. One year they dug
a grave for their sister's baby: "The frost goes down about

two and a half feet in North Dakota. We used to get dyna-
mite and shoot the charge into the grave and take it out with
pick and shovel." Grave digging didn't bother him, this man
said, and one day he mentioned the grave of an older brother:

Tom's grave was out there, and I was curious, so I said, "Let's see
what's in Tom's grave." We got in there. It was next to the baby's
grave. So we looked in there. Sure, I opened the casket and we
looked in. Black, about this long, and all of a sudden, poof, the
fumes from the corpse. There was no corpse there, just ashes,
ashes, just like you make a loaf of bread and it all gets black. Not
any bigger than a loaf of bread. All dried up and decomposed and
then it collapsed, it fell down. It shrinks together and then when
the air hits it, boom. Then they fly up a little bit. I never told anybody we did it. I figured it was nobody's business. I was curious.
We were all curious. I expected to see a body in there, but there
was no body in there, just a smooth, oblong loaf. [S ms.]

This boy's curiosity led him also to "operate" on gophers:

I used to operate on gophers, cut their hearts out, cut them open
after I gave them ether. I'd watch their heart beat. Did you ever
watch a heart beat? It's very interesting, and you'd be surprised
how long they live even when the air was dry in the summertime.
We used to lay them on the fence and cut them open and watch
their heart beat, but they never felt it because they were under
ether all of the time. They died that way. You could feel the palpita-
tion of their hearts. We were curious, that's why we did it. [S 27]

Medicine, we have seen, had hardly been professionalized
in rural settlement regions, even though these were the
years in urban areas when hospitals, medical schools, and
an organized American Medical Association were growing
increasingly influential. But rural North Dakota families
were more likely to be served by midwives and neighbors
than by doctors. Common sense, traditions of herbal medicine, and some superstition prevailed. Children were heirs
to their parents' medicinal practices:

Old Lady Shroat, she was the midwife. She was a big fat woman, and boy she used goose grease on us when we had a cold and she used to rub our back. You were lying on your belly, and she'd rub her hands over your back and boy by the time you got through with her you had plenty, yes sir. She was big, strong. We got sulphur and lard treatment for itch too. They had all kinds of old-time remedies. Some worked and some didn't. [S 27]

I had warts all over my hands once. Somebody told me to tie knots in a string for as many warts as I had, and I counted them and I had one hundred and forty. So I tied the knots and they said to bury them in manure and I did and my warts went away. Not immediately, but a little at a time. They were on the top of my hand. It worked, maybe it was faith. [S ms.]

One of the strongest impressions these children had about their parents, and about their fathers especially, was of their violence toward children. Children (by now in their seventies and older) remembered and did not forgive the beatings. A granddaughter said, "My father said Grandpa was strict; he would hit him right on his head, and he would fly clear across the room. He had to sleep in the barn one night because he was naughty. My father never hit us because he said he got enough of it when he was young, and made up his mind he was never going to hit his children, and he never did" (L ms.). But other such abuses drove another son to lasting resentment:

I could have gone to my dad's funeral but I couldn't go but I would never miss my mother's funeral. I could have gone there but it was a cold day, and I didn't go, but I went to my mother's regardless of what kind of weather it was. You see that was how much closer I was to my mother than I was to my dad. In the first place, Mother was kind hearted. She was a woman, kind hearted like a woman. And she was sympathetic with kids. And my dad, it was all business. He didn't give a damn about the kids, that's the way it looked. [S ms.]

Violence toward children did not invariably end in the second generation, however. A son who became a preacher inflicted both pain and fear on his children. A sister described dinner at his house, presided over by a second wife, the first having died:

Molly has certainly been wonderful to John's children. She has been a sweet lady. She must have endured a lot with him. We were at their house one time, and it was prayer time. He was praying at the evening meal, and no one dared move until he gave a sign. He said his prayer first, and sometimes they were long prayers, and I would look and the kids would be looking at the food, and Lewellyn would look out from underneath, and he wasn't listening to that prayer. Then when John was through he would help himself, and then the rest of them could take some.

The children "had to get permission for a second helping. They didn't dare talk at the table either." The children were nearly afraid to eat. She saw the father

give Alathea a bloody nose at the table once at our house. If they didn't have anything on their plate, he would ask if they would like another helping. They wouldn't dare reach for another one. Every one of them stuttered, no wonder. Scared to death. He was strict. I don't think he should have been a minister, that was too hard on him. His nerves were so bad. I remember Molly had to puree all of his vegetables, put them through a strainer. He always drank a mixture of milk and water. Had a nervous stomach. When I was in Waco, there was a piece of dust or lint on the floor, and all he did was look at Aunt Molly and point it out. I think that is why he was sick all of the time, because he was so fussy. [L ms.]

How to account for such strange goings-on? One answer I think lies in the language. We are hearing highly particular details, perhaps because that is the way conversation tends to move, especially when it dwells on the past. Childhood itself is the time of particularity—smells, textures, fears, and joys are what we remember if we remember anything, not a family's overall connection to their community. And once the particulars are named, it is easy for them to look a bit odd.

While these recountings by second-generation members

of settler families describe persons in the context of community—the small towns of Ashley, Anamoose, and Larimore— descriptions of the same towns written without particulars make them appear entirely ordinary. Thus Ashley was described in the issue of the *North Dakota Magazine* for September 6, 1906. The style is boosterish journalism; the article ignores ghosts and eviscerated gophers in favor of the numbers of buildings and their position on the block. In 1906, Ashley thought well of itself:

Ashley, the county seat and the oldest town now in the county, is surrounded by a thrifty German settlement. The court house there was originally built by the farmers and later on donated to the county and enlarged until now the county has a very comfortable court house. The town has two newspapers, the McIntosh County Republican and the Ashley Tribune, both printed in German and English. There are also five general stores, two hardware stores, three implement houses, two banks, three elevators, three hotels, two blacksmiths, four churches, opera house, two livery barns, two drug stores, flour and feed stores, one seventy-five barrel flouring mill, three lumber yards, furniture factory and store, harness store, creamery, shoe store and a cement factory. The population of Ashley is nearly 800.[2]

No one Florence Clifford interviewed gave so platted an account of the town in which the Lippert's had their store.

Anamoose also has been praised in a county history, in an article written by one of the sons of the family who owned the hotel. Anamoose began in 1898 as a stop along the Soo railway. It "grew rapidly and in ten years or so there were four blocks in the business section on main street. There were five grocery stores. The Schoessler Brothers store was on the south end of the south block on the west side of Main Street. On the north end of the same block was the William Frankhauser and August Becker store, a large two-story cement block building, the upper part of which was used for banquets, roller skating and other entertainment." The four business blocks included three banks, two

law offices, six elevators, several hardware stores, two farm
machinery stores, three lumber yards, a drug store, a school,
five churches, a cement block factory, and two livery barns.
The town prospered: "In 1916 N. J. Walper built a power
plant on the Schoessler Brothers lot and the same year the
Waldemar Hotel was erected on the Frankhauser and Becker
site. This was a brick building with 25 rooms, kitchen and
dining room facilities and a large banquet room. Half of the
lower part of the building was occupied by the Anamoose
Cash Store." There were several fires over the years. "In
spite of these setbacks this city thrived and in 1916 had a
population of about 800 people" as well as telephone service, a water works, sewage, and electricity.[3]

The manner of reporting cannot, however, be entirely responsible for the strangeness we find people describing in
these small towns. Part of the cause lies also in the relative
isolation of towns. News analyst Eric Severeid, for instance,
who grew up in Velva, North Dakota, recalled how, in school,
he traced with his fingers "that rectangle at the top of the
map"; and in the novel *Beyond the Bedroom Wall*, Larry
Woiwode has one of the characters refer to North Dakota as
the "attic" of the United States. Remoteness may well exac-
erbate strangeness. And yet, boosterish articles to the contrary, people's accounts insist repeatedly that life in such
towns can appear strange. The story of the haunted bed, for
instance, told in so matter-of-fact a manner, puzzles me.
When both priests and spiritualists fail, the ghost is set to
rest by removing the bed. It would seem that in this community, there is considerable tolerance for unusual behavior
(no one is criticized for the misfortune of living in a haunted
house), but tolerance is limited, and ultimately what does
not fit in is "got rid of." Whatever dimension of religious and
imaginative experience a priest or spiritualist might represent, that realm is not tested for long. It is this avoiding a
larger meaning, of not generalizing upon experience, that
leaves episodes without context, and therefore seeming a bit
askew. Some of that effect may also come, as I have suggested, because of the anger with which the now elderly

children were remembering their parents, as though they placed emphasis on the strange, the bizarre, the grotesque almost out of revenge. The mercilessly documentary recollections—like the description of the prospective suitor's photograph—go to the heart of differences between the second generation and the first, as though these children of late pioneering were getting back at parents for putting them through so much.

Thus, when turn-of-the-century towns are described in their generality, they appear platted and orderly, right angles declaring order in so precarious an environment: six elevators, three hotels, four churches for populations of 800. This sense of order, of remembering where everything was, must have a good deal to do with the public impression that small towns and their rural agrarian surroundings indeed are orderly, calm, and essentially wholesome. But looked at more particularly, the same mappings turn up emotional dimensions that render the scene differently, as in discovering bread-loaf-shaped ashes in a dug-up grave, or spying on coffee laced with breast milk. Indeed the apparent calm of towns like Anamoose rested partly, I should think, upon tolerance for such seemingly odd behavior as sparrow-eating or having small boys nip off the heads of fledglings. Order rested also upon firm paternal control at home. Henry the Eighth, the boys called their father, and such violence at the ready never drew them affectionately toward him. However we interpret these testimonials, in what they chose to tell, these children of first-generation settlers implied considerable skepticism if not overt resistance to the progressive optimism that infests the public records, some of which they even wrote themselves.

It would seem that there is a connection also between what they have described of their experiences many years ago and reports of events from small towns that increasingly make their way from back pages of newspapers to front-page headlines, as these have in North Dakota and northern Minnesota in the last few years: U.S. marshals killed near an interstate highway by rural residents who call themselves a *posse comitatus;* a farming community racked by accusations of incest and child abuse; a clergyman of a rural church shot to death by his wife, who was convinced that he would kill her; a father who led a large community search party for his disappeared daughter and who was finally convicted of her rape and murder. Events like these certainly contradict the sort of rural images that sell dry cereals and sleeping pills. I think, however, that they are not as aberrant as they may appear, and there is a historical continuity between them and such a far more benign event as the episode of the haunted bed. Both are being enacted and recounted by residents of the towns themselves; they are not the imaginings of artists or observations of outsiders.

Partly, residents of small towns manage that accommodation by seeing the grid of their town a bit aslant. They tell of the violence their fathers used to control children's behavior, their mothers daring to do little more than stand by; and of strange and deviant behavior, sometimes couched as a tall tale or ghost story. And over and over they dramatize how immediate the effect inevitably was of any disaster: grass fire, drought, flood, a drop in wheat prices, illness, accident, death. There is little, physically, economically, and emotionally, to cushion such damage. I do not think it is too much to suggest that the excesses we are seeing these days in some rural communities—the virulent anti-Semitism, the survivalist mentality—have a history. They are quantitatively but not qualitatively different from the degree of strangeness that small towns always have harbored as a matter of course, and which has remained in the memories of the towns' children.

9

Children of the Middle Border

This study began in a desire to know more about how the settlement experience affected the children of those who first ventured onto homesteads, farms, and ranches in the American Plains and western regions (found in North Dakota). Doing it "for the children" was a reason many gave for the extraordinary journeys from Europe and the eastern and midwestern states. But the question of what it was like for children suggests also the reverse: how was the settlement of the region affected by children? Accounts of settlement childhoods—from the private writings of their parents, from their reminiscences when adults, and from such public records as newspapers or orphanage newsletters—also describe the maturation of towns. It was the second generation who solidified the communities their parents founded, and whether those children were willing to stay or also moved on to seek fortunes somewhere else decided which towns and agricultural regions would thrive and which would remain fragile and eventually disappear. The Upper Plains states continue to export young people; the habits of hard work and independence they learned from their parents' farms or small businesses serve them well in finding occupations in cities. Rural communities cannot offer enough to the most talented in the way of opportunities in professions or in social and cultural stimulation. Young people keep moving away.

Parents who migrated had to worry first about survival; for poor parents, survival could turn desperate. But their children, aware as they were of those often precarious beginnings, needed to continue their own lives in this place their parents had brought them to. If obvious prosperity sometimes eluded the parents, their children often found, as adults, that they indeed were better educated, better housed and fed, and that their work was less physically laborious than what they had experienced as children. Their generation marked the history and character of the region almost more than their parents' had. For the children, brought up in the ways of their parents, nevertheless separated themselves from the "old" ways enough to be thought "American." They also helped their parents learn English and adapt as far as they could to "American" ways (a difference that typically had less to do with nationality or ethnicity than with class aspirations). Daughters wore short dresses in preference to their mothers' long white aprons. In the Lima family, the son at age seventeen escaped to gold fields in Idaho, and the daughter, after college, returned to her native Cooperstown to teach school and live near her father. Among the relatives with whom Florence Clifford carried out interviews, some had left the state, and some stayed, but few did not have painful memories of growing up in small settlement towns. Listening to the children's assessments about settlement, the verdict, we have to say, is mixed.

The first settlement generation, at least in the Upper Plains states, was primarily interested in economic improvement, and they were passionate about owning land. Prosperity and land, the one to be realized through the other, became so fused with ideals of freedom and opportunity that they defined the mythology of American history. Yet single-mindedness about wealth and land could mean paying less attention to the values inherent in education, art and theater, the publication of fiction and poetry, medicine, conservation of natural resources, even religion. These came later. Later also, attention turned to those not primarily engaged in acquiring land and wealth. Children, most women, and aging and infirm people had to wait.

This waiting may account for differences in attitudes and experiences between first- and second-generation residents. Even among children who stayed, many did not really continue their parents' ambitions. Smaller towns began to empty not long after their brief years of prosperity—towns of no more than eight hundred persons, who at the time of World War I could boast of hotels, opera houses, newspapers, churches, grain elevators, and numerous businesses. Many homestead farms consolidated under the ownership of the more wealthy landowners. Do these movements away from the aspirations of the first settlers mean that their efforts failed? Or did the children who left, or turned from owning land to careers in professions, politics, and the arts represent not a failure of vision or nerve, but an extension of the aspirations of their parents to something more public, more social, and possibly more lasting? Such questions arise from the evidence available about children's experiences on the frontier, and they may suggest ways of using the recent history of the region, however brief, to interpret its present.

If that interpretation now is for the most part unclear, ambiguous, and fraught with sentimentality and neglect, meanings of the settlement experience were no better understood by those who underwent it. It is difficult to find critical assessments by persons who wrote or spoke in interviews of their families' ventures; they hardly analyzed what they regarded in progressive terms almost unanimously. If anyone expressed hesitation, it was for personal reasons—Martha Lima wishing she could be with her family again in Norway. But few individuals, even in the face of their own often excruciating hardships, suggested they might have made a mistake. And virtually no qualms were expressed for Indian people they were displacing or the children who often died and seldom achieved even as much education as their parents had in the less promising regions they came from.

In their old age, many children of settlers, as we have

seen, enjoyed reminiscing about their pioneering experiences. Social organizations, historical societies, and local
and regional publications sought out accounts and continue
to do so as the region passes its hundredth anniversary of
settlement and statehood. These writings and oral histories
seem remarkable for the manner in which they avoid recon-
sidering the past as anything but an unmitigated success regardless of circumstances. Native and foreign immigrants
alike endorse and praise "America" in patriotic slogans,
even though the same accounts may catalog little relief from
suffering that national or local governments may have been
responsible for. In the 1950s a magazine called *The Farmer*
asked readers to submit pioneering accounts. Mrs. W. B. of
Rolla, on the edge of the Turtle Mountain Chippewa Indian
Reservation in north-central North Dakota, tells of familiar
hardships (she asked to be identified in publication only by
her initials). She expresses the family's fears and early fail-
ures like this:

I was born in California in 1880 and came with my parents in
1889 to this great golden west of today, and us white people wasn't
welcome with the Indians of that time, and we had to take and give
from them so we could develop this great country into agriculture
of progress. So we settled in Rolette County. I remember as a little
girl, father filed on land, bought a team of oxen, 1 cow and 3 horses
to level the land, raise a little grain crop. Drought for several years
made it very hard for families to go through these years. To top it
off [we were] in fear of those Indians that was on war path at every
moment. They had their war dance in great number to decide what
should be done to chase us out of the country or waiting for a
settlement with the government. One night Dad had all things
ready to leave in the morning in the wagon—horses, what we could
bring along the easiest way. Brother and sister and I kept on watch
all night long for any sign of disturbance (war). I was so afraid that
just to talk about it [put me] on edge to collapse, and I still have that
same feeling about war.

After living in this Rolette County for 61 years, it is still rumors
of war, war, but not with Indians any more. I remember one Sunday going to church some people driving oxen, on a big wagon at-

tending services and us we had horses and buggy. One time my brother hitched a big ox with long horns on the buggy and told Mother to dress me up with my best, that he was to take me to church, and so she did with a red embroidery silk dress, tafetta, and we thought it was fun. And as years went by and us whites that stuck to the good and bad of the country, made a very prosperous country that we are proud to live in. A lot of change since those years of 90s. Most people have modern homes even on the farm. My husband and I often recall of all the hardship he had while farming in those pioneer days. We also had some recreation on 4th July during the day and dancing in the evening in private home or in grainary. That was fun then, and we were well satisfied the way it was and just as happy as it seemed everybody felt that he was equal to the next neighbor, and live like this is what I recall of my (our) life as pioneers of the west. I hope that I gave you right impression of the early settling of the west. If you use this letter in the Farmer journal please use only my Initials.[1]

Indians took the blame for the many fears that had to have been part of settlement experience—harsh climate; remoteness; lack of roads, transportation, schools, and other services; inadequate housing; and generally the loss of a more comfortable life, which this family, for one, apparently had known in California. Hysteria about Indians on the warpath may not be surprising, considering that many people had children in tow, but expressions about "us white people" prove how deeply embedded racist feelings are in the imagery of "the great golden west" and how unreflectively at least this woman accepted such attitudes. She did not connect the hardships she experienced with the lives of Indian people around her.

Yet Mrs. W. B.'s sense of history and ethics are not really more confused than some writings by more practiced authors. A book for children, *An Orphan for Nebraska*, by Charlene Joy Talbot,[2] is about eleven-year-old Kevin O'Rourke, who sets sail from Ireland to New York with his mother after the death of his father. The mother dies aboard ship, leaving Kevin orphaned to seek his fortune in New York by way of selling newspapers and visiting an uncle, who is in jail for murder—he killed the foreman on his building crew for calling him "Paddy." While living at the Newsboys' Lodging House, Kevin hears that the Children's Aid Society is taking groups of orphaned children from New York City by train to towns in the Midwest and Far West. At railroad stations along the way they are to be claimed for adoption by people willing to care for them or, as it typically turned out, desiring essentially indentured workers. The plight of "orphan train" children, as they came to be known, is the impetus for the book. In Nebraska, Kevin, the last to be chosen, is taken on by the town's newspaper publisher, but as soon as the train moves on, the story becomes another boys' adventure, a sort of *Huckleberry Finn* of the Central Plains.

Kevin learns quickly the duties of a printer's devil; he rides horseback back and forth to the printer's homestead; he weathers a blizzard and goes to school. Euclid Smith, his benefactor and employer, is not married, and the two enjoy a close, relaxed, bachelor household. This is threatened, however, by the discovery that Mr. Smith is engaged to be married to a schoolteacher from Philadelphia, and she is expected, come spring, to venture out for a wedding. Kevin is saved from near despair, however, by her not emerging from the train on which she was due to arrive, leaving Kevin and Euclid Smith to continue their idyll. The entrepreneurial West as represented by Euclid Smith's *Cottonwood Clarion* depends on male society undisturbed by threats of female domesticity. Women and girls are absent in the book: Kevin's mother is dead (conveniently having taught him how to cook first); the few girls on the orphan train are taken up by families looking for domestic help and disappear from the story. Abandoned slum children; policies of the Children's Aid Society, which thought that the country was more wholesome than the city and is alleged to have removed some children from parents who did not want to give them up; the employment of children in rural areas—these and other issues connected to the orphan train schemes become lost in the requirements for a boys' adventure book.

Hamlin Garland, one of the most respected and sympathetic writers of the settlement West, expressed great ambiguity about his childhood, even though it led him to professional success as a writer. Garland resented his father's moving the family to ever remoter and harsher places in a continuing hope for prosperity that never came, and he felt great pity and guilt about his mother's life. At the time of the parents' last remove to South Dakota, Garland went in the opposite direction, to Chicago, to begin his career, and when eventually he achieved success and prosperity bought back the farm his parents had left in Wisconsin and settled them on it. But by then his mother had had her first stroke and never fully recovered. Garland's autobiographical novels, *A Son of the Middle Border* (1914) and *A Daughter of the Middle Border* (1921), as well as his short book, *A Pioneer Mother* (1922), express the guilt and sorrow he felt about his mother's suffering during the moves west.

A scene in *A Son of the Middle Border,* which takes place before one of the family's departures, dramatizes the difference between his mother's and his father's feelings about leaving, differences that can be documented in countless personal accounts, especially by women. The family has been singing the song "O'er the Hills in Legions Boys":

My father's face shone with the light of the explorer, the pioneer. The words of this song appealed to him as the finest poetry. It meant all that was fine and hopeful and buoyant in American life, to him—but to my mother's sweet face a wistful expression deepened and in her fine eyes a reflective shadow lay. To her this song meant not so much the acquisition of a new home as the loss of all her friends and relatives. She sang it submissively, not exultantly, and I think the other women were of the same mood though their faces were less expressive to me. To all of the pioneer wives of the past that song had meant deprivation, suffering, loneliness, heart-ache.[3]

For the boy, the various moves and the sense of living always on the "border" meant physical labor that was hard enough to threaten the imagination: "For seventy days I walked behind my plow on the new farm while my father finished the harvest on the rented farm and moved to the house on the knoll. It was lonely work for a boy of eleven. . . . There is a certain pathos in the sight of that small boy tugging and kicking at the stubborn turf in the effort to free his plow. Such misfortunes loom large in a lad's horizon." So large, in fact, that the plot of the book is the "lad's" escape from the plow he knows would destroy him. He also, though less acutely, senses his mother's resistance, and her despair in this environment: "I am not sure that haying brought to our mother anything like this rapture, for the men added to our crew made the duties of the kitchens just that much heavier. I doubt if the women—any of them—got out into the fields or meadows long enough to enjoy the birds and the breezes. Even on Sunday as they rode away to church they were too tired and too worried to react to the beauties of the landscape."[4]

Garland's objections have a more personal than political conviction when he writes, "This wasteful method of pioneering, this desolate business of lonely settlement took on a new and tragic significance as I studied it." On leaving South Dakota he reflected, "It seemed a treachery to say good-bye to my aging parents, leaving them and my untrained sister to this barren, empty, laborious life on the plain whilst I returned to the music, the drama, the inspiration, the glory of Boston."[5] Nevertheless, return he did. In 1889 he went again briefly to see the ravages of that waste: "My heart filled with bitterness and rebellion, bitterness against the pioneering madness which had scattered our family, and rebellion toward my father who had kept my mother always on the border, working like a slave long after the time when she should have been taking her ease."[6]

Hamlin Garland's feelings about land, his agrarian boyhood, his escape from the tyranny of the plow and desolating landscape, and his protective affections for women all spring from the troubling guilt he felt about his mother. The life she led was mistaken, yet from it also were nurtured his opportunities. Of all the family, he was the clearest beneficiary of everything that passed for sacrifice in the family's ventures westward. If nothing else, the years of his growing up when his mother suffered so, provided subjects for the books he wrote. Garland described his feelings after his mother's death:

> My first morning in the old Homestead without my mother was so poignant with its sense of loss so rich with memories both sweet and sorrowful, that I shut myself in my study and began a little tribute to her, a sketch which I called "The Life of a Pioneer." Into this I poured the love I had felt but failed to express as fully as I should have done while she was alive. To make this her memorial was my definite purpose.
>
> As I went on I found myself deep in her life on the farm in Iowa, and the cheerful heroism of her daily treadmill came back to me with such appeal that I could scarcely see the words in which I was recording her history. Visioning the long years of her drudgery, I recalled her early rising, and suffered with her the never-ending round of dishwashing, churning, sewing, and cooking, realizing more fully than ever before that in all of this slavery she was but one of a million martyrs. All our neighbors' wives walked the same round. On such as they rests the heavier part of the home and city building in the West. The wives of the farm are the unnamed, unrewarded heroines of the Border.[7]

Yet for all his claim to empathy with his mother, when he came to write about her in *A Pioneer Mother,* he abstracts her to a monument: "She was neither witty, nor learned in books, nor wise in the ways of the world, but I contend that her life was noble. . . . There was something in her unconscious heroism which transcends wisdom and the deeds of those who dwell in the rose-golden light of romance. Now that her life is rounded into the silence whence it came, its significance appears."[8] Garland has not remembered here that to ourselves we are not "unconscious" nor waiting to die so that someone else may see shape to our life and give it

"significance." But that is how Garland wrote about his mother, as he did aging farmers on their front porches.
He appears baffled by her inner life:

I don't know what her feelings were about these constant removals to the border, but I suspect now that each new migration was a greater hardship than those which preceded it. My father's adventurous and restless spirit was never satisfied. The sunset land always allured him, and my mother, being of those who follow their husbands' feet without a complaining word, seemed always ready to take up the trail. With the blindness of youth and the spirit of seeking which I inherited I saw no tear on my mother's face.[9]

Garland's descriptions of his mother center upon her attention to him. He wondered about her pride at hearing his graduation address "for she never expressed her deeper feelings. She seldom kissed her children." Attributing the fact to poverty and her hard work, Garland describes the dreariness of the home surroundings: "I cannot recall a single beautiful thing about our house, not one." The house was "only a warm shelter, where my mother strove to feed and clothe us."[10] Hamlin's buying the Wisconsin farm for his parents, his frequent visits, and his writing about their lives, especially his mother's, all seem to me to be efforts to assuage the guilt he felt toward them and the disconnectedness that kept him apart from a way of life they had cast him into:

I have a purpose in this frank disclosure of my mother's life. It is not from any self-complacency, God knows, for I did so little and it came so late—I write in the hope of making some other work-weary mother happy. There is nothing more appealing to me than neglected age. To see an old father or mother sitting in loneliness and poverty dreaming of an absent son who never comes, of a daughter who never writes, is to me more moving than Hamlet or Othello. If we are false to those who gave us birth we are false indeed.

But if elderly parents are cared for, he concludes, "Then
will the debt be lessened—for in such coin alone can the
wistful hearts be paid."[11] This son of the middle border felt
the debt overwhelmingly because he could not continue his
parents' lives, as so many sons and daughters of settlers
have felt they could not, and yet he knew he was indebted to
them personally and professionally. Their lives were the
subjects of his books, as well as the start of his own life.

The "middle border," as Hamlin Garland calls the rather
undefined central section of the continent, settled later than
the West Coast and the mountains, always has been a difficult region for people to claim allegiance to. One is a little
ashamed to admit to being "from" the Plains. It is the place
where jokes are made about stolid, not very bright souls.
The concentration on particulars can leave one puzzled.
A freshman college student in a class I taught wrote of his
great-grandparents' having homesteaded while sharing a
house with a friend. The house was built on the boundary
between the two plots—one room for the family on their
land, another room for the friend on his adjoining allotment.
Eventually the friend married and wished to live apart from
the family, so the house was sawed in two, and each half was
moved more centrally into the owner's territory. This appeared to me so amazing a solution that I asked the student
whether he did not find it odd. No, he said; he only regretted
not knowing what had become of the front door.

Other writers from this middle border continue to feel as
ambivalent about their origins as Hamlin Garland did, and
just as critical of the region's inhospitality toward women.
Patrick Morrow grew up in Kenmare, North Dakota. His
Irish Catholic grandparents homesteaded near there, and
his father was born a year after the family's arrival. Kenmare
was named after a town in Ireland and overlooks a lake
from its hillside setting—one of the more picturesque North
Dakota spots. "Colonies of Dunkards" settled here, a guide-
book says, in a region strong in Irish-English connections.
Donnybrook is nearby, as well as Bowbells, named by Cock-

ney settlers ("Cockney" referring generally to those born in London within the sound of the bells of the Church of St. Mary Le Bow). But not only the hilly setting makes Kenmare lovely and reminiscent of the British Isles. The town is designed around a grassy square on which stands a Dutch windmill—both pleasing surprises.

Morrow has published two books set in Kenmare. *Growing Up in North Dakota* (1980) recounts his father's youth and departure from North Dakota. *Seventeen North Dakota Tales* [12] is about people Morrow knew, or heard about, or was related to. He is not in North Dakota now, but in Auburn, Alabama, where he has been teaching regional literature, including books set in North Dakota. Some of the seventeen tales are whimsical or curious small-town anecdotes, literary versions of the goings-on in Ashley or Anamoose—a canvas catcher's mitt his mother sewed for him; the preponderance of eighth-grade boys named Halley listed on a school bulletin board, fourteen years after Halley's Comet; an infant's death popularly attributed to an "enlarged thymus." There are tall tales, a ghost story, and tales of the innocent made fools of. During the summer of 1983, Morrow returned to Kenmare for a reunion of high school classes. At the Friday banquet, Morrow reports, his father, sitting with the pre-1930 graduates, made the best speech of the evening: "Tonight, as I look out there and see all your faces, it reminds me of getting in front of the class to recite—some sixty years ago. All I could think of was how beautiful you girls were, and I wanted to hug and kiss every one of you. . . . Tonight you are all still beautiful, and I'd still like to hug and kiss every one of you." Morrow dramatizes, but he does not comment upon, the sentimentality toward women his father displayed—cruder, but not so different from Garland's.

At this reunion Morrow met again some of his Kenmare relations. In "Feminism on the Frontier" he explores the lives of three aunts—Mary, Mathilda, and Catherine—and their mother, Elizabeth. These women might have been constructed from Hamlin Garland's mother. Elizabeth, we learn, had been abandoned by her husband and urged her daughters to escape the confines of Kenmare. While his father's growing up was fairly adventurous, Patrick Morrow realized that the women in his family had led more constricted lives, were even more hemmed in by the conformity and boredom of the small town. Looking at the town and thinking of these women, he paints a dour picture: "I was most struck that summer in Kenmare by the absolute lack of any cultural dimension to the place. Kenmare is not exactly anti-intellectual. Rather, life consists of only two parts. Mom tends to home and church, Dad tends to business and the field. Art, literature, serious music, and creative individual expression form what might today be called a zero set"— much as Garland remembered the lack of adornment, of anything beautiful in his mother's house. And like Garland, Morrow appears to have realized late, but with some force, the deprivations suffered by women he was close to.

Morrow and Garland are right—the arts do not thrive in rural communities. There is a suspicion that art lies, it does not report the material truth so needful to survival: it would not solve the puzzle about the door on the severed house. The arts necessitate a degree of abstraction that the children of settlers, and their children, find difficult yet to undertake. This literalness, or materiality, is a habit of mind so deep in the social and political consciousness that those who do not share it find little alternative but to depart. I wonder, however, what Patrick Morrow would think of Kenmare if he were teaching at one of the colleges in North Dakota instead of in Alabama. I have no explanation, but in the years of my own teaching here, time and again particularly talented students turn out to be from Kenmare, and my prejudices lead me to expect something extraordinary of anyone from that place. For that matter, students from all over the state tend still not to appreciate how talented they are, but when they have completed their university course, they still must leave—for Minnesota, even Alabama. As Morrow recognized in his aunts and grandmother, strong talents can begin here, to flourish somewhere else.

Patrick Morrow and Hamlin Garland are among writers

who express the ambivalences of many from the Upper
Plains states and feel themselves the beneficiaries of one or
two generations of hard-working, sacrificial settlers. There
are others, although not many—like Louise Erdrich, Lois
Phillips Hudson, and Larry Woiwode in *Beyond the Bedroom Wall*—and all of them have left the region, writing
their major books elsewhere. What these professional writers share with less practiced although not entirely less elo-
quent residents is a serious division of mind about their
origins. Those who come after the first generation deeply
want to praise and honor and memorialize their past. Except
in writings about Indian populations, they seldom speak
against the idea of migration and settlement. On the other
hand, memories of deprivations will not leave them, and
when they look around, many see little more than ugli-
ness. They speak and write as though they are sad and
angry, wanting at the same time to be proud and progressive-
minded. The German-Russian woman who thought she
would have achieved something if only she could get her off-
spring "over fool's hill" did not count on what they might
find on the other side.

Notes

Chapter 1

1. Burnett, *Destiny Obscure*, p. 12.
2. Ibid., p. 10.
3. Marshall, "Unheard Voice," p. 326.
4. Edward J. Lander Papers 1889–1931, University of North Dakota Libraries, OGL 3.

Chapter 2

1. Aries, *Centuries of Childhood*, p. 33.
2. Lineage of the Bischoff, Pankow, and Schumacher Families, c. 1979, xerox typescript, University of North Dakota Special Collections, p. 71.
3. Ibid.
4. *Jamestown Capital*, n.d.
5. Lineage of the Bischoff, Pankow, and Schumacher Families, p. 57.
6. Ibid., p. 83.
7. Ibid., p. 61.
8. De Mause, "Evolution of Childhood." De Mause focuses on what he calls psychogenic changes in personality "occurring because of successive generations of parent-child interactions." Child-rearing practices, he says, "are the very condition for the transmission and development of all other cultural elements, and place definite limits on what can be achieved in all other spheres of history. Specific childhood experiences must occur to sustain specific cultural traits, and once these experiences no longer occur the trait disappears" (p. 503). Better lives for children come about, he says, the more parents empathize with their children and the less they exert on them their own anxieties and desires. Progress can be traced historically. In ancient times children were seen as both loving and bad—changeling tales reflect hostility to adult desires. Saint Augustine thought children suffered from demons, and some, he wrote, "die of this vexation" (p. 521). "It is, of course, not love which the parent of the past lacked, but rather the emo-

tional maturity needed to see the child as a person separate from himself" (p. 519). In the Bible "you find lots on child sacrifice, on stoning children, on beating them, on their strict obedience, on their love for their parents, and on their role as carriers of the family name, but not a single [passage] that reveals any empathy with their needs." Jesus' request to "suffer little children" "refers to exorcising by laying on of hands the evil in children" (p. 519). Children's clothing styles until the mid-nineteenth century depict children becoming parents to their parents, dressed in the style of their grandparents' generation: "The mother is literally reborn in the child, children are not just dressed as 'miniature adults,' but quite clearly as miniature women, often complete with decollete" (p. 520). Infanticide, which increases as one goes back in time, De Mause thinks was attributable not to women's "hostility to the child itself, but rather to the need to sacrifice the child to propitiate their own mothers" (p. 527). Foundling homes in eighteenth-century eastern European villages hired "killing nurses." The convenience of swaddling clothes meant that adults "hardly had to pay any attention to infants once they were tied up" and may have resulted in cases of physical retardation. It is a brutal history.

De Mause describes in sequence six "modes" of parent-child relations. Antiquity to the fourth century A.D. he calls the Infanticidal Mode, when parents resolved anxieties by killing their children, and the sodomy of children was tolerated. Chaucer's "Tale of Patient Griselde" illustrates the Abandonment Mode (to the thirteenth century), a period when children were thought to have souls and therefore were not killed outright, but sent away instead to wet nurses, monasteries, or nunneries. The Ambivalent Mode came next, lasting through the seventeenth century, when a child still was thought "a container of dangerous projections," but manuals nevertheless were written with instructions for molding a child to something better. Cults of Mary and Jesus helped to soften harsh treatments of children. The eighteenth century brought the Intrusive Mode, when physical abuse continued to decline, and children were taught to obey by means of threats and impositions of guilt. A strong mind was to be trained to control the will: "The child was so much less threatening that true empathy was possible, and pediatrics was born, which along with the general improvement in level of care by parents reduced infant mortality and provided the basis for the demographic transition of the eighteenth century" (p. 554).

The mid-nineteenth to mid-twentieth century De Mause says experienced the Socialization Mode, when parents tried to train children to conform and spent less effort to conquer the evil within them. Fathers took more interest in children's daily affairs. Our present time, which uses the Helping Mode, was shaped by books and educational experiments, most notably, in his view, by the work of A. S. Neil, who thought that children should not be disciplined at all. The Helping Mode "involves the proposition that the child knows better than the parent what it needs at each stage of life, and fully involves both parents in the child's life as they work to empathize with and fulfill its expanding and particular needs." Parents should be "servants" to a child. The result of such an upbringing, in De Mause's observation, is "a child who is gentle, sincere, never depressed, never imitative or group-oriented, strong-willed, and unintimidated by authority" (p. 556). De Mause was writing in the early 1970s, when reaction to the Vietnam War and other forces favored a great variety of liberalizing trends in human relationships, including child-raising.

9. Postman, *Disappearance of Childhood.* Having chronicled this progressive and generally hopeful evolution of childhood, Postman then documents its "disappearance," which was activated by further technological invention: the Morse code and electricity. These brought "mass" communication, culminating in television, where again, as in the Middle Ages, the image is all. On the TV screen we "read" pictures but actually need not read at all. No analysis is necessary, or possible, and, as in the Middle Ages, identical information is made available to all—adults as well as their children, who watch eight or more hours of television a day. There are no secrets anymore. Illness, violence, death, sexuality (traditionally the major subjects of taboo) are casual subjects in advertising and news. Small children can see, in living color, starved babies in Africa without having been prepared for such news by schooling. News is whatever "comes on" the screen.

This "a-literate" environment, Postman says, marks the end of childhood. We should not be surprised, he maintains, that with its disappearance, children are suffering more severely than they have at any time since the Middle Ages, and in similar ways: through sexual abuse, abandonment, economic exploitation, and a return to illiteracy. There is an astonishing increase in the crime rate of young children: between 1950 and 1979 serious crimes by children under fifteen years old rose 11,000 percent, and non-violent crimes by 8,300 percent (p. 134).

10. Lineage of the Bischoff, Pankow, and Schumacher Families, p. 2.

11. "*Der Stammbaum,*" North Dakota Historical Society of Germans from Russia, February 1979, p. 9.

12. Bremner, *Children and Youth,* p. 687.

13. *U.S. Statutes at Large* 39, ch. 432, pt. 1. Quoted in Bremner, *Children and Youth,* pp. 675–76.

14. Quoted in Bremner, *Children and Youth,* pp. 712–13.

15. Owen R. Loveboy, "What Remains of Child Labor," *New Republic* 9 (November 11, 1918). Quoted in Bremner, *Children and Youth,* pp. 705–706.

16. Thomas J. Parkinson, "The Federal Child Labor Law," *Child Labor Bulletin* 7 (2): 89–90 (August 1918). Quoted in Bremner, *Children and Youth,* p. 711.

17. Lowell Mallett, "The Sequel of the Dangenhart Case," *American Child* 6 (January 1924): 3. Quoted in Bremner, *Children and Youth,* pp. 716–17.

18. *U.S. Statutes at Large* 43, pt. 1. Quoted in Bremner, *Children and Youth,* p. 670.

19. Quoted in Bremner, *Children and Youth*, p. 737.
20. Sara A. Brown, *Missouri Review of the World* 46 (July 1923):515–20. Quoted in Bremner, *Children and Youth*, p. 633.
21. Quoted in Bremner, *Children and Youth*, p. 748–49.
22. "Child Labor Still a Living Issue," *Ohio Woman Voter* 4 (December 1925):2.
23. "Bettina," *Plainswoman*, May 1983, vol. 7, no. 8, pp. 5–6.
24. Martha Gray Wales, p. 13.
25. Ibid.
26. Coe, *When the Grass Was Taller*, pp. 8–9.
27. Wales, p. 15.
28. Ibid., p. 18.
29. Ibid.
30. Ibid.

Chapter 3

1. Lucille Gullickson, a journalist for the *Center Republican*, has collected contemporary newspaper accounts about the Hazel Miner incident and interviewed family members and friends. Her compilation, the basis of the information that follows, is published in Bjorn Benson, Elizabeth Hampsten, and Kathryn Sweney, eds., *Day In, Day Out: Women's Lives in North Dakota* (Grand Forks: University of North Dakota, 1988), pp. 97–103.
2. Hazel Satterthwaite Evans, "A Storm Experience in 1920," typescript. Used by permission of the author.
3. Ben Walsh, "I Attended a Country School," 1980. University of North Dakota Libraries, OGL 589. Original held by the author, Courtenay, North Dakota.
4. "Autobiography of Gabriel Lundy (1886–?)," typescript copy 1968, University of North Dakota Libraries, OGL 494.
5. Colleen A. Oihus, "Stephanie Prepiora: The First Seventy Years," paper submitted to the course "Methods in Cultural Anthropology," April 22, 1976, at the University of North Dakota. The major portion of the paper is Stephanie Prepiora's reminiscence, edited by Colleen Oihus. Updated and printed in Minto, North Dakota, in March 1989 as Stephanie Prepiora, "'Miss Prep': A Biographical Sketch of Stephanie Prepiora," editorial assistance by Colleen Oihus. Excerpts here are from the earlier version.

Chapter 4

1. Robert W. Graham, who moved from Ontario to Benson County, North Dakota. University of North Dakota Libraries, OGL 597.
2. Christian Welsch, "A Voice from the Past: A German-Russian Life," *Journal of the American Historical Society of Germans from Russia* 4 (1): 51 (Spring 1981).
3. Monsignor George P. Aberle, *Pioneers and Their Sons: 165 Family Histories* (Dickinson, North Dakota: n.p., n.d.).

4. *Stark County Heritage and Destiny* (Dickinson, North Dakota: Stark County Historical Society, c. 1978), p. 69.

5. Marie Johnson Enochson, "Memories of Life in the Wild Rice Community of North Dakota," undated manuscript, University of North Dakota Libraries, OGL 647.

6. Letter of February 1, 1932, to her daughters. Contributed by Brenda E. Caranicas, School of Nursing, Minot State College, Minot, North Dakota, November 1, 1984.

7. Charles H. Skalet and R. E. Fuglestad, transs., "Torkel Fuglestad, 1856–1954," manuscript, 1937. Original held by the Norwegian-American Historical Association, Northfield, Minnesota. University of North Dakota Libraries, OGL 646.

8. Manuscript supplied by Janet Kruckenberg, Wahpeton, North Dakota.

9. Lineage of the Bischoff, Pankow, and Schumacher Families, p. 102.

10. "Sarah Pickwell Reid, 1843–1902," manuscript, c. 1900. University of North Dakota Libraries, OGL 428.

11. February 26, 1891, pp. 126–27.

Chapter 5

1. Text transcribed and edited by Cynthia Kristjanson, Grand Forks, while a student in the course "Rural Women," fall 1980, University of North Dakota, and in her possession.

2. Manuscript, 1933, State Historical Society of North Dakota, Heritage Center, Bismarck.

3. Letters edited from typescript by Gretchen Beito, Thief River Falls, Minnesota, while a student in the course "Rural Women," fall 1980, at the University of North Dakota, and in her possession.

4. The letters have been edited by Frances M. Wold and published in *North Dakota History* (Winter 1980).

5. Josiah B. Chaney and Family Papers, Minnesota Historical Society. The journal has been published in *Plainswoman* 8, no. 7 (April 1985) pp. 3–6.

6. A typescript copy of the diary, part of the Edmund F. Ely papers, A/E52, in the Archives and Manuscripts Division of the Minnesota Historical Society, was copied by Veronica Houle from the original, which is in the custody of the St. Louis County Historical Society.

Chapter 6

1. Ruth Bond's essay is in the possession of Jean Guy, Bismarck, North Dakota.

2. The interviews are recorded in the Historical Data Project files, North Dakota State Historical Society, Bismarck, North Dakota.

Chapter 7

1. The discussion that follows is based on the Martha and Ole Lima correspondence, 1886–1902, University of North Dakota Libraries, OGL 638.

The original letters are held by the Norwegian-American Historical Society, Northfield, Minnesota.

Chapter 8

1. Florence Clifford, *We Didn't Want for Anything: Katharina Morlock and Johann Lippert's Family in North Dakota; Great Ones for Telling Stories: Josephine Delvo and Johann Howitz's Family in North Dakota; and Over Fool's Hill, Rosine Hirsch and Johann Schmidt's Family in North Dakota,* ed. Elizabeth Hampsten (Grand Forks, North Dakota: Privately printed, 1984). Page references are to the booklet of the family beginning with that letter.

2. Quoted in Nina Farley Wishek, "Along the Trails of Yesterday: A Story of McIntosh County," *Ashley Tribune*, 1941.

3. Typescript in the possession of Thomas J. Clifford, Grand Forks, North Dakota.

Chapter 9

1. The Farmer Collection, 1949–1958, Archives and Manuscripts Division of the Minnesota Historical Society, St. Paul.

2. New York: Atheneum, 1979.

3. Hamlin Garland, *A Son of the Middle Border* (New York: The Macmillan Co., 1917), p. 63.

4. Ibid., p. 139.

5. Ibid., p. 367.

6. Ibid., p. 402.

7. Ibid., p. 219.

8. Hamlin Garland, *A Pioneer Mother* (Chicago: The Bookfellows, 1922), p. 5.

9. Ibid., p. 9.

10. Ibid., p. 13.

11. Ibid., p. 21.

12. Sioux Falls: Center for Western Studies, Augustana College, 1985.

Selected Bibliography

Aries, Philippe. *Centuries of Childhood: Social History of Family Life.* New York: Alfred A. Knopf, 1962.

Bremner, Robert. *Children and Youth in America: Their Labor History.* Cambridge: Harvard University Press, 1971.

Burnett, John, ed. *Destiny Obscure: Autobiographies of Childhood, Education and Family from the 1820s to the 1920s.* New York: Penguin Books, 1982, 1984.

Coe, Richard N. *When the Grass Was Taller.* New Haven: Yale University Press, 1984.

De Mause, Lloyd. "The Evolution of Childhood," *History of Childhood Quarterly, Journal of Psychohistory* 1 (4): 503–75 (Spring 1974).

Garland, Hamlin. *A Son of the Middle Border.* New York: Macmillan, 1917.

———. *A Pioneer Mother.* Chicago: The Bookfellows, 1922.

Marshall, James. "An Unheard Voice: The Autobiography of a Dispossessed Homesteader and a Nineteenth-Century Cultural Theme of Dispossession." *Old Northwest* (n.d.), pp. 303–29.

Postman, Neil. *The Disappearance of Childhood.* New York: Delacorte Press, 1982.

West, Elliot. "Heathens and Angels: Childhood in the Rocky Mountain Mining Towns." *Western Historical Quarterly,* April 1983, pp. 146–64.

Index